The Transfer of Economic Knowledge

The Transfer of Economic Knowledge

Edited by

Ernst Mohr

Director, Institute for Economy and the Environment,
University of St. Gallen, Switzerland

Edward Elgar

Cheltenham, UK • Northampton, MA, USA

Published by
Edward Elgar Publishing Limited
Glensanda House
Montpellier Parade
Cheltenham
Glos GL50 1UA
UK

Edward Elgar Publishing, Inc.
136 West Street
Suite 202
Northampton
Massachusetts 01060
USA

A catalogue record for this book is available from the British Library

Library of Congress Cataloguing in Publication Data
The transfer of economic knowledge / edited by Ernst Mohr.
        p.   cm.
    Papers presented at a colloquium held at the University of St.
Gallen in June 1998.
    Includes index.
    1.   Economics—Congresses.   2.   Economic policy—Congresses.
I. Mohr, Ernst.
HB21.T73   1999
330—dc21   98–53415
                                                                                   CIP

ISBN 1 85898 855 1

Printed and bound in Great Britain by Biddles Ltd, Guildford and King's Lynn

Contents

List of figures   vii
List of tables   viii
Notes on the contributors   ix
Acknowledgements   xv
Introduction   xvii
Ernst Mohr

PART I   THEORETICAL PERSPECTIVES AND THE TRANSFER
          PROCESS

1   Public choice and alternative policy perspectives   3
     James M. Buchanan
2   On the political economy of economic policy advice   13
     Gebhard Kirchgässner
3   The use and misuse of theory in the transfer process   32
     Anne O. Krueger

PART II   ASPECTS OF INSTITUTIONAL POLICY ADVICE

4   The culture of economic policy advice: an international
     comparison with special emphasis on Europe   47
     Charles Wyplosz
5   Economic policy advice: opportunities and limitations   74
     A.W. Bob Coats
6   Economic knowledge transfer by research institutes in Germany:
     some reflections   90
     Heinz König

PART III TEACHING AND APPLICATION OF ECONOMICS

7   The making of applied economists: challenges for undergraduate
     curricula   103
     Manfred Gärtner
8   Financial innovation, the transfer of knowledge, and implications
     for postgraduate education   125
     Heinz Zimmermann

9   The new media: chances and challenges for suppliers of
    economic education   151
    Heinz Hauser and Sascha Spoun

PART IV   INTERDISCIPLINARY PERSPECTIVES OF THE
          TRANSFER PROCESS

10 The relevance of psychological aspects for policy design   165
    Bruno S. Frey
11 Interpreting institutions: the case of international public law   186
    Ernst Mohr

Index   207

Figures

1.1 Promarket and antimarket perspectives on policy issues 6
7.1 Economics majors in the US, 1948–1996 106
7.2 Students enrolled in economics in Germany, 1972–1996 107
7.3 Percentage of students enrolled in economic science in Switzerland, 1980–1996 108
7.4 Majors in business, economics and all fields at the University of St. Gallen, 1970–1997 110

Tables

4.1   Supply of policy advisers   56
4.2   Demand for policy advice   59
4.3   The public side of economics   63
10.1 Social capital according to the World Values Survey
      (averages 1990–1993)   169

Notes on the contributors

James M. Buchanan, Nobel Laureate in Economics, is Professor emeritus of Economics and Advisory General Director at the Center for Study of Public Choice at George Mason University. Formerly, he was Professor of Economics at Virginia Polytechnic Institute and State University and at the University of Virginia. His research focuses on political economy, constitutional economics and economic philosophy. His numerous publications include: *The Calculus of Consent: Logical Foundations of Constitutional Democracy* (with G. Tullock, University of Michigan Press, 1962), *The Limits of Liberty: Between Anarchy and Leviathan* (University of Chicago Press, 1975), *The Power to Tax* (with G. Brennan, Cambridge University Press, 1980), *The Reason of Rules: Constitutional Political Economy* (with G. Brennan, Cambridge University Press, 1985) and, recently, the volume *Politics by Principle, Not Interest: Toward Nondiscriminatory Democracy* (with R.D. Congleton, Cambridge University Press, 1998).

A.W. Bob Coats is Professor emeritus of Economics and Social History at the University of Nottingham (UK). Formerly he held the position of Research Professor of Economics at Duke University (US). He is a Distinguished Fellow and Past President of the American History of Economics Society. He was Associate Editor of the *History of Political Economy* journal and is on the editorial boards of various other economic journals. His fields of interest include the history and methodology of economics with a focus on the sociology and professionalization of the economic profession, especially with regard to the role of economists in governments and international agencies. A collection of his papers can be found in two volumes: *On the History of Economic Thought: British and American Economic Essays vol. 1* (Routledge, 1992) and *The Sociology and Professionalization of Economics: British and American Economic Essays vol. 2* (Routledge, 1993). A third volume, *The Historiography and Methodology of Economics: British and American Economic Essays vol. 3* is forthcoming. Other publications include *The Post-1945 Internationalization of Economics* (ed., Duke University Press, 1977) and *The Development of Economics in Western Europe Since 1945* (Routledge, in press).

Bruno S. Frey is Professor of Economics at the University of Zurich and Director of the Institute for Empirical Economic Research. After his PhD studies in Basle and Cambridge (UK) and his habilitation he was Associate Professor at the University of Basle. From 1970 to 1977 he was Professor at the University of Constance. He was then appointed as a member of faculty of the University of Zurich. He holds an honorary doctorate from the University of St. Gallen. Frey's work covers a broad range of topics. He has written more than 300 articles and numerous books especially in the fields of institutional economics, fiscal federalism, the psychological foundation of economics, and environmental economics. Among his books are: *Muses and Markets: Explorations in the Economics of the Art*s (with W. Pommerehne, Blackwell, 1989), *Economics as a Science of Human Behaviour: Towards a New Social Science Paradigm* (Kluwer, 1992) and *Not Just for the Money: An Economic Theory of Personal Motivation* (Edward Elgar, 1997). Recently he coauthored *FOCJ. A New Proposal for Federalism in Europe* (with R. Eichenberger, 1998).

Manfred Gärtner is Professor of Economics at the University of St. Gallen and a member of the *Forschungsgemeinschaft für Nationalökonomie* (Institute of Economics). Past positions include a lectureship in Economics at the University of Basle. His areas of research include the theory of public choice, international monetary economics and the economic theory of trade unions and labour markets. Among his publications are: 'Political and industrial change in a model of trade union militancy and real wage growth', *Review of Economics and Statistics*, **67**, 1985, pp. 322–7, 'Intervention policy under floating exchange rates: an analysis of the Swiss case', *Economica*, **54**, 1987, pp. 439–53 and 'Political business cycles when real activity is persistent', *Journal of Macroeconomics*, **18**, 1996, pp. 679–92. Books in the field of macroeconomics are: *Macroeconomics under Flexible Exchange Rates* (Harvester Wheatsheaf, 1993), *A Primer in European Macroeconomics* (Prentice-Hall, 1997). Recently he published *Principles of Economics* (with K. Case, R. Fair and K. Heather, Prentice-Hall, 1998) and 'Who wants the euro – and why? Economic explanations of public attitudes towards a single European currency', *Public Choice*, **93**, 1997, pp. 487–510.

Heinz Hauser is Professor of Economics at the University of St. Gallen. He is Director of the Swiss Institute for International Economics and Applied Economic Research (SIAW) in St. Gallen and Chairman of the Community of European Management Schools (CEMS). His research focuses on international economics, European integration, international trade policy and the World Trade Organization (WTO). His publications include: *EWR-Vertrag, EG-Beitritt, Alleingang. Wirtschaftliche Konsequenzen für die Schweiz* (with S. Bradke, Rüegger, 1991), *Das Neue GATT. Die Welthandelsordnung nach Abschluss der Uruguay Runde* (with K.-U. Schanz, Oldenbourg, 1995), 'Swiss

Trade Policy and the 1996 WTO Review', in *The World Economy, Global Trade Policy 1997* (with R. Straw, Blackwell Publishers, 1997) and 'The WTO Dispute Settlement System: Playing the Game', discussion paper, Department of Economics, University of St. Gallen, 1998 (with M. Büttler).

Gebhard Kirchgässner is Professor of Economics and Econometrics at the University of St. Gallen. He is Director of the Swiss Institute for International Economics and Applied Economic Research (SIAW) in St. Gallen. Formerly he was Professor of Economics at the University of Osnabrück. His special research interests are political economy, environmental and energy economics, the methodological foundation of economics, and applied econometrics. His publications include: 'U.S.–European interest rate linkage: a time series analysis for West Germany, Switzerland, and the United States', *Review of Economics and Statistics*, **69**, 1987, pp. 675–84 (with J. Wolters), *Homo oeconomicus. Das ökonomische Modell individuellen Verhaltens und seine Anwendung in den Wirtschafts- und Sozialwissenschaften* (J.C.B. Mohr, 1991), 'Testing weak rationality of forecasts with different time horizons', *Journal of Forecasting*, **12**, 1993, pp. 541–58 and 'Constitutional economics and its relevance for the evolution of rules', *Kyklos*, **47**, 1994, pp. 321–39. Recently he has published 'The double dividend debate: some comments from a politico-economic perspective', *Empirica*, **25**, 1998, pp. 37–49 and 'Ecological tax reform and involuntary unemployment: simulation results for Switzerland', *Schweizerische Zeitschrift für Volkswirtschaft und Statistik*, **134**, 1998 (with U. Müller and M. Savioz).

Heinz König is Professor of Economics and Econometrics at the University of Mannheim. From 1991 to 1997 he was Scientific Director of the Center for European Economic Research (ZEW) in Mannheim. He is also Past President of the German Economic Association. His fields of interest include labour economics and industrial organization. Among his publications are: *Einführung in die Spektralanalyse ökonomischer Zeitreihen* (with J. Wolters, Anton Haun, 1972), 'On the formation of price expectations: an analysis of business test data by log-linear probability models', *European Economic Review*, **16**, 1981, pp. 103–38 (with M. Nerlove and G. Oudiz), 'Price flexibility, inventory behavior and production responses', in W.P. Heller et al. (eds), *Essays in Honor of Kenneth J. Arrow, vol. 2, Equilibrium Analysis*, pp. 179–218 (with M. Nerlove, Cambridge University Press, 1986), and 'Labor utilization and nonwage labor costs in a disequilibrium macro framework', *Scandinavian Journal of Economics*, **94**, 1992, pp. 71–83 (with H. Entorf and W. Pohlmeier). Recently he has coauthored 'Employment, investment and innovation at the firm level', in *The OECD Jobs Study: Investment, Productivity and Employment; 5*, pp. 67–84 (Paris, 1995).

Anne O. Krueger is Herald L. and Caroline L. Ritch Professor in Humanities and Sciences, Director of the Center for Research on Economic Development and Policy Reform and a Senior Fellow, Hoover Institution, at Stanford University. She was Arts and Sciences Professor of Economics at Duke University, Vice President 'Economics and Research' at the World Bank and Professor of Economics at the University of Minnesota. She holds honorary PhDs from Hacettepe University in Turkey, Monash University in Australia and Georgetown University, and is a Distinguished Fellow and Past President of the American Economic Association. Anne Krueger specializes in international economics and economic development. She has done research and consulting in a number of developing countries, and has written a number of books and numerous articles on problems of the international economy, including US international economic policy. Recent books are: *The WTO as International Organization* (University of Chicago Press, 1998), *Regionalism versus Multilateral Trade Arrangements* (co-ed., University of Chicago Press, 1996), *The Political Economy of US Trade Protection* (ed., University of Chicago Press, 1996), *Trade Policy and Developing Countries* (Brookings Institution, 1995) and *American Trade Policy: A Tragedy in the Making* (American Enterprise Institute, 1995). Her present work includes further research in the fields of policy reform in developing countries, the political economy of policy formulation and US international economic policy towards the developing countries.

Ernst Mohr is Professor of Economics at the University of St. Gallen and Director of the Institute for Economy and the Environment (IWÖ-HSG). Formerly, he was Head, Research Department 'Resource Economics', at the Kiel Institute for World Economics. His fields of interest include environmental economics, international economics and cultural economics. His publications include: *Economic Theory and Sovereign International Debt* (Academic Press, 1991), 'Sustainable development and international distribution: theory and application to rainforests', *Review of International Economics*, **4**, 1996, pp. 152–71, 'Pooling sovereign risks: the case of environmental treaties and international debt', *Journal of Development Economics*, **55**, 1998, pp. 171–88 (with J. Thomas) and 'The window of opportunity for rainforest protection: the time remaining in the Rio-process', *International Environmental Affairs*, **10**, 1998, pp. 40–63 (with J. Janssen).

Sascha Spoun is a PhD student at the University of St. Gallen. His research fields are the processes of internationalization and public management. He has published *Universität und Praxis. Tendenzen wissenschaftlicher Verantwortung für Wirtschaft und Gesellschaft. Der Universität St. Gallen zum 100-Jahr-Jubiläum* (co-ed., Verlag NZZ, 1998) and *Internationalisierung von*

Universitäten – Eine Studie am Beispiel der Community of European Management Schools (PhD thesis at the University of St. Gallen, 1998).

Charles Wyplosz is Professor of International Economics at the Graduate Institute of International Studies, University of Geneva. Formerly, he was Professor of Economics at the European Institute of Business Administration (INSEAD) at Fontainebleau (France) and the Ecole des Hautes Etudes en Sciences Sociales in Paris. He is a Research Fellow of the Centre of Economic Policy Research (CEPR), London. His research focuses on monetary and exchange rate economics, the macroeconomics of transition processes, the European Monetary Union and unemployment problems. His publications include: 'Capital control and balance of payment crises', *Journal of International Money and Finance*, **5**, 1986, pp. 167–79, *Macroeconomics, A European Text* (with M. Burda, Oxford University Press, 1993), 'Gross worker and job flows in Europe', *European Economic Review*, **38**, 1994, pp. 1287–1315 (with M. Burda), 'Two cases for sand in the wheel of international finance', *Economic Journal*, **105**, 1995, pp. 162–72 (with B. Eichengreen and J. Tobin), 'Equilibrium exchange rates in transition economies', *IMF Staff Papers*, **44**, 1997 (with L. Halpern) and 'EMU: why and how it might happen', *Journal of Economic Perspectives*, **11**, 1997, pp. 3–22.

Heinz Zimmermann is Professor of Economics and Finance at the University of St. Gallen. Also he holds a lectureship at the University of Basle. He is Director of the Swiss Institute of Banking and Finance (s/bf-HSG) in St. Gallen. He specializes in finance, especially with regard to asset pricing, portfolio theory, derivatives, risk management and empirical research. Current research is on the impact of global economic conditions on international stock and bond markets, and on the interest sensitivity and cost of capital of financial institutions. His publications include: 'Stock offerings in a different institutional setting: The Swiss case, 1973–1983', *Journal of Banking and Finance*, **12**, 1988, pp. 353–78 (with C. Loderer), 'The structure of European stock returns', *Financial Analysts Journal*, **48**, 1992, pp. 15–26 (with M. Drummen), *Pensionskassen Schweiz: neue Strategien für wachsende Leistungsansprüche* (Züricher Kantonalbank, 1992), 'Constant return participating (CRP) portfolio insurance strategies', *Journal of Derivatives*, **4**, 1996, pp. 80–88 and *State Preference Theoric und Asset Pricing: eine Einführung* (Physica-Springer, 1998).

Acknowledgements

On the occasion of the centenary of the University of St. Gallen, Switzerland, several research colloquia were held in June 1998. This volume contains the proceedings of one colloquium, entitled 'The State and Development of the Transfer Process of Economic Knowledge' and hosted by the University of St. Gallen's Department of Economics. The colloquium brought together members of the Economics Department with distinguished economists from abroad and other Swiss universities to discuss issues surrounding the question 'how economic knowledge is or should be put to use'.

In preparing the colloquium and this volume I have incurred many debts. Chief among them is to the authors, who stuck firmly to the project over an unusually long period of personal commitment at a time when the outline of the project was still uncertain. Thanks to them also for the timely submission of their contributions and their cheerfulness in revising their manuscripts where needed.

Special thanks also go to the chairmen of sessions, Jörg Baumberger, Philipp Guyer, Peter Moser and Jean-Robert Tyran. They worked through the manuscripts speedily before the colloquium, and introduced them to participants during the event. They chaired the sessions superbly.

I also owe thanks to all colleagues in the Department of Economics for endorsing the project. Thanks also go to the *St. Galler Stiftung für Internationale Studien* for their generous financial support of the colloquium.

Johannes Anderegg, Director of the centenary celebrations, and Barbara Stamm coordinated the various colloquia and made them a joint and pleasant event. Johannes Schmidt helped me organize the colloquium and Claus Wepler assisted me in the preparation of the proceedings. Without their constant personal engagement this undertaking would not have been possible.

Ernst Mohr
St. Gallen, September 1998

Acknowledgements

Introduction

Ernst Mohr

We economists are accustomed to relating input and output using the concept of the production function. Thereby we express our firm belief that what comes out of a production process differs in a significant way from what is put in. No matter what industry we analyse, the production process is of importance to us.

However, this does not adequately describe the attitude of most economists towards their own industry. It is possible to think of the knowledge which emerges from research as an input in a production function, and its effect on the course of society as an output. However, the transfer process of economic knowledge from its generation to societal use appears to be of little interest to many economists. It is as if economists conceive their own industry as one in which input is output, one in which the transfer process of economic knowledge can be safely neglected. And contrary to the criteria by which many of them prefer to judge the societal contribution of other industries, they are content with measuring their input.

That perspective is almost certainly false. This volume is a collection of papers which address various aspects of the transfer process of economic knowledge. Their common denominator is the conclusion that this process matters. A better understanding of the process is therefore not only of scientific interest as such, but may also help to improve the output of the economics profession. The papers contained in this volume seek to strengthen that understanding.

The transfer process can be affected by a number of factors. One is the scientific and other discourse within academia itself. This aspect is addressed in Part I of this volume. Other factors affect one of various channels by which economic knowledge is transferred. One channel is 'up' to the government. Part II addresses issues of government consulting and economic policy advice. Another channel of transferring economic knowledge is 'down' into the private sector, an important part of which is brought about by teaching university students and training practitioners and post-graduates. These issues are addressed in Part III. A final aspect of the transfer of economic knowledge relates to the 'lateral' transfer to and from other scientific disciplines. This is the subject of Part IV.

*   *   *

Part I, 'Theoretical Perspectives and the Transfer Process', starts with 'Public choice and alternative policy perspectives' by *James M. Buchanan*, who discusses four distinct perspectives on the performance of alternative organizations of economic activity which embody different scientific theories concerning the working of markets and politics. He argues that these perspectives identify separate prior understandings of general constitutional issues that participants in ultimate organizational discussions will employ. Buchanan claims that these competing priors are not limited to nonscientific members of political constituencies but necessarily govern also the debate among legitimate members of the scientific establishment.

Chapter 2, 'On the political economy of economic policy advice' by *Gebhard Kirchgässner*, also argues that one cannot expect from economic theory the elimination of all degrees of freedom in scientifically sound policy advice. Kirchgässner claims that consistency with the mainstream economic approach to modelling individual behaviour requires that the economist as analyst should regard the economist as policy adviser as a self-interested individual, who exploits scientific degrees of freedom when acting as adviser. After supporting this claim empirically he ends on a more optimistic note, arguing epistemologically that it is not necessary for the proper working of science that scientists are altruists but that it suffices that the organization of the scientific discourse between egoistic scientists produces sound results. Finally, he argues that such discourse is more likely to produce better policy decisions in a direct rather than in a representative democracy.

In 'The use and misuse of theory in the transfer process', *Anne O. Krueger* looks at the historical performance of a particular set of theories in the 'production process' of economic policy. The case she examines is development theory and policy. She differentiates between useful theory, good and bad theory, and shows how each of them has affected the formulation of development policy. Krueger argues that even some good theory was not useful and helped to perpetuate policies which are now believed to be inferior. To some degree, she attributes this misapplication of good theory to well-established and beloved practices in scientific research and policy formulation, such as simplification in modelling or the quest for exceptions from the validity of established theorems.

*   *   *

Part II, 'Aspects of Institutional Policy Advice', starts with 'The culture of economic policy advice: an international comparison with special emphasis on Europe' by *Charles Wyplosz*. At the outset he gives an overview of the institutional landscape in Europe, focusing on the situation of policy advisers with direct access to policy makers but without holding a permanent position in the institution which they advise. Starting from the profile of an 'ideal' adviser, Wyplosz then analyses actual European supply of and demand for economic policy advisers. This comparative investigation is based on information generated from a questionnaire, polling internationally renowned policy-orientated economists throughout Europe. His analysis reveals a substantial heterogeneity throughout Europe in supply of and demand for economic policy advisers as well as in terms of the institutional environments in which they are embedded.

Chapter 5, 'Economic policy advice: opportunities and limitations', by *A.W. Bob Coats* complements the Wyplosz chapter in focusing on the US and British situations. The institutional environment in which policy advice takes place in these countries contains more elements from 'inside' government, compared to the European continental situation at large. With that focus, Coats addresses the questions who are the people that are engaged in policy making, and how are their activities affected by the institutional settings in which they work?

'Economic knowledge transfer by research institutes in Germany: some reflections' by *Heinz König* is a case study which deepens the Wyplosz analysis by looking in greater detail into the specific situation in a particular European country. He focuses on the situation of five German economic research institutes, cofinanced by the Federal and the respective State governments, and on the criteria applied and proposals made by the German Science Council, in the context of an evaluation of these institutes. König discusses financing and design issues of economic research institutes in Germany and compares the quality of empirical economics in Germany with the Anglo-American situation.

*   *   *

Parts I and II of this volume have a focus on the transfer of economic knowledge into the public domain. However, perhaps less prominent yet important transfers of economic knowledge involve other domains. Part III, 'Teaching and Application of Economics', takes up the issue of transferring economic knowledge into the private domain, and not necessarily for the purpose of indirectly feeding back on the public policy process. The starting-point is the observation that the majority of students of economics will subsequently not proceed to a career as a professional economic policy adviser, or as a professional economist at large, but will pursue other activities.

Chapter 7, 'The making of applied economists: challenges for undergraduate curricula' by *Manfred Gärtner* develops principles for undergraduate curricula recursively from the special situation in which economics graduates will find themselves when entering the nonacademic labour market. He argues that the problem with economics teaching lies less in the way economics is taught than in what is being taught. Gärtner cautions against an ever-increasing exposure to latest generation theories and argues the case for training students to be able to communicate with superiors and peers, in terms of older or more basic theories than those taught now.

'Financial innovation, the transfer of knowledge, and implications for post-graduate education' by *Heinz Zimmermann* is a case study of the evolution, dissemination and success of finance theory in practice, paying special attention to the Swiss situation. He explains how the development and transfer of the theory of finance was affected by deregulation, new regulation and technological innovation. He explains for the case of derivatives and risk management how knowledge acts as an innovative force. Zimmermann also explains, using the capital asset pricing model (CAPM) and option pricing theory as an example, why it is possible that one theory can revolutionize an entire sector of the economy and another, equally sound theory, has almost no impact at all. He concludes by developing a curriculum for postgraduate and executive education in finance.

'The new media: chances and challenges for suppliers of economic education' by *Heinz Hauser* and *Sascha Spoun* addresses the question of how the new communication media will affect the distribution and interpretation of knowledge. Although the issue is more general, it equally applies to the transfer process of economic knowledge. The authors take up the industrial organization perspective and ask what will be the likely changes in the market structure if new communication technologies have an uneven impact on different segments of the economics industry and modes of delivery. They predict a radical change in the industry and a shift away from traditional university education. But they also suggest how universities can maintain a market share in the dissemination of economic knowledge.

*   *   *

Part IV, 'Interdisciplinary Perspectives of the Transfer Process', concerns the scientific exchange across disciplinary boundaries and how it does or should affect the transfer of economic knowledge. 'The relevance of psychological aspects for policy design' by *Bruno S. Frey* addresses economic policy again. By presenting evidence from experimental economics, generated by himself and others, he argues that orthodox economic policy recommendations are seriously fraught with systematic and possibly undesired consequences. Frey attributes this to a 'crowding effect' by which the intrinsic motivation of individuals is systematically affected by changes in external (policy) intervention. He thereby argues that economic policy formulation can be improved by heeding well-identified and empirically supported psychological factors.

Finally, 'Interpreting institutions: the case of international public law' by *Ernst Mohr* investigates difficulties of cross-disciplinary communication. It argues that the fate of economic arguments in the transfer process also hinges on how they are received by other disciplines which offer 'competing' views. It is claimed that some unnecessary problems are encountered by economists because of their inclination to interpret the object of interest of other scientific disciplines as economic institutions. The relationship between economics and international public law serves to substantiate this claim.

PART I

Theoretical Perspectives and the Transfer Process

1. Public choice and alternative policy perspectives

James M. Buchanan

IN DEFENCE OF MARKETS

In a review of Robert Kuttner's book, *Everything for Sale* (1997), Jagdish Bhagwati (1997) suggests that modern critics of markets neglect two separate arguments that have proved persuasive as counters to the market failure theses that dominated thought in the mid-century decades. The first argument, which may broadly and inclusively be associated with 'Chicago', itself embodies two distinct strands of inquiry. There is, first, the exhaustive empirical work that has demonstrated that departures from the idealized conditions for market equilibrium, as detailed in textbooks, need not measure up to much in value shortfall. And there is, second, the belated recognition, seminally attributable to Coase (1960), that freedom of contract along with enforceability of rights offer ever-present avenues of market-like escapes from putatively imposed restrictions.

The second inclusive argument that lends support to market organization of economic activity does not concentrate initial attention on the efficacy of markets, *per se*. Instead, the argument analyses the workings, and possible failures, of the alternatives to markets, which, of necessity, are political. Bhagwati identifies two strands of the inclusive argument here. He could have added a third, and important, component. There is, first, the Hayekian recognition of the severe limits on knowledge that could be available to any political agents or agencies, no matter how benevolent the motivation. There is, second, the more directed public choice emphasis on the incentive incompatibilities that must characterize any location of decision making in others than those who must bear the costs and enjoy the benefits of action. And, finally, there is the logical force of the Arrow impossibility theorem (see Arrow 1951) which demonstrates that any aggregation of individual preference orderings through collective structures for decisions may yield inconclusive outcomes.

The two separate pro-market arguments sketched out earlier may be summarized by the two short statements: (i) markets work (Chicago school) and (ii) politics fail (Hayekian–Austrian, public choice, Arrow).

IN OPPOSITION TO MARKETS

I propose now to move beyond the modern arguments in defence of markets and attempt to make a comparable classification of the opposition to and criticism of markets. There is, first, the position or perspective effectively represented by Kuttner – one that may be referenced by the term 'residually socialist' with the 'residual' qualifier added to indicate persistence of basic socialist attitudes well after the great revolutions of 1989–91. This perspective interprets the market economy as a complex network of power relationships among persons and organizations, with few coordinating or equilibrating properties and with little or no direction towards the generation of maximal aggregate value or even tolerable justice in the distribution of rewards. The market economy, in this perception, fails, and massively so, in any efforts to use resources most effectively and in offering its bounty equitably. Sophisticated representatives of this set of attitudes may fully appreciate the efficiency-generating properties of the stylized models that are analysed in the advanced textbooks and taught in the academies. But they tend to reject, and categorically, any correspondence between these stylized models and the economic reality that may be observed. These critics might, therefore, agree to a proposition that states: 'Yes, markets would be fine, if they worked as they should'.

A second antimarket argument is quite different; this argument concentrates attention on the disruptive forces of markets, the selfsame 'creative destruction' that Schumpeter (1949) isolated as the market's distinguishing feature. These critics suggest that the market does, indeed, treat pushpin to be as good (or bad) as poetry. As such, the market remains wholly indifferent to conventions, traditions and longstanding cultural values. This argument rejects the market as a morally acceptable organizing principle precisely because it does work in accordance with its central logic. So long as there are potential profits to be made, entrepreneurs will move to exploit opportunities.[1]

The second strand of inquiry and criticism sketched out earlier may loosely be labelled communitarian, although the argument merges readily into one that becomes more elitist–paternalistic than might be suggested by the emphasis on community, as such. In one sense, the condemnation of the market by these critics arises, not so much in opposition to the market order itself, but against the public's preferences that the market must satisfy.

Similarly to the classification on the promarket side, we may summarize the antimarket arguments in the two statements: (i) markets fail and (ii) markets disrupt social order.

PERSPECTIVES ON POLICY: A PROVISIONAL MATRIX

I have briefly described four distinct attitudes or perspectives on the organization of economic activity through market or market-like institutions, where each perspective is understood to embody the presumption that the legal framework or protective political order is in place. It becomes almost absurd to refer to market successes or failures in the total absence of any operating legal framework. The differences among the perspectives described above relate to the efficacy of organizational arrangements between the poles of the 'ordered anarchy' that fully operative markets describe and the extensively regulated regime under the watchful eye of the benevolent collective authority – the regime that is apparently the end-state ideal of the antimarket advocates.

A helpful means of understanding the ultimate policy thrusts of the separate perspectives may be offered by the construction of a matrix representation which relates each of the perspectives to predicted stances on identifiable constitutional dimensions. Consider Figure 1.1, where the rows of the matrix classify the positions discussed – two of them as broadly promarket and two of them as broadly antimarket. In each cell of the matrix, there is placed a predicted stance on the part of the agent for the more generalized perspective defined by the relevant row. The ability to enter any such predictions at all is predicated on the presumption that such generalized perspectives are, indeed, distinguishable apart from particular applications. That is to say, participants in ultimate organizational discussions are presumed to 'bring to' the ongoing dialogue a set of attitudes towards alternative organizational arrangements, a prior understanding, of sorts, of the predicted working properties of structural alternatives. This basic presumption rules out only the total pragmatist (if one could exist) who literally approaches each and every organizational decision without any priors.

I have used the term *perspective* to refer to the separate promarket and antimarket evaluative stances. Some clarification is perhaps necessary, since the term perspective implies some base point or location from which reality is observed. As I use 'perspective' here, several elements may enter in the definition, over and beyond those that emerge from some inferred locational relationship between the observer and that which is observed. A perspective must be informed by a theory or theories as to how the observed arrangements work, as well as how alternatives might be predicted to operate. Such theories are independent of the preferences or even the interests of the observer (see Vanberg and Buchanan 1989). On the other hand, theories may incorporate both genuinely scientific and evaluative–interpretative components. The distinction between an inclusive interpretative framework, sometimes called an ideology, and the set of falsifiable hypotheses that combine to describe any theory of social interaction

		Free external trade (1)	Open entry domestic markets (2)	Rules vs. discretion (3)	Generality in taxation – spending vs. targeted or discriminatory programmes (4)
Promarket	Markets work (1)	I Support	II Support	III Mildly support	IV Mildly support
	Politics fails (2)	V Support	VI Support	VII Strongly support	VIII Strongly support
Antimarket	Markets fail (3)	IX Support	X Support with exceptions	XI Strongly oppose	XII Strongly oppose
	Markets disrupt social order (4)	XIII Oppose	XIV Oppose	XV Support	XVI Ambivalent

Figure 1.1   Promarket and antimarket perspectives on policy issues

may be difficult to determine. And the feedbacks on the interpretative framework exerted by the cumulative testing of empirical hypotheses need not be direct.

The influence of scientific error in evaluation cannot, however, be left out of account. The matrix is constructed on the presumption that agents for the separate perspectives interpret the reality they observe differently but do so in the context of theories that are themselves internally coherent in some fundamental sense. Such a presumption is vulnerable in all settings, and critically when evaluation by others than members of the scientific community must be considered. And who is to be eligible for membership in such a community? How are the charlatans to be identified before being thrown out of the temple? Considerations such as these become especially important in those situations where organizational decisions are made through procedures that are broadly 'democratic' in the sense that explicit or implicit choices must be made by nonscientific members of political constituencies. The consensus attained by scientists on particular constitutional issues may be effectively countered by interest-motivated arguments that explicitly exploit vulnerability to error in basic theories. Adequate consideration of the prospects for scientific error would require that we add yet another dimension to the matrix. By restricting discussion to the matrix in hand we are, necessarily, limiting debate to those among and between legitimate members of the imaginary scientific

establishment, who may or may not be effective in determining ultimate
constitutional outcomes.

MATRIX ENTRIES EXAMINED

It will now be useful to examine particular matrix entries more carefully.
Consider Column 1. Note that a general thrust towards free trade, towards
freedom of persons and firms within the polity to exchange with persons and
groups outside the polity limits, will likely receive general support from three
of the four agents that represent the separate perspectives. Only the communitarian
critic seems likely to oppose, and perhaps strongly so, extensions of the free trade
nexus across boundaries, that is, to take a protectionist position explicitly, on
the grounds that such extensions will disrupt patterns of behaviour, disturb
locational concentrations and reduce values of human capital that are embedded
in professional skills.

Much the same predictions may be made with reference to the entries in
Column 2. Only the entry in Cell X (Row 3, Column 2) might be seriously
challenged. Those agents whose overall perspective suggests the presence of
ubiquitous market failure, as generated by quasi-autonomous centres of private
power throughout the market nexus, should lend support to policies aimed at
opening entry into all markets. Such policies can only operate to reduce
concentrations of market power, an objective that is shared with promarket
advocates. But these market-failure critics will not support the opening of
internal markets if existing or status quo barriers are publicly initiated and
enforced.

The entries in Columns 3 and 4 are noteworthy for the categorical differences
between the predicted reactions of agents representing the perspectives that define
Row 2 and Row 3 and, further, by the prospect that communitarian critics of
market order may join forces with market advocates in support of rules that limit
political discretion. The public choice perspective (Row 2) places strong
positive evaluation on rules because of the prediction that these rules, if
effectively constitutionalized and enforced, place limits on the damage-causing
potential of majoritarian politics, including both minority exploitation and
cyclical instability. By contrast, precisely because rules do, in fact, limit the range
and scope of political action, those whose market-failure diagnoses suggest the
need for continuous hands-on intervention in economic processes through
monetary, fiscal and regulatory instruments (micromanagement and fine tuning)
must strongly oppose any such constraints. The communitarian, even as the
market is severely criticized as a disruptive allocative process, may tend to support
monetary-fiscal regulatory rules because these rules, in themselves, embody quasi-
permanence with some predictability–stability.

The entries in Column 4 are, in many respects, similar to those in Column 3. Policy thrusts that invoke the generality norm tend, in themselves, to constrain discretionary political authority. In this respect a generality principle is akin to a rule. Piecemeal interference with the functioning of markets, through targeted tax, spending and regulatory schemes are restricted when any generality requirement is in place. For the market-failure perspective, a generality principle will act to prevent hands-on particularized direction and guidance, through collective institutions, which are considered essential to make decentralized organization tolerable.

Note that, in both Columns 3 and 4, the 'markets work' perspective (Row 1) is listed as 'mildly supportive'. Both monetary-fiscal rules and a generality requirement may be evaluated as efficiency enhancing. Especially in its extreme versions, however, this perspective embodies the prediction that markets will act to circumvent almost any efficiency-restricting institution. The communitarian perspective in Column 4 is marked as 'ambivalent', suggesting possible opposition to generality principles in application to targeted programmes aimed at sustaining cultural values (for example antipornography laws, public funding of symphony orchestras and so on) but, by contrast, suggesting support for the generality norm in so far as its effect is to increase overall predictability in patterns of collective action.

POLICY PERSPECTIVES AND THE PROPOSITIONS OF ECONOMIC SCIENCE

I suggested earlier that the perspectives described embody scientific theories concerning the workings of markets and politics. This claim may seem to run counter to everyday opinion to the effect that there are unique truths in science and that competent scientists will come to agreement on basic propositions about the reality that they observe. Inference from such opinion would be that there should exist, at most, a single perspective that could claim to be scientifically grounded. The observed fact that professional social scientists seem to take categorically distinct perspectives on the same observed social reality may seem to suggest the overt intrusion of values – some failure to adhere to the fact–value boundary that allegedly separates science from nonscience.

Such an inference is only partially legitimate and the necessary inclusion of evaluative interpretation into the formation of the separate perspectives on market-political efficiency need not, itself, imply an absence of genuinely scientific propositions that may be present in the positions taken by all agents. The basic propositions of economic science (see Buchanan 1997) can be agreed upon by all agents who represent the separate perspectives.

Consider a familiar policy-relevant example. A major retail chain (for example, Wal-Mart) announces plans to open an outlet in a small community. The economies of scale will allow for lower product prices, yielding net benefits to consumers. At the same time, profit margins for existing small independent retailers will be squeezed, perhaps to the extent that several such firms will be forced into liquidation. These propositions, generated by elementary economics, may be uniformly accepted in all of the perspectives. But the policy stance taken differs as between the promarket and antimarket positions. Should the prospective entry of the outlet be politically thwarted? The differences may stem, in part, from divergent predictions concerning sequences of events after the prospective entry. The 'markets work' perspective may incorporate the proposition that residual contestability will ensure against undue exploitation, whereas the 'markets fail' perspective may reckon that threat of potential re-entry is insufficient protection. In a sense, these differences are scientific, but they cannot be reconciled, either by resort to empirical falsifiability tests or by logical chains of causation.

Agents of both the 'politics fail' perspective (Row 2) and the 'markets disrupt order' perspective (Row 4) approach the policy issue quite differently from the other two perspectives noted. The 'politics fail' vantage point concentrates attention on the inefficacy of any political institution in translating public preferences into collective action. Whose interests are most likely to be served by political authority, whose interests should be served, and how is any genuine 'public interest' to be discovered? Scepticism about politics tends to call any interventionism into question.

The communitarian perspective, by comparison, locates its evaluative judgement at a much more basic level than any of the other three perspectives. There is no need for an agent representing this position to carry out the economic conjectures that suggests either market success or failure. And there need be little direct concern with the workings of politics, as such. The communitarian-paternalist rejects any and all proposed changes from an institutionalized status quo, quite independently of propositions of economic science, which remain irrelevant, even if fully acknowledged in some cognitive sense.

CONSTITUTIONAL POLICY

The illustrative example introduced in the preceding section is misleading because it seems to direct attention to a particularized issue of policy: should political action be taken to prevent the large retail chain from opening the outlet in the community? As generally analysed and as depicted in the matrix construction, however, the separate perspectives identify predicted stances or positions on general constitutional issues rather than on detailed policy options.

By presumption, the ultimate choices are those among *policy regimes*, or policy constitutions, rather than those among particular options or alternatives within existing regimes. The issue addressed is how the separate agents might come down on a general policy regime of free trade versus protectionism (Column 1), and not at all on whether or not a specific quota or tariff should be raised or lowered on, say, beans from Mexico. Similarly, for Columns 2, 3 and 4, where the dimensions for choice are all constitutional in nature: open or closed entry in domestic markets, rules versus discretion, general versus discriminatory treatment.

Important implications of the classificatory schemata summarized in the matrix involve the role of particularized policy choices within the alternative perspectives in confrontation with the constitutional dimensions depicted. Note especially that, at least for the structural classifications listed, the promarket perspectives include *no* role for issue-by-issue policy choice (and, by inference, policy advice) on any dimension. (In a generalized regime of free trade, issues about particularized tariff treatment do not arise.) By comparison, the 'markets fail' perspective would require specific policy choices in the absence of rules. Policy choices arise within an overall regime only if there remains period-by-period, issue-by-issue policy discretion in the authority of political agents. Monetary policy, as such, becomes meaningful only in the absence of a monetary rule; discriminatory treatment of a class, group or category, either favourable or unfavourable, is possible only when a generality norm is not in effect (see Buchanan and Congleton 1998). The construction itself suggests that there may exist self-selection bias in the adoption of perspectives. Persons who imagine themselves in roles of policy makers, or advisers to policy makers, will be attracted to those perspectives that allow those roles to remain active. In other words, 'natural policy works' may place themselves in the socialist camp, not so much because of some abiding faith in collectivized nostrums but simply because they want to exert 'hands on' controls over activity, either directly or vicariously. Natural bureaucrats need bureaux to control. Where would a tariff commission be without tariffs?

Much the same incentive bias may be extended to the motivations of persons who seek political office as elected representatives. Those who seek, constitutionally, to restrict the range and scope of political authority are unlikely to covet political office, as such. Such considerations as these suggest that the perspective depicted in Row 3 in Figure 1.1, referenced earlier as 'residual socialist', may be stronger than its underlying ideational base because of the self-selection bias. Those who identify with this perspective include both (i) those whose interpretative theories suggest that politicized direction of economic activity is relatively superior and (ii) those whose interests prompt them to seek roles that allow participation in political authority. Such a juxtaposition of theories and interests does not occur elsewhere in the intersection of perspectives and constitutional choices depicted in the whole matrix. The general philosophical implication is that the observed politicization of economic activity is perhaps more extensive than the strength of the ideas upon which it is based.

PUBLIC CHOICE REVISITED

To this point, I have identified the 'politics fail' category as one of four perspectives on the relative efficacy of market-like and politics-like institutions for organizing economic activity. In this section, I propose to concentrate attention on this perspective, both because it is highlighted in my title and because it is the perspective that best reflects my own location in the matrix. As I noted earlier, there are three distinct strands in the inclusive umbrella argument summarized under the 'politics fail' rubric.

There is, first, the Hayekian (Austrian) emphasis on the severe epistemological limits of any efforts to impose collective controls over markets. There is, second, the incentive incompatibility that must be present whenever political agents are designated to act as choosers for others. And, finally, there is the difficulty in any aggregation of separate individual preferences over collective alternatives. 'Politics fail', then, due to informational, incentive and aggregation problems.

By contrast, at least at an elementary level of inquiry, 'markets work' because (i) participants can utilize localized information, (ii) those who choose suffer the consequences of choices and (iii) outcomes emerge from interactions among separate choosers, thereby removing any necessity of preference aggregation.

Note that the agent who reflects the 'politics fail' perspective need not advance any claim to the effect that markets work perfectly or even work closely in accordance with any idealized model. The market, as actually observed, may remain imperfect, and – indeed – the 'markets fail' perspective may become quite persuasive. And, at some point, the elementary three-point comparison sketched out above may be swamped by accumulating evidence of market failures. A combination of the 'politics fail' and 'markets fail' perspectives is not at all inconsistent, and indeed such a combination is almost necessary if failure is, in each case, measured against some idealized standards for performance. In this situation, the constitutional regime choice becomes strictly pragmatic and involves some ordering of imperfectly working alternatives.

Considerable progress in the ongoing dialogue–discussion may be made if the insights of theoretical welfare economics, which identifies market failures, and public choice theory, which identifies political failures, are integrated into a genuinely constitutionalist approach that transcends the overly simplified classificatory scheme of the matrix illustration. Markets may, indeed, 'fail' in any meaningful normative sense until and unless their operations are confined within rules that must, themselves, be politically originated and enforced.

Markets work only within the parameters of an effective legal order, which includes protection of person, property and enforcement of contracts, and which may also include rules that prohibit voluntary agreements made in restraint of trade. Similarly, the failures of politics can be substantially mitigated by the presence of enforceable constitutional limits. Differential political exploitation can be prevented and political instability reduced by appropriately drawn constitutional boundaries on collective action.

I do not suggest that a constitutionalist approach can, finally, accomplish complete reconciliation between the 'markets fail' and the 'politics fail' perspectives. None the less, a *modus vivendi*, of sorts, may be reached which brings the three top rows of the matrix into meaningful dialogue, which might, hopefully, involve direct or indirect participation by a relatively large constituency. Such a constitutional approach may do little to modify the stand of the communitarian who finds both markets and democratic politics to be morally unacceptable. Even for the agent of such a perspective, however, a constitutional emphasis may prompt some effort at articulation concerning just how much liberty citizens are to be allowed. And, who knows, a properly designed framework of rules that restricts both market and political excesses, may dampen many of the overtly meddlesome communitarian urges.

NOTE

1. My professor, Frank Knight, at the University of Chicago in the late 1940s, was fond of saying that he could never distinguish among the market's critics between those whose objections stem from the market's failure to work as it should and those whose objections stem from the market's successes in doing what it is supposed to do.

REFERENCES

Arrow, K. (1951), *Social Choice and Industrial Value*, New York: Wiley.
Bhagwati, J. (1997), 'What's wrong with the visible hand?', *Times Literary Supplement*, 21 November.
Buchanan, J.M. (1997), 'There is a science of economics', in J.M. Buchanan, *Post-Socialist Political Economy – Selected Essays*, Cheltenham, UK and Lyme, US: Edward Elgar, pp. 9–19.
Buchanan, J.M. and R.D. Congleton (1998), *Politics by Principle, Not Interest: Toward Nondiscriminatory Democracy*, Cambridge: Cambridge University Press.
Coase, R.H. (1960), 'The problem of social cost', *Journal of Law and Economics*, **3**, pp. 1–44.
Kuttner, R. (1997), *Everything for Sale*, New York: Knopf.
Schumpeter, J.A. (1949), *Theory of Economic Development*, Cambridge, MA: Harvard University Press.
Vanberg, V. and J.M. Buchanan (1989), 'Interests and theories in constitutional choice', *Journal of Theoretical Politics*, **1** (1), pp. 49–62.

2. On the political economy of economic policy advice

Gebhard Kirchgässner[*]

INTRODUCTION

Usually, economic theorizing employs the economic model of behaviour, 'homo economicus', assuming that individuals (economic agents) are self-interested rationally acting utility maximizers.[1] This is first of all assumed to hold for all individuals acting in markets. On the contrary, when analysing behaviour in nonmarket decision situations, traditional economic theory used other assumptions, such as benevolent or altruistic behaviour. This held, for example, for the traditional economic analysis of the family. During recent decades, however, economic theory became imperialistic, as more and more areas of human behaviour were analysed using the economic model.[2] Rational, self-interested behaviour is not only assumed in 'the economic analysis of law', on behalf of agents making contracts, but also in 'the economics of crime and punishment', on behalf of criminals, be they thieves or murderers.[3] 'The economics of the family', going back mainly to Becker (1981), has shown that also within the family a considerable amount of observable behaviour can be explained as exchange relations and, therefore, can be traced back to individual utility-maximizing behaviour. Even the arts have been analysed using the economic model of behaviour, an area, which according to their self-image, is far from being ruled by economic considerations.[4]

With respect to politicians, traditional economic theory assumed that they behave like benevolent dictators whose only intention is to maximize social welfare.[5] Their main task was considered to be the detection of market failure and to eliminate it using policy measures. Thus, the problem of policy advice was mainly reduced to helping politicians to perform this job well. The main question was how the necessary information could be delivered to the politicians to enable them to improve social welfare. 'Public choice' or 'the new political economy' has broken radically with this point of view. First of all, Arrow

* I thank Lars P. Feld, Ernst Mohr (both University of St. Gallen) and Nils Karlson (City University of Stockholm) for helpful comments.

(1951) has shown that it is highly problematic to talk about something like 'social welfare' with respect to a democratic system. For a democracy, the social welfare function which (implicitly or explicitly) is assumed to exist whenever the term is used in discussions about public policy, does not exist in general. Moreover, following Schumpeter (1942), Downs (1957) and Buchanan and Tullock (1962), public choice has reinvented the notion that there is not only market failure but also government failure. The latter results not so much from informational problems but mainly from the fact that politicians – like all other individuals – mainly strive for their own utility and much less for social welfare, whatever this might be. Thus, public choice considers politicians like all other individuals as self-interested, rationally acting utility maximizers.

Taking this into consideration, the task of economic policy advice becomes much more difficult. To transmit information to the politicians on what is to be done in a specific situation to reach a certain objective is not the only problem the policy adviser has to solve. In addition, the information has to be presented in such a way as to create incentives for the politicians to actually use this information. Thus, the process of transforming scientific advice into economic policy has to be taken into consideration as well.[6]

Despite the fact that (not only, but also public choice) economists are rather critical of others, especially of political authorities, they are – probably like all other people – rather uncritical of themselves. They not only often believe that they have lots of information, much more than they actually do, but they also consider themselves as being objective and standing above the daily political discussions and political ideologies. The latter they derive from their authority as scientific economists.[7] However, economists are self-interested, rationally acting individuals in the same way as all other human beings. This also holds when they give policy advice. The money they earn if they produce reports, used by their clients to strive for their own objectives, is not necessarily a sign of corruption. However, it can hardly be denied that scientists are often paid for producing exactly the statements their clients want to hear, and that they know about this and put up with it.[8] It does not help to argue – often mainly for the salving of their own conscience – that this money is spent for a good purpose (according to their opinion). In addition, they often do not want to be reminded later of what they have written in earlier reports.

The general public has a more realistic picture of economists as policy advisers, than they have themselves. The same economic agents, who in modern economic theory are usually assumed to have rational expectations, which implies that their expectations are on average correct, accuse economists who are policy advisers of being biased and sometimes even of being corruptible. They certainly have a point, and are not totally wrong. Today it is possible to find, in support of nearly any political position, a professor of economics willing to write a scientific report. For example, with respect to an ecological tax reform in Switzerland we have the report produced by Prognos (1993) on behalf of the Swiss Federal Department of the Interior, which predicts large employment gains. Erdmann (1997) produced a report on behalf of the *Wirtschaftsförderung Schweiz* (Society for the Development of the Swiss Economy), an organization supporting the interests of Swiss employers. He cautions about possible large employment losses. Studies produced in a programme of the *Schweizerischer Nationalfonds* (Swiss National Science Foundation), come to the conclusion that small but positive employment gains are to be expected.[9] Another example is the discussion about the cantonal monopolies in housing insurance for fire and natural (elementary) damages. Such monopolies exist in 19 out of 26 Swiss cantons, whereas this market is left to private companies in the remaining seven cantons (as well as in the Principality of Liechtenstein). For several years, there has been an ongoing public debate on whether these monopolies should be privatized or not. On behalf of the cantonal monopolies, Ungern-Sternberg (1994) produced a report which showed that these monopolies provide their services at lower costs than the private companies do (and can do). The latter, however, asked Schips (1995) for a report and he claimed just the opposite.[10] In the meantime, several independent studies have been written, which show that in this debate Ungern-Sternberg is right and Schips is wrong.[11] Nevertheless, Schips (1997) still sticks to his earlier position.

When asked, economists who are engaged in political debates nearly always claim that their statements are purely scientific and that their clients did not influence their results at all. This may be true in many cases. However, it would be just the opposite of the usual economic procedure if we strongly believed in such affirmations. Economists usually take into account the behaviour of economic agents and not their verbal statements, and they try to draw conclusions about the preferences of the individuals from their *actual* behaviour.[12] The reason for this is that talk is in many cases cheap, but acting is costly. Thus, in general, individuals are more honest when acting than when talking. This holds for economists as for all other human beings. If we judge by behaviour and not by verbal statements the impression of bias can, however, not be put aside easily.

One might try to distinguish between two kinds of policy advice. The first kind is on behalf of (political) parties and interest groups or directly on behalf of the government. The second kind is done by 'independent' institutions, such as (scientific) institutes for economic policy research, the *Sachverständigenrat* (Council of Economic Experts) in the Federal Republic of Germany, the scientific councils of the different departments of the German government or several *Enquete-Kommissionen* (*Enquete*-Committees) of the German parliament or the *Kommission für Konjunkturfragen* (Committee for Business Cycle Questions) of the Swiss *Bundesrat* (Federal Government).

Despite the fact that this is only a (small) part of the policy advice activities of economists, the statements and reports of these institutions are often highly debated. In Germany (and elsewhere) it is possible to link formally independent economic research institutes to specific political positions. It was not by chance that the *Deutsches Institut für Wirtschaftsforschung (DIW)* (German Institute of Economic Research) in Berlin produced a report (DIW 1994) on the economic consequences of an ecological tax reform on behalf of Greenpeace, and not the *Institut für Weltwirtschaft* (Kiel Institute of World Economics). If this report had been produced by Kiel, the study would probably have predicted a reduction in employment as a consequence of such a reform. The *DIW*, however, predicts an increase of 800 000 jobs.[13] Moreover, the reports of the *Sachverständigenrat* are also sometimes contested. This is made clear not only by numerous deviating statements by the members nominated by the trade unions, but also by 'antireports' which are sometimes produced (privately) and, last but not least, by the scientific discussion about these reports.

A closure of this apparent discrepancy between the self-assessment of many economists who are in the business of policy advice and the assessment by the general public can only take place if we dissociate from the picture of the ideal scientist and apply the economic model of behaviour to ourselves as well. That is, we must assume that economists are self-interested rationally acting utility maximizers, too. Economic theory supposes that this is a useful assumption for analysing human behaviour. Thus, there is no reason to except economists from this assumption.[14] This implies not only that their information is limited as well, but also (and more importantly) that strong monetary incentives can cause economists to defend (nearly) any even arbitrary political position.

Taking this into account, does economic policy advice then make any sense at all? Or is everything lost in the battle of interest groups, as Krelle (1979) suspects? The fact that there is a demand in the political process for scientific advice does not necessarily imply that there is also a demand for something like 'scientific truth' or 'objective knowledge'. It cannot be ruled out that the only purpose of enrolling economists as policy advisers is to serve the political positions of various interest groups.

In this chapter an answer to these questions is attempted. First, we ask what is the role of the scientist in this process? This is done on the basis of a specific position of the philosophy of science, critical rationalism. In the following section it is asked why is it possible that different economists so often defend quite contrary positions with the claim of scientific truth? Finally, we discuss how it is possible that despite all these problems the process of policy advice may lead to something like 'objectivity' and why even economists who are not corruptible in most cases promote the objectives of their clients.

SOME REMARKS FROM THE PHILOSOPHY OF SCIENCE

Despite the fact that their reports are often accused of being biased the public prestige enjoyed by economists, as well as by other (social) scientists, is higher than that of ordinary people. Economists benefit from the reputation of others, especially natural scientists. These are seen to be (at least in comparison to others) objective and to feel an obligation to produce 'objective knowledge' more than others. That this reputation spills over to social scientists is a main reason for the demand for reports of (social) scientists from special interest groups trying to pursue their goals in the political process. If a certain position is presented by a scientist, there is usually a greater acceptance by the general public than if it is presented only by a special interest group. Behind this widely held opinion is the image of the ideal scientist who is striving only for truth. This ideal image, which has been brought to us (besides others) by Max Weber (1919), is hardly compatible with politically acting scientists. This does not imply that scientists are not allowed to make political statements, but when they act as citizens they should not enjoy special privileges from their status as scientists.

How is this picture compatible with scientists giving contradictory answers to specific factual questions? For example, the question of what political measures should be taken to reduce high unemployment in Germany is answered quite differently by the *Institut für Weltwirtschaft* in Kiel and by the *DIW* in Berlin. Because of the complexity of this problem and the theories we have to apply if we want to answer this question, obtaining different answers might be understandable. Quite generally, univocal statements seem to be more difficult to obtain in social than in natural sciences. This excuse is, however, not valid if two professors of economics make quite different statements with respect to the question whether the cantonal monopolies or the private insurance companies in Switzerland had lower rates for fire and natural damages insurance. It should be possible to give a univocal answer to such a factual question.

The differentiation between facts and standards, which lies behind this argumentation, and the request for *Wertfreiheit* (freedom from value judgements) of the (social) sciences, which is based on this differentiation, are today largely undisputed in economics as well as in large areas of the philosophy of science. Thus, even if the reality is different, striving for objectivity might nevertheless be seen as a (moral) claim on the individual scientist. Max Weber (1919) at least suggests this. However, it is always possible to make nearly arbitrary moral claims on individuals or groups. What is relevant is the foundation of such claims; but (in a liberal society) everybody can decide for him- or herself whether he or she intends to follow such a claim.

One might argue that this is not a problem of individual attitudes of scientists but that this is a 'systemic request': objectivity of individual scientists might be

seen as a necessary condition for scientific progress. However, Karl R. Popper
has a quite different opinion:

> It is a mistake to assume that the objectivity of a science depends on the objectivity
> of the scientist. And it is a mistake to believe that the attitude of the natural scientist
> is more objective than that of the social scientist. . . . [T]he objectivity of science is
> not a matter of the individual scientists but rather the social result of their mutual
> criticisms, of the friendly–hostile division of labour among scientists, of their co-
> operation and also of their competition. (Popper 1962, p. 95)

Does this thesis not contradict, however, the position of Albert (1956, 1963),
who claims that *Wertfreiheit* of the sciences is a 'methodological principle'? Is
it not necessary that scientists strive for objectivity at least in their internal
scientific discourse, even if they attempt to influence political decisions (for
example by producing scientific reports) according to their individual preferences?

To get a satisfactory answer to this question, it is necessary to take into account,
as Popper emphasizes, that science is not the business of separate individuals
but that it is a social process, in which some scientists make conjectures and others
criticize these. Some of these conjectures will (at least temporarily) survive the
criticisms and be taken as approved hypotheses, while others will be refuted
because of logical deficiencies or incompatibility with the available empirical
data. It is not decisive whether the individual scientist is objective or not, but
that the scientific discourse takes place in a climate where criticisms are not only
allowed but even desired. Only criticisms of our conjectures enable us to detect
their weaknesses and to proceed to better conjectures. In this respect, there is
no difference between natural and social scientists. If we had to rely on the
objectivity of the individual scientist to make scientific progress, then the
possibilities for progress would be rather limited, because scientists – like all
other human beings – are generally biased in favour of their own ideas. Whether
scientific progress is possible in a society depends much more on the (rational)
organization of the scientific process than on the intentions of the individual
scientists. Nevertheless, in an open discourse, scientists have strong incentives
to strive for objectivity in order not to be refuted (too swiftly) by other
participants. This is the only way to acquire a reputation and – this way – also
to pursue other (individual) objectives.[15]

Thus, for the concept of critical rationalism it is less important that individual
researchers try to reject their own hypotheses and theories, than that the scientific
process is organized in a way that such rejections are possible and even probable.
Actually, no scientist wants his or her hypotheses and theories to be rejected.
Usually, scientists attempt just the opposite: they collect all the evidence in favour
of their theories, and sometimes they even suppress contradictory evidence. If
there is no other way left, they 'extend' their theories to make them compatible
with empirical evidence which previously seemed to be in contradiction.

Because scientists behave this way, it is important that the scientific discourse is organized so as to make rejections of hypotheses possible and to provide incentives that such discourses take place. For this we need 'theoretical pluralism'. In such a discourse, it might even be desirable that individual scientists defend their theories as vehemently as possible. This is how to discover the limits and strengths of the theories. Lakatos (1970) has pointed out the fact that it might be harmful for scientific progress if theories are drawn back 'too fast' whenever empirical evidence against them has been presented. The best conditions for scientific progress are given when both refutation and defence of theoretical propositions are possible.

Scientists also try to test their theories and hypotheses. Before they present a hypothesis to the scientific community, they usually try to minimize the probability that this hypothesis will be rejected by others. Thus, they themselves ask what possible objections could be raised against their work. They will, for example, make experiments, perform statistical analyses or collect additional data. Because they want to defend their ideas, they are forced to first perform hard tests in order not to be refuted (too easily). The motivation for this behaviour depends again, however, on the organization of the scientific process.

If in the internal scientific process objective results are obtained through discussion and mutual criticism, and evolve only to a much lesser extent out of the scientists' quest for truth, why should this be different when science becomes 'political', that is, in the realm of scientific policy advice? Scientists (largely) behave according to the economic model of behaviour just like everybody else; their scientific work is one (and often a very important) possibility of pursuing their personal interests. In this process, they make mistakes, try to manipulate results or at least to present their results in a way that is compatible with their personal interests. Limits to this behaviour arise predominantly from the public discussion, and only to a lesser extent from their own conscience. In most situations it is (at least implicitly) accepted that they primarily present evidence which is in favour of their own political intentions. But manipulations which are detected can strongly damage an economist's reputation. In the worst case (for themselves) they might even become unacceptable as an adviser for those interest groups which are politically close to them. Thus, quite independently of whether an intrinsic motivation is present, economists have a self-interest in maintaining the scientific standards of their profession when they act as policy advisers as well.

But even if economists keep up these standards, the examples given above indicate that it is possible to have totally different opinions with respect to economic policy questions. How can this be the case if economists have (at least in principle) a theoretical common ground? Economic theory does not seem to be as strong as we would like it to be. Thus, the question has to be addressed of how strong the propositions are which can be derived from economic theorizing.

ON THE POWER OF STATEMENTS OF ECONOMIC THEORY

Whenever economists give advice about how to solve actual economic problems, they typically give answers which imply changes in relative prices. To reduce unemployment trade unions must make moderate wage claims and taxes and charges on labour must be reduced in order to lower the price of and increase the demand for labour.[16] And to reduce air and water pollution, ecological taxes and/or tradable permits are the usual prescription in order to impose a positive price on environmental media.

There are two basic assumptions behind such proposals:

1. *Stability*: The economic system is stable in the following sense: small changes in policy instruments lead to only small changes in the economic objective variables.
2. *Substitution*: Increases (reductions) in the (relative) price of a good lead to reductions (increases) in the (relative) demand for this good and increases (reductions) in the demand for other goods: the good which is now (relatively) more expensive will be (partially) substituted by goods which are now (relatively) cheaper.

Whether the economic system is stable in this sense is quite independent of the question whether this system tends to reach full employment or not. Equilibria with (involuntary) unemployment can be stable in this sense as well. The assumption of stability stated above is much weaker, in that it only excludes chaotic behaviour of the economic system. If we had to take into account chaotic behaviour, economic policy would be a gamble: small changes in government expenditure or even an infinitesimally small change in a single tax rate could lead to a massive recession, but also to a strong economic upswing.[17]

The assumption of substitutability implies that the (aggregate) demand functions for individual goods have a negative slope: an increase (reduction) of the price leads to a reduction (increase) in the quantity demanded. This assumption is so fundamental for economic theorizing that Weizsäcker speaks of the 'confidence in the working of the substitution principle' as the basic common conviction of economists (Weizsäcker 1976, p. 69; own translation).

Is this basic common conviction covered by economic theory? This question might sound ridiculous. It should be possible to suppose that economists take into account the relevant results of economic theory when giving policy advice. Until about 25 years ago, it was possible to assume (with more or less bad conscience) that these assumptions were safe. Since then, however, it has been shown that they are not necessarily covered by economic theory. Thus, the question of whether it is possible to give economic policy advice based on economic theory is no longer a trivial one. Why this is the case is first explained in general and then illuminated with three examples.

Let us first ask whether aggregate demand functions have a negative slope. Somewhat more precisely, the question is whether we get aggregate demand functions for individual goods with a negative slope if all economic agents behave 'rationally' in the sense of the economic model of behaviour. A general answer to this question cannot be derived from partial analyses but, if the feedback of the actions of individual actors is taken into account, by the theory of general equilibrium. This was the question Sonnenschein (1972, 1973) addressed in the early seventies. He has shown that by employing the usual assumptions about individual preferences in an exchange economy, the demand function for an individual good can (locally) have any slope.[18] To exclude this possibility, rather restrictive assumptions about individual preferences are necessary. This also holds if one tries, as Hildenbrand (1983) did, to impose restrictions on the possible distribution of preferences (and initial endowments).

With respect to the assumption of stability it has been shown that such economies can have multiple equilibria. If such multiple equilibria exist they cannot be globally stable, and some equilibria are not even locally stable: small deviations from one equilibrium can lead to a totally different new equilibrium.[19] This implies, however, that the two basic assumptions about the structure of the economic system, which are typically employed whenever policy advice is given, are not covered by general equilibrium theory.

Thus, the attempt has failed to derive univocal results about the basic structure of exchange economies, which extend the existence and optimality conditions of equilibria, by reliance only on the general primitives of economic analysis. If one takes into account these 'nonresults', it is no surprise that it is possible to derive nearly any result by employing the corresponding assumptions. This is shown by three examples:

1. Since the seminal work of Pigou (1920) it is well known among economists that it is possible to internalize external effects using (Pigou-) taxes. Today, the most important and threatening external effects relate to our natural environment. As has been mentioned above, for a long time economists have been requesting the introduction of ecological taxes. This request is based on the idea that the imposition of a positive price for the private usage of nature would reduce pollution and, therefore, would improve the situation of the natural environment. However, Braulke and Endres (1985) have shown that this is not necessarily the case. The introduction of ecological taxes is logically consistent with an extension of pollution. Thus, the theoretical basis for the introduction of such taxes seems to vanish.

2. To preserve the stocks of nonrenewable natural resources, an increase in recycling activities is generally requested. Jäger (1976), however, has shown that because of declining prices, extended recycling might even lead to an increased exploitation of natural resources.
3. It is hardly disputed that high taxes provide incentives to evade taxes and to work in the shadow economy. The higher the marginal tax rate on legal income, the more it becomes profitable to withhold taxes from the fisc and to take the corresponding risk. Allingham and Sandmo (1972), however, have shown that under plausible assumptions about the risk aversion of individuals just the opposite can happen. Higher taxes imply a smaller disposable income of the taxpayers. Hence, if risk aversion increases, then with decreasing income people will be more hesitant to take the risk induced by tax evasion and by working in the shadow economy if tax rates are increasing. Thus, the income effect overcompensates the substitution effect: higher taxes lead to a decline of the shadow economy.

These examples show that despite the factual consensus between most economists, economic theory cannot provide a theoretical foundation for policy advice, at least not immediately.[20] Thus, economic theory seems to be at best of limited help for economic policy. This even holds for microeconomics, where there is a large consensus among economists: the validity of the dominant theory is hardly disputed. How much less help can we expect from macroeconomics, where the basic consensus, which lasted up to the beginning of the seventies, has long ago broken apart?[21]

But even if it is assumed that stability is given and the substitution principle holds, we are still far from an ideal situation. Many economic policy measures have income and substitution effects which go in opposite directions. The overall effect is theoretically ambiguous. This is the underlying problem in the above-mentioned example of the shadow economy. In such a situation, economists – following Weizsäcker (1976) – usually argue for the dominance of the substitution effect. There are, for example, two effects if we ask for the impact of wage increases on mass unemployment in Switzerland or Germany today. Following the OECD, one of the reasons for low employment is the weakness of domestic demand.[22] The income effect of a wage increase strengthens domestic demand, which leads – *ceteris paribus* – to an increase in employment. On the other hand, a wage increase raises labour costs, which leads to a (partial) substitution of labour by other production inputs. At the same time, the costs of domestic compared to foreign production increase, which also leads to a substitution process. These two processes cause a reduction in the demand for labour, and therefore also a reduction in employment. Thus, the overall effect of a wage increase on employment is theoretically ambiguous. If one believes in the disposable income argument of wages, usually employed by trade unions, then the income effect dominates, employment increases and unemployment is reduced. Most economists, however, believe (as the employer organizations do) that the substitution effect dominates: a wage increase raises – *ceteris paribus* – unemployment.

However, in many cases the argumentation of economists is not consistent. With respect to the employment effect of an ecological tax reform they often use a quite opposite argument. If such a reform reduces the tax burden on labour by increasing taxes on energy, the demand for labour increases because of the substitution effect and the demand for energy is reduced. Thus, employment increases. At the same time, however, the narrower tax base of energy compared to (labour) income leads to an increase in the excess burden which reduces real income. This reduces the demand for labour. If it is consistently argued that the substitution effect is dominant, then such a reform should lead to a reduction in unemployment. Actually, however, many economists exercise caution, claiming that the reform can lead to job losses.[23] Thus, they (implicitly or explicitly) assume that the income effect dominates. Despite the fact that it is almost exactly the same question as the one on how changes in the gross wage rate influence employment, the same economists argue in the first case for a dominant substitution effect and in the second case for a dominant income effect.[24] Because it is theoretically open which effect dominates and because it is difficult to present reliable empirical evidence with respect to these questions, such statements cannot easily be rejected as being wrong. Therefore, whenever the income and the substitution effects go in opposite directions, it is possible for different economists to make opposite statements without violating the rules of the scientific game.

ON THE PROCESS OF POLICY ADVICE

Thus, we are in a situation where we can find economists providing scientific support for nearly every political position. Apart from other factors, this is possible because economic theory is compatible with nearly all (factual) statements and because, what we did not discuss here, the corresponding empirical research is often difficult to perform and its results are open to, and also require, interpretations. Under these circumstances, can we expect that (not only ideology but also) information is transmitted in the process of economic policy advice? Or do we have to assume that (most) economists in this business are corruptible because they deliver the results demanded by their clients?

If information is (also) to be transmitted in the process of policy advice, it must be ensured that the discussion is public and that the respective material is publicly available. As to empirical questions, this includes the exact specification of the data employed as well as their sources.[25] Only under these circumstances are competing interest groups, as well as the general public, able to discuss different statements critically. This discussion is, however, necessary to enable participants in the political discourse to distinguish between factual statements and political (ideological) positions. Of course, both have their legitimate place in this discourse, but it should always be possible to differentiate between them, irrespective of how difficult this might seem to be in a concrete situation. In so far, the concept which assumes that the public discourse and not the individual motivation of scientists is crucial in order to get 'objective' information is fully based on the principle of *Wertfreiheit* as proposed by Max Weber, Hans Albert and others.

With respect to economic policy recommendations, it is safe to say that in most cases experts have a personal interest in reaching (almost) exactly those results they actually achieve, which implies that they are biased in favour of their clients. This contradicts the notion of the ideal scientist presented above, whose only objective is to find 'truth'. It is a fact, however, that clients (often very carefully) look for (potential) experts who can be expected to produce exactly the results desired by clients themselves. Because experts know these expectations, it can be assumed that the results sought by the customer are at least not completely contrary to the experts' own ideological views. In the end, they have to identify themselves with these positions if their report is published.

On the other hand, that experts come to different conclusions does not imply that the results are casual or arbitrary. Even if the statements of the experts are quite different, a critical discussion is still possible which uncovers mistakes and tricks of individual experts and, therefore, allows for a more objective evaluation of the situation from the outside. The main purpose of such a discussion is to show how the different arguments are related to specific interests, even if they are garnished with the rhetoric of social welfare. Such a clarifying discussion is certainly not for the benefit of all participants, but it can help other independent people or the political authorities to make 'reasonable' political decisions. This holds more so in a direct than in a (purely) representative democracy, because the public political discourse is of greater importance if people have (the possibility of) the final decision.[26]

Moreover, it can even be helpful for the political discourse and the following decision if the experts of both sides try to make convincing points. In the same way as it can be detrimental for scientific progress if a theory is withdrawn 'too fast' in a scientific discourse, it makes sense in a political discourse that both sides present all their arguments. Only then do voters (and their representatives in the parliament) really know about what they have to decide.

This might be taken for granted. But it can nevertheless be objected that in many cases scientists strive for truth, and that this is their only motivation. Moreover, economists as experts do not always write what their clients expect. This can be denied just as little as the observation that, besides truth, scientists often strive for quite other objectives and that their reports made on behalf of special interest groups usually reflect what those groups expect. What follows from this for the concept presented?

First, it has to be taken into account that the incentives of scientists depend on the environment in which they operate. Other conditions hold in the 'scientific game' than in the 'political' or the 'policy advice game'. Generally, the scientific game is more transparent and has a longer-run perspective. Thus, the striving for objectivity is stronger in (purely) scientific activities than in the policy advice game, but it can exist in the latter as well. Moreover, there are many arguments in the utility functions of economists; (monetary) income is a very important one, but, still, only one among many others.[27]

Reputation in the scientific community certainly plays an important role for scientists. They are usually not willing to risk this reputation because of negligible financial rewards. Thus, it would not be rational, even for self-interested scientists, to be corrupted by small amounts of money, and to produce results which can be rejected easily.[28] This holds the more, the easier information spills over from the political to the scientific area, that is the easier other scientific colleagues get knowledge of political advice statements which are scientifically not sound. Thus, striving for objectivity can be generated by self-interest, even if it might appear or be interpreted differently: as intrinsic motivation. On the other hand, among scientists, there is also genuinely non-self-interested (altruistic, intrinsically motivated) behaviour. In some situations such behaviour can even be very relevant for society.[29]

Nevertheless, in order to find answers to the question of how the process of policy advice has to be organized such that not only ideology but also information is transmitted, it makes sense to follow the concept of constitutional economics and assume self-interested behaviour of all participants. This holds even if the majority of scientists were purely intrinsically motivated, solely striving for objective knowledge.[30] In analogy to the constitutional considerations of Popper (1945, p. 121), the relevant question is this: how can we organize the institutions of scientific policy advice in a way that bad or incompetent experts can be prevented from doing too much damage? A somewhat nicer formulation is this: the rules of the policy advice game should be built in a way that even those scientific experts who are more interested in their own (monetary) income than in truth will produce objective knowledge. As has been shown above, a precondition for this is the open discussion of research methods and results.

With respect to the question of the objectivity of scientific reports it has additionally to be taken into account that scientific experts, who get their mandate from interest groups, are in many cases neither able nor willing to do anything else other than to support the political objectives of their clients. This holds even if they are in no way corruptible. First, a report not in support of the political objectives of the client will – with high probability – never be presented to the general public. This alone ensures that the published reports will (largely) support the objectives of the client. Second, an expert who presents results which contradict the objectives of his or her client might get no further mandate. Consequently, the selection of the experts by clients leads to a substantial convergence of interests of clients and experts. We observe a similar process in the market for scientific reports as, following Adam Smith ([1776] 1976), it has already been described by Alchian (1950) and Friedman (1953). First, the self-interest of the experts provides incentives for them to help their clients to reach their political objectives. Second, even if all experts only support those political objectives of which they are personally convinced and which they believe to be justified (in a moral way), the selection mechanism generates an assignment between clients and experts such that, finally, the political objectives of clients and experts largely correspond. In this game all experts may survive, but only under the protection of specific clients; 'objectivity' can be reached only approximately, and only through public discourse.

On the other hand, whenever they are engaged as experts, most scientists have not only scientific but also political objectives. Thus, they have strong private incentives to look for clients whose political objectives correspond to their own. As citizens they have the right – as all others do, too – to pursue their own objectives in the political process. They will only be successful if they accept themselves as active players in the democratic process and if their political objectives are not too far away from those of their clients.[31] Therefore, there is a convergence of interests between clients and experts in the process of scientific policy advice. It originates not only from the demand but also from the supply side, and the experts do not have to be corruptible for such a convergence to occur.

CONCLUDING REMARKS

The fact that economists as policy advisers usually produce those results which are expected from their clients does, therefore, not necessarily show that economic experts (or at least a large number of them) are corruptible. They might be no more (but also no less) corruptible than other citizens. This fact is also compatible with their striving for objective knowledge, as long as it is acknowledged that economists (like all other citizens) have political objectives, and that it is legitimate that they also attempt to pursue these political objectives with their scientific work. Thus, it has always to be taken into account that their (scientific) statements are biased, because, among other things, they have only a selective perception of reality, and this selection is influenced by their political objectives. From this it follows that objectivity can hardly be expected to be generated by single (isolated) individuals. It has to be produced in an open political discourse. And it may evolve out of this discourse because of the countervailing interests which are represented in this discourse. What holds for the scientific process holds for the political process *a fortiori*. The better and more open the discourse is organized, the larger is the probability that it helps to find some truth and that we get 'better' political decisions. And because this process is much more general and open in direct than in (purely) representative democracies, we can assume that, on average, the decisions are better in a direct than in a representative democracy. Truth and objectivity do not necessarily disappear in the struggle of interests in the process of economic policy advice, but they are also not as easily reached as the traditional theory of economic policy advice believed and as many economists engaged in this process want us to continue to believe today.

NOTES

1. For a presentation of this model, see Kirchgässner (1991).
2. See, for example, Stigler (1984), Hirshleifer (1985) or Kirchgässner (1988).
3. On the 'economic analysis of law' see, for example, Posner (1972); on the 'economics of crime and punishment', see Becker (1968) and Ehrlich (1975).
4. See Frey and Pommerehne (1989).
5. Today, this still holds for a large part of modern public finance such as, for example, the theory of optimal taxation. See for this the dispute between Richter and Wiegard (1993, 1994), on the one side, and Blankart (1994), on the other.
6. See, for example, Meier and Mettler (1986).
7. See, for example, Hesse (1994), p. 18.
8. It often does not need very much to cause economists (and other scientists) to act in the interest even of organizations which have nothing to do with economics as a science at all. For example, conferences organized as well as books edited by and with contributions of prominent economists have been financed by the 'Professors' World Peace Association', an organization, financed by the Mun-Church, which has as its main purpose the improvement of the public image of this organization (see also Blankart 1987, p. 669).
9. See the survey in Kirchgässner (1997).
10. See also the reply by Ungern-Sternberg (1995).
11. See Kirchgässner (1996), Felder (1996), Felder and Brinkmann (1996), Proeller (1996) as well as the statement of the Swiss official *Preisüberwacher* ('government price surveillance') in his report of 19 July 1996. Finally, even the Swiss Supreme Court in Lausanne decided on this matter on 27 February 1998, and it came to the conclusion that the cantonal monopolies contribute to social welfare because they have – *ceteris paribus* – lower rates for their services than the private insurance companies (Decision 2P.32/1997).
12. The basic paper (with respect to the theory of consumer behaviour) is Samuelson (1948).
13. See Bonus (1981) for a description of the positions of these two institutes, which he links with 'supply theory' and 'demand theory' and the perspectives and experience associated with these.
14. There is also empirical evidence that economists behave more in accordance with this model than does the average individual, especially that economists are more self-interested and less altruistic than others. Experiments with the ultimatum game show, for example, that students of economics show much stronger freerider behaviour (as predicted by economic theory) than other students. See for this Carter and Irons (1991).
15. This is in analogy to the role of the (self-interested) entrepreneur in the market and his or her contribution to the social result. As Adam Smith has already written: 'It is not from the

benevolence of the butcher, the brewer, or the baker, that we expect our dinner, but from their regard to their own interest. We address ourselves, not to their humanity but to their self-love, and never talk to them of our own necessities but of their advantages' (Smith [1776] 1976, p. 27).

16. See, for example, Sachverständigenrat (1996, pp. 180 ff.).
17. For the relevance of chaos theory for economics see, for example, Baumol and Benhabib (1989).
18. See Ingrao and Israel (1987, pp. 315 ff.) as well as Balasko (1988, pp. 120 ff.). Further work in this area and generalizations of the results of Sonnenschein can be found in Mantel (1974), Debreu (1974) and Mas-Colell (1977).
19. See Ingrao and Israel (1987, pp. 329 ff.).
20. This is claimed, for example, by Friedman (1985, p. 3).
21. The situation of macroeconomics is described, for example, by Mankiw (1990).
22. See, for example, OECD (1997, pp. 20 ff.).
23. See, for example, Richter (1997, p. 124): 'A tax on productively used energy endangers jobs' (own translation).
24. The main difference is that in the second case the price of a second production factor increases, which strengthens the substitution effect even further.
25. The specific problem that data from surveys are not reproducible (for technical or financial reasons) is not discussed here.
26. See Frey and Kirchgässner (1993).
27. Nevertheless, how important the income motive can be, even if it tends to destroy reputation, is shown, for example, by the 'self-service' of the editors of the *Journal of Industrial Economics* (see Ungern-Sternberg 1995a).
28. On the other hand, it is really astonishing how little money is often necessary to induce economists (but also other scientists and politicians) to risk their reputation (and their future career).
29. See Kirchgässner (1996a).
30. On the position of constitutional economics see, for example, Buchanan (1987, 1987a).
31. See also Meier and Mettler (1988, pp. 141 ff.).

REFERENCES

Albert, H. (1956), 'Werturteil und Wertbasis: Das Werturteilsproblem im Lichte der logischen Analyse', *Zeitschrift für die gesamte Staatswissenschaft*, **112**, pp. 410–39.
Albert, H. (1963), 'Wertfreiheit als methodisches Prinzip', in E.v. Beckerath, H. Giersch and H. Lampert (eds), *Probleme der normativen Ökonomik und der wirtschaftspolitischen Beratung*, Berlin: Duncker & Humblot, pp. 32–63.
Alchian, A.A. (1950), 'Uncertainty, evolution, and economic theory', *Journal of Political Economy*, **58**, pp. 211–21.
Allingham, M.G. and A. Sandmo (1972), 'Income tax evasion: a theoretical analysis', *Journal of Public Economics*, **1** (November), pp. 323–38.
Arrow, K.J. (1951), *Social Choice and Individual Values*, New York: Wiley.
Balasko, Y. (1988), *Foundations of the Theory of General Equilibrium*, Orlando: Academic Press.
Baumol, W.J. and J. Benhabib (1989), 'Chaos: significance, mechanism, and economic applications', *Journal of Economic Perspectives*, **3** (1), pp. 77–105.
Becker, G.S. (1968), 'Crime and punishment: an economic approach', *Journal of Political Economy*, 76, pp. 169–217.
Becker, G.S. (1981), *A Treatise on the Family*, Cambridge, MA: Harvard University Press.
Blankart, Ch.B. (1987), 'Review of: G. Radnitzky and P. Bernholz (eds), *Economic Imperialism: The Economic Method Applied Outside the Field of Economics*, (New

York: Paragon House, 1987)', *Journal of Institutional and Theoretical Economics*, **143** (4), pp. 669–73.

Blankart, Ch.B. (1994), '"Neue Finanzwissenschaft": Eine alternative Sicht', *Zeitschrift für Wirtschafts- und Sozialwissenschaften*, **114** (2), pp. 245–54.

Bonus, H. (1981), 'Das wissenschaftliche Gutachten in der Politik: Information, öffentliche Meinung, Verantwortung', in M. Timmermann (ed.), *Nationalökonomie morgen: Ansätze zur Weiterentwicklung wirtschaftswissenschaftlicher Forschung*, Stuttgart: Kohlhammer, pp. 263–98.

Braulke, M. and A. Endres (1985), 'On the economics of effluent charges', *Canadian Journal of Economics*, **18** (4), pp. 891–7.

Buchanan, J.M. (1987), 'The constitution of economic policy', *American Economic Review*, **77** (3), pp. 243–59.

Buchanan, J.M. (1987a), 'Constitutional economics', in J. Eatwell, M. Milgate and P. Newman (eds), *The New Palgrave, A Dictionary of Economics*, Vol. 1, London: Macmillan, pp. 585–8.

Buchanan, J.M. and G. Tullock (1962), *The Calculus of Consent: Logical Foundations of Constitutional Democracy*, Ann Arbor: University of Michigan Press.

Carter, J.R. and M.D. Irons (1991), 'Are economists different, and if so, why?', *Journal of Economic Perspectives*, **5** (2), pp. 171–7.

Debreu, G. (1974), 'Excess demand functions', *Journal of Mathematical Economics*, **1**, pp. 15–21.

Deutsches Institut für Wirtschaftsforschung (DIW) (ed.) (1994), *Wirtschaftliche Auswirkungen einer ökologischen Steuerreform*, Berlin: Duncker & Humblot.

Downs, A. (1957), *An Economic Theory of Democracy*, New York: Harper & Row.

Ehrlich, I. (1975), 'The deterrent effect of capital punishment: a question of life and death', *American Economic Review*, **65** (3), pp. 397–417.

Erdmann, G. (1997), *Volkswirtschaftliche Auswirkungen von Lenkungsabgaben auf Energieträger in der Schweiz*, Bern: Haupt.

Felder, St. (1996), 'Fire insurance in Germany: a comparison of price-performance between state monopolies and competitive regions', *European Economic Review*, **40** (3/5), pp. 1133–41.

Felder, St. and H. Brinkmann (1996), 'Deregulierung der Gebäudeversicherung im Europäischen Binnenmarkt: Lehren für die Schweiz?', *Schweizerische Zeitschrift für Volkswirtschaft und Statistik*, **132** (3), pp. 457–72.

Frey, B.S. and G. Kirchgässner (1993), 'Diskursethik, Politische Ökonomie und Volksabstimmungen', *Analyse und Kritik*, **15**, pp. 129–49.

Frey, B.S. and W.W. Pommerehne (1989), *Muses and Markets: Explorations in the Economics of the Arts*, Oxford: Basil Blackwell.

Friedman, L.S. (1985), *Microeconomic Policy Analysis*, New York: McGraw-Hill.

Friedman, M. (1953), 'The methodology of positive economics', in M. Friedman, *Essays in Positive Economics*, Chicago: University of Chicago Press, pp. 3–43.

Hesse, H. (1994), 'Als Wissenschaftler in der Politik?', in Universität Hannover (ed.), *Vorträge im Fachbereich Wirtschaftswissenschaften*, Vol. 20, Hannover, pp. 17–37.

Hildenbrand, W. (1983), 'On the Law of Demand', *Econometrica*, **51** (4), pp. 997–1019.

Hirshleifer, J. (1985), 'The expanding domain of economics', *American Economic Review*, **75** (6), pp. 53–68.

Ingrao, B. and G. Israel (1987), *La mano invisibile*, Rome: Gius, Laterza et Figli Spa, (translated in English as: *The Invisible Hand, Economic Equilibrium in the History of Science*, London: MIT Press, 1990).

Jäger, K. (1976), 'Eine ökonomische Theorie des Recycling', *Kyklos*, **29** (4), pp. 660–77.

Kirchgässner, G. (1988), 'Ökonomie als imperial(istische) Wissenschaft', *Jahrbuch für Neue Politische Ökonomie*, 7, pp. 128–45.

Kirchgässner, G. (1991), *Homo Oeconomicus: Das ökonomische Modell individuellen Verhaltens und seine Anwendung in den Wirtschafts- und Sozialwissenschaften*, Tübingen: J.C.B. Mohr (Siebeck).

Kirchgässner, G. (1996), 'Ideologie und Information in der Politikberatung: Einige Bemerkungen und ein Fallbeispiel', *Hamburger Jahrbuch für Wirtschafts- und Gesellschaftspolitik*, 41, pp. 9–41.

Kirchgässner, G. (1996a), 'On minimal morals', University of St. Gallen: mimeo, October.

Kirchgässner, G. (1997), 'Environmental policy in Switzerland: methods, results, problems, and challenges', in Ph. Bacchetta and W. Wasserfallen (eds), *Economic Policy in Switzerland*, London: Macmillan, pp. 184–212.

Krelle, W. (1979), 'Schlußwort', in C.C. von Weizsäcker (ed.), *Staat und Wirtschaft*, Berlin: Duncker & Humblot, pp. 851–5.

Lakatos, I. (1970), 'Falsification and the methodology of scientific research programmes', in I. Lakatos and A. Musgrave (eds), *Criticism and the Growth of Knowledge*, Cambridge: Cambridge University Press, pp. 91–195.

Mankiw, N.G. (1990), 'A quick refresher course in macroeconomics', *Journal of Economic Literature*, 28 (4), pp. 1645–60.

Mantel, R.R. (1974), 'On the characterization of aggregate excess demands', *Journal of Economic Theory*, 7 (3), pp. 348–53.

Mas-Colell, A. (1977), 'On the equilibrium price set of an exchange economy', *Journal of Mathematical Economics*, 4, pp. 117–26.

Meier, A. and D. Mettler (1986), 'Einfluss und Macht in der Wirtschaftspolitik', *Schweizerische Zeitschrift für Volkswirtschaft und Statistik*, 122 (1), pp. 37–59.

Meier, A. and D. Mettler (1988), *Wirtschaftspolitik: Kampf um Einfluß und Sinngebung*, Bern and Stuttgart: Haupt.

Organization for Economic Cooperation and Development (OECD) (1997), *Études économiques de l'OCDE 1996–1997: Suisse*, Paris: OECD.

Pigou, A.C. (1920), *The Economics of Welfare*, London: Macmillan.

Popper, K.R. (1945), *The Open Society and its Enemies, Vol I: The Spell of Plato*, London: Routledge & Sons.

Popper, K.R. (1962), 'Die Logik der Sozialwissenschaften', *Kölner Zeitschrift für Soziologie und Sozialpsychologie*, 14, pp. 233–48; quoted from the English translation 'The logic of the social sciences', in Th.W. Adorno et al. (1976), *The Positivist Dispute in German Sociology*, New York: Harper Torchbooks, pp. 87–104.

Posner, R.A. (1972), *Economic Analysis of Law*, Boston: Little Brown & Company.

Proeller, I. (1996), *Kriterien für die Beurteilung eines Privatisierungsentscheids am Beispiel der Gebäudeversicherungsanstalt*, Diploma thesis, University of St. Gallen.

Prognos (1993), *Bewertung der wirtschaftlichen Auswirkungen einer CO_2-Abgabe*, report for the Swiss Department of the Interior, Basel.

Richter, W.F. (1997), 'Über die Ineffizienz einer nationalen Energiesteuer', *WiSt* (26), pp. 124–30.

Richter, W.F. and W. Wiegard (1993), 'Zwanzig Jahre "Neue Finanzwissenschaft", Teil II: Steuern und Staatsverschuldung', *Zeitschrift für Wirtschafts- und Sozialwissenschaften*, 113, pp. 337–400.

Richter, W.F. and W. Wiegard (1994), 'Erwiderung zu den Kommentaren von Charles B. Blankart und Fritz Söllner', *Zeitschrift für Wirtschafts- und Sozialwissenschaften*, 114, pp. 255–66.

Sachverständigenrat (1996), *Jahresgutachten 1996/97*, Bundestagsdrucksache No. 13/6200, 18 November.
Samuelson, P.A. (1948), 'Consumption theory in terms of revealed preference', *Economica*, **15**, pp. 243–53.
Schips, B. (1995), 'Ökonomische Argumente für wirksamen Wettbewerb auch im Versicherungszweig "Gebäudefeuer- und Gebäudeelementarschäden"', University of St. Gallen: mimeo, January.
Schips, B. (1997), 'Anmerkungen zur Kontroverse über die Vorteilhaftigkeit der kantonalen Monopole in der Gebäudeversicherung im Vergleich mit den zu erwartenden Ergebnissen bei Wettbewerb in diesem Versicherungszweig', ETH Zürich: mimeo.
Schumpeter, J.A. (1942), *Capitalism, Socialism and Democracy*, New York: Harper & Brothers.
Smith, A. (1776), *An Inquiry into the Nature and Causes of the Wealth of Nations*, reprinted in W.B. Todd (ed.) (1976), *The Glasgow Edition of The Works and Correspondence of Adam Smith*, Oxford: Clarendon Press.
Sonnenschein, H. (1972), 'Market excess demand functions', *Econometrica*, **40** (3), pp. 549–63.
Sonnenschein, H. (1973), 'Do Walras identity and continuity characterize the class of community excess demand functions?', *Journal of Economic Theory*, **6** (4), pp. 345–54.
Stigler, G. (1984), 'Economics, the imperial science?', *Scandinavian Journal of Economics*, **86** (3), pp. 301–13.
Ungern-Sternberg, Th. v. (1994), 'Die kantonalen Gebäudeversicherungen: Eine ökonomische Analyse', *Cahiers de recherches économiques No. 9405*, Université de Lausanne: Département d'économétrie et économie politique.
Ungern-Sternberg, Th. v. (1995), 'Kritische Überlegungen zu dem Gutachten von Professor Schips über die kantonalen Gebäudeversicherungsmonopole', *Cahiers de recherches économiques No. 9502*, Université de Lausanne: Département d'économétrie et économie politique, February.
Ungern-Sternberg, Th. v. (1995a), 'Running down non-profit organizations: the case of the *Journal of Industrial Economics*', *Cahiers de recherches économiques No. 9510*, Université de Lausanne: Département d'économétrie et économie politique, September.
Weber, M. (1919), *Wissenschaft als Beruf*, München and Leipzig: Duncker & Humblot.
Weizsäcker, C.C. v. (1976), 'Die Welt aus der Sicht der Ökonomen', in H. Körner et al. (eds), *Wirtschaftspolitik: Wissenschaft und politische Aufgabe*, Bern: Haupt, pp. 67–83.

3. The use and misuse of theory in the transfer process

Anne O. Krueger

INTRODUCTION

As all economists know, having the appropriate analytical framework is essential for good policy analysis. Indeed, all policy formulation is based on *some* analytical framework, implicit or otherwise, as Leontief long ago pointed out.

However, the art of good theory is to choose the simplest possible set of assumptions to capture the essentials, both in order to understand the workings of the economy in the situation at hand and in order to gain intuition as to the robustness of the results that emerge from the model.

But, by the nature of theory, the real world never fits the theoretical model exactly. As such, application of theory requires judgement as to which model is appropriate, and what, if any, modifications need to be made to bring the model into line with the reality of the situation under review.

The art of good policy analysis then becomes choosing the right model to take into account those complexities that are relevant (and perhaps missed in simple models) when applying it. But since no simple theory ever fits perfectly (or it would not have been simple), the policy analyst's judgement must be called into play in selecting the right model.

These two criteria – simplicity of theory and fitting the problem at hand – are, to a considerable degree, in conflict. The world is complex, and many apparently sound policies have foundered for lack of recognition of some seemingly minor peculiarity of the functioning of a particular economy. On the other hand, complex models provide little guidance because it is difficult, if not impossible, to infer their robustness to changes in parameters, misspecifications and changes in the underlying parameters facing the economy.

Moreover, any simple model can be attacked as being unrealistic by those seeking alternative policies: there are always aspects of reality not captured by models. And any complex model is suspect, because it will still inevitably fail to take into account all those aspects of the economy that the opponent of the policy believes are important, as well as the robustness considerations already mentioned.

This is well illustrated by considering the role of computable general equilibrium (CGE) models, which are one of the most promising tools economists have for evaluating the impacts of alternative policies. Those models, which are data-intensive, have the potential for addressing complex policy questions where simple analytics cannot even 'sign' an outcome. But they are also sensitive to the assumptions made by the model builder.

This was well documented in the results reported in Fretz, Srinivasan and Whalley (1986): they asked several researchers to build CGE models to estimate the effects of a 50 per cent tariff cut. Some authors derived effects that were 'large'; others, effects that were 'small' (ibid., p. 21). Understanding the reasons for these differences was challenging, and subject to interpretation by those who worked the models through carefully.

There is, moreover, a huge difference between the mindset of researchers and that of policy makers. Researchers, by the very nature of their task, question (and try to build on by amending) existing wisdom. As such, finding an exception to an existing model, or showing that a change in the underlying assumptions alters the results, is a significant contribution to knowledge.

Policy makers, by contrast, must act on the best available knowledge. The market under consideration may not be perfectly competitive, but is it close enough to that condition so that one may assume that price equals suppliers' marginal costs? Or there are inevitably some imperfections in the labour market: the key question is whether those imperfections are sufficiently important to make it wise for the policy maker to abandon the assumption of a well-functioning labour market.

These dilemmas arise in all fields of policy analysis, but nowhere more so than in the arena of development policy formulation. There are several reasons for this. First, development economics began at a time when emotions ran high over the independence of developing countries from colonial powers and when the ideology surrounding 'economic independence' and the desire for industrialization and modernization ran high. Second, especially in the eyes of rich people from industrialized countries, the world of the 'poor peasant' was far removed from anything with which they had any familiarity: ideas about illiterate peasant 'irrationality', lack of response to incentives, 'structural rigidities' and so on were accepted even more uncritically than they would have been if they had been made about the behaviour of people in an industrialized country. Third, there was little systematic empirical evidence and bodies of data about developing countries.

Under those circumstances, it was easy to adopt 'stylized facts' that were, in many instances, wrong. Models built upon these facts provided a rationalization for policies (industrialization through import substitution and government 'direction' of the economy) that most of the 'modernizing elite' in developing countries wanted in any event to follow. And, once those policies were in place, they were naturally supported by those who were benefiting from them. As such, the ideas which had perhaps originally started as 'best-guess' behavioural assumptions quickly became supported by vested interests which had been built up around them.

There is thus an apparent paradox: we desperately need excellent theory to underpin policy analysis; and yet good theory is liable to rejection or misapplication on the part of people benefiting from policies supported by other dogmas or wanting to carry out a particular set of policies in any event.

In this chapter, I attempt to assess the role of theory – use and abuse – in transferring knowledge of economics and economic policy from industrial to developing countries. Any such assessment must, of necessity, be at least partly subjective, both because it is difficult, if not impossible, to ascertain what finally determines policy choices (or even inclinations on the part of individual decision makers and analysts) and partly because there is little systematic literature. This chapter is therefore more in the nature of a 'think-piece', and is based more on anecdotal evidence and personal experience than is normally desirable. It is conjectural in tone, in the hope of provoking further thought and research. The disclaimer is stronger and different: 'the author does not bear responsibility for the ideas expressed herein'.

It should be noted that my assignment is to consider the role of theory. If one were to consider the role of numbers, and the contributions of econometrics and other quantifications, there would be some differences from what follows. Elsewhere (Krueger 1997), I have pointed to the important contribution of basic empirical work in overturning some of the inappropiate 'stylized facts' on which theory was based in the 1950s and 1960s. And since good theory must be well grounded in the relevant stylized facts there are important interrelations between theoretical and empirical developments, another subject not touched upon here.

A starting-point is to identify the theory that has been most useful. Thereafter, I consider varieties of abuses of theory, and reasons for them.

USEFUL THEORY

Underlying Analytical Framework

At a fundamental level, the microeconomic theory that guides policy makers must come down to models relating to four things: (i) what rational resource allocation at a point in time, and intertemporally, would be; (ii) the degree to which private decision making achieves static and dynamic efficiency (that is, rational allocation and rational savings and investment decisions); (iii) the determinants of the behaviour of public sector decision makers with regard to these same variables; and (iv) the interactions between private and public decision makers.

There is, of course, macroeconomic theory as well as microtheory. Much of the theory that is relevant for policy is fairly simple: the role and effects of fiscal deficits; the interrelations between seigniorage, domestic credit creation and inflation; alternative exchange rate regimes and the consistencies of alternative monetary and fiscal policy regimes with them; and so on. With experience of rapid and sustained inflation – especially in Latin America – and its costs, however, theory has been widely accepted and there has been little abuse.[1] I thus stay with microeconomic theory.

There is little quarrel among economists with respect to what rational resource allocation at a point in time and over time would look like.[2] When there are departures from constant returns to scale and perfect competition (and thus the presence of externalities), it is evident that an allocation that relied entirely on private marginal decision making would be nonoptimal unless these departures could be captured (*à la* Coase theorem) by other market participants. The same is true of informational asymmetries if they are severe enough, and if the costs of distortions introduced in attempting to correct them do not outweigh the benefits of reducing informational distortions.

However, important questions arise as to when these imperfections arise, how great they are, and whether governments can reduce them at sufficiently low cost to make intervention increase social welfare. It is at this juncture that the next questions arise.

The theory that arises to show rational resource allocation is excellent. It can be used to derive highly policy-relevant cost–benefit analysis, evaluate alternative tax structures and derive optimal trade policy.[3]

If an economist/policy analyst accepts that theory and in addition believes that private individuals (and profit-making institutions such as corporations) are rational economic agents, it is a short step in policy analysis to use basic theory to ask, when outcomes do not seem to accord with what one might have expected or desired, what it is in the incentive system that led to the apparently nonoptimal outcome. Often, the answers (such as lack of enforceable property rights, government regulations and inappropriate tax structures) emerge as a consequence simply of using the simple individual maximization paradigm and asking what the individual decision maker is responding to.[4]

However, there have long been many sceptical of the underlying premises of the model. This was true of the early beliefs regarding 'irrational peasants', already noted. It was, and to a greater degree, still is true of the belief that individuals may not rationally maximize intertemporally and that the government has a major role to play in affecting intertemporal resource allocation.[5]

View of Government

As experience with development policy has accumulated, many analysts have increasingly questioned the determinants of public sector behaviour. There are again two conflicting views: on one hand there are those who see the state, or the government, as a benevolent social guardian. This group typically believes in a strong role for government in correcting private market failures.

An alternative view is that of the predatory state – one in which certain groups capture the apparatus of the state and employ it for their own ends. Lal and Myint (1996) distinguish between bureaucratic–authoritarian states, in which bureaucrats essentially work the system for their own interests, and factional states in which a weak coalition must 'reward' its members in order to maintain power. In both cases, the behaviour of government bears little resemblance to the benevolent social guardian maximizing some variant of a Benthamite social welfare function.[6]

Finally, there is the question of interactions between policies, governments and the private sector. There are many instances where well-intentioned policies had effects quite different from those initially intended as the regulated 'captured' the process, or as interest groups sprang up to seize the benefits of measures intended for another group.

The transfer of ideas about economic policies in the development process began after World War II in the aftermath of the Great Depression. It was a time when there was disillusionment with the private sector's tendency to maintain full employment. Keynesian economics had developed and was used to demonstrate an active role for the state in maintaining full employment. It was also a time when, partly for the same reasons, public ownership of many activities – including steel mills, railroads, oil, airlines and even automobile factories – was not seen as significantly different from private ownership.[7]

Given misimpressions about the rationality (or lack thereof) of private behaviour, the potential for disinterested action on the part of governments and suspicions of the market, it is not surprising that initial policies in developing countries were, judged by present-day standards, woefully inconsistent with aspirations for rapid growth. Policy shortcomings arose not only because of the ideas but also because there were few civil servants and government ministers with experience and training: the administrative capacities of governments were greatly overtaxed.[8]

From thereon out, experience with development policies and their implementation and the outcomes of alternative policies (especially in the East

Asian newly industrializing countries) resulted in bringing about change, both in policy and in theory.

To some degree, theory was used to support change. In part, however, theory was used to obstruct it. In what follows, several of the abuses of theory that were important for perpetuating policies that are now generally believed to be inferior are discussed.

MISAPPLICATION OF GOOD THEORY[9]

Failure to Appreciate Simplifying Assumptions

Misapplication of good theory was significant.[10] Perhaps the identification of comparative advantage with the two-factor, two-good model, and the implication that developing countries would for ever have to specialize in primary commodity production if they maintained free trade was the most abused idea.

Proponents of open trade regimes failed to refute the allegation that free trade would for ever leave developing countries specialized in production of agricultural commodities.[11] It was not until the 1970s (see Jones 1971 and Krueger 1977) that models – motivated in part by the East Asian experience – were developed in which three factors of production (land, labour and capital) were allocated among sectors, each of which could produce many commodities. As the three-factor models demonstrated, comparative advantage lies within manufacturing and within agriculture, and not between them. Thus, poor unskilled labour-abundant countries have a comparative advantage in labour-intensive agricultural *and* unskilled labour-intensive manufactured commodities while countries with a much higher land–labour ratio have a comparative advantage in more land-using agricultural commodities and their comparative advantage in manufacturing lies more in goods with higher capital–unskilled labour ratios. It is an interesting, and probably unanswerable, question as to whether the basic tenets of comparative advantage were rejected by policy makers in developing countries because the modernizing elite were determined to protect domestic industry, or whether it was a conviction that development could not take place with continuing primary commodity specialization. But, either way, the basic comparative advantage argument for free trade was certainly misused.

A second serious misapplication of good theory arose because of the nonoperational nature of the theory itself, and the failure to identify circumstances under which policy implementation might be incentive compatible *and* potentially increase welfare. A key culprit in this case was the interpretation of the 'infant industry' argument. It was widely used as a rationale for import substitution, and generally recognized as a 'legitimate' case for a departure from free trade.

One can hardly argue with the proposition that the presence of a positive externality gives rise to a basis for intervention; if the externality is dynamic and temporary, then temporary intervention, such as infant industry protection (preferably, of course, through production subsidies), can be called for.

The problem with the argument, as a basis for policy, is that it fails to provide any guidance as to how to distinguish between an infant that will grow up and a would-be producer seeking protection because protection will be privately profitable to him or her. It is not even clear how one could begin, empirically, to identify the domain of the externality. Moreover, even if there were a producer or producers whose increased production would generate dynamic externalities, it does not follow that any level of protection is warranted. And there is nothing in the infant industry argument to provide guidance for quantifying or estimating the likely magnitude of the externality. Finally, there is nothing in theory that suggests how one might protect infant industries in ways that do not provide incentives for behaviour that perpetuate high costs: if public policy states that high-cost producers will receive protection, it is not in producers' interests greatly to strive for cost reductions.

Indiscriminate protection in developing countries was defended on 'infant industry' grounds with arguments of capital market failure, labour market failure (as the costs of training, presumably, would be borne by first entrants into industries and then not recouped as others hired workers away), costs of investments in technology and uncertainty all used. It was not until Robert Baldwin's (1969) seminal article that it was demonstrated that, even when the presumed imperfection existed, it was unlikely that infant industry protection would help correct it. As Baldwin cogently argued, later entrants to an industry might speed up their investments if protection made domestic production more profitable and the first entrant might even be worse off! It was only after critical examination of these circumstances that the defenders of the infant industry case for import substitution became less vehement.

The infant industry argument is also an excellent example of a theory that is nonoperational because criteria for bureaucrats to identify cases have not been put forward. Quite aside from the unpredictability and unmeasurability of the future time path of costs in new factories and the moral hazard associated with asking individual entrepreneurs to indicate how much protection they need, there is nothing to my knowledge in the literature specifying how the policy maker might instruct a bureaucrat to identify (much less measure) a dynamic externality if it were present, how an incentive-compatible mechanism might be devised for improving welfare, how the bureaucrat might measure the height of warranted protection, or how policy makers might credibly commit to temporary protection. Even *ex post*, it is not entirely clear how one might identify an industry as a successful infant: simply because a firm became profitable and exported does not prove that there was either an externality or a dynamic process at work![12]

Negative Results

Much of the theorizing that took place was concerned with what I call 'negative results'. That is, analysts sought to find reasons why, for example, an exception to free trade should be made. Once the principle of comparative advantage was laid down as a basis for policy, there was little left for theorists to prove supporting an open trading system, so the challenge to theorists was to find conditions under which the free trade precept did not hold. As theory, these findings were significant. But for policy, they were unhelpful, and probably served to perpetuate inappropriate policies.

In most real-world circumstances, one strongly suspects that protection exists where theoretical exceptions do not justify it and that moves to first-best policies would on average lower, and not raise, protection. However, in practice, every negative result was used as yet another rationale for trade policy intervention. When strategic trade theory first began developing, with its implied argument that a country with a potential new industry might capture rents by being first, many in the policy community seized on the argument as yet another basis on which developing countries might protect their industries. This, despite the fact that the strategic industries were generally high-tech where there was no evidence whatever that the arguments might be relevant for developing countries.[13]

Another example will illuminate the argument. Whereas theory suggests criteria for departures from *laissez-faire* free trade which would normally result in different levels of protection for different industries, a widely-used prescription for policy makers is that, if there is to be protection, a uniform tariff is usually preferable to any alternative structure. This proposition rests on several considerations. First, only a uniform tariff can generate a uniform rate of effective protection in the import-competing sectors and, if different goods are subject to different rates of tariff, the resulting differences in effective rates of protection will lead to resource misallocation even within the import-competing industries and have no relation to underlying 'dynamic' or market failure considerations. Second, a uniform tariff simplifies customs administration, making evasion and/or bribery of customs officials more difficult than a varying rate structure. Third, a uniform tariff greatly reduces the opportunities for resource losses in rent-seeking and lobbying. Fourth, given international prices, international value added is more likely to be maximized under a uniform tariff structure than under a variable one.

None of these arguments is sufficient to prove that a uniform tariff is optimal. And, indeed, it is straightforward to develop models in which a uniform tariff is nonoptimal, especially in the presence of income distribution considerations. In theory, the costs of protection can be minimized by imposing higher tariffs or taxes on goods whose supply and demand is relatively more price inelastic.

Those arguments, as put forward, are all couched in terms of demonstrating the 'falsity' of the proposition that a uniform tariff is preferable to variable tariff rates and that there is a departure from uniformity that can potentially improve welfare. But the difficulty with that formulation is that it does not provide a criterion for which departures from uniformity might improve welfare, because a model considering, for example income distribution considerations, cannot simultaneously address issues of corruption and administration. And the fact that income distribution considerations can warrant a nonuniform tariff structure does not prove that any nonuniform tariff structure is preferable to a uniform one! As such, a negative result gives little or no guide for policy. None the less it arms lobbyists and others with ammunition to discredit technocrats' efforts to maintain a less irrational structure of protection.

In that regard it is often overlooked that most policy implementation is carried out by government officials who cannot be expected to have advanced degrees, and sometimes even undergraduate degrees, in economics. In many instances (including formulas for optimal tariff differentiation), the degree of sophistication needed to interpret research results is well beyond that which most bureaucrats will have. As pointed out by Harry Johnson:

> The fundamental problem is that, as with all second-best arguments, determination of the conditions under which a second-best policy actually leads to an improvement in social welfare requires detailed theoretical and empirical investigation by a first-best economist . . . It is therefore very unlikely that a second-best welfare optimum will result based on second-best arguments. (Johnson 1970, p. 101)

Good Theory Assuming Counterfactual Situations

The final abuse of theory was primarily a fault of inappropriate stylized facts. None the less, in many instances, analysts *assumed* signs of variables that were certainly questionable, modelled the situation neatly and then drew policy conclusions that could hold only if the posited signs were valid. Yet their claims often went beyond the assertion of that 'if these facts . . . then' variety.

As an example to illustrate the point, I have deliberately chosen a good, widely-cited paper, because the paper represents good theory, but interprets it, for policy purposes, with dubious 'stylized facts'. Anand and Joshi (1979) considered a world, such as that envisaged by Hagen (1958) in which workers in the advanced sector receive a higher wage than those in the rest of the economy due to unions or other (presumably unalterable) circumstances. They then asked whether maximizing international value added for given employment of domestic resources is an appropriate criterion when income distribution considerations cannot be separated from productive efficiency considerations.

In their setup, the clear answer is no, because tradables are produced by the advanced (presumably unionized) sector, and hence maximizing international value will pull more resources into that sector at the cost of a deteriorating income distribution. Interestingly, they do not address the question of whether the advanced sector is labour- or capital-intensive. If, as is true for outer-orientated developing countries, the exportables are labour-intensive relative to import-competing activity, removing protection to induce a move of more workers to the 'advanced' high-wage sector would presumably increase wages of those workers and also those in the rest of the economy: a more equal income distribution would be obtained at the expense of lower real wages for all. Without regard to factor intensity, however, Anand and Joshi conclude that:

> The motivation behind the theory of distortions has been to criticise and to guide trade and industrialisation policies . . . Our analysis emphasises the need for caution . . . Departures from technical efficiency may be called for as part of the rational response by governments to the limitations they face in carrying out desirable income distribution policies . . . (Anand and Joshi 1979, p. 350)[14]

Anand and Joshi assumed that moving towards economic efficiency in tradables requires paying higher wages because of a distortion. Yet, in fact, the evidence suggests that it has been the highly protected, import-competing industries, which have been able to pay above-average wages: removing protection has led to rapid expansion of employment in labour-intensive industries. If the latter stylized fact is correct, and if income distribution considerations are important, it would suggest that the policy implications of the Anand–Joshi analysis are the opposite of what they conclude: namely, that policy makers should encourage, even beyond the optimum, a shift of resources out of protected industries (presumably by removing protection) and into exportable industries.[15]

Capture of Policy

Finally, many policies that were initiated and promulgated by well-intentioned individuals behaving as benevolent social guardians were 'captured' by those who benefited from them. Bureaucratic capture was mentioned at the outset, but it is worthwhile noting that bureaucratic opposition to reforms has been a central element of the difficulties encountered in many developing countries attempting to change policies.

Once ideas are 'legitimate', those whose interests are served use those ideas, regardless of whether they apply in the relevant situation. Armies of bureaucrats, politicians, businessmen and -women and labour union members in many countries have been at the forefront of those opposing change. They may oppose it as being 'too rapid', or because the country is not yet 'ready' or for other reasons relating to theory.[16] The real reasons, of course, have to do with self-interest, but would not be as persuasive in the public policy debate.

FACTORS LEADING TO CHANGE

The above discussion has focused on ways in which theory has been abused in its application in developing countries. As pointed out initially, however, some abuse is inevitable. And, in order to end on a more positive note, it should be recognized that ideas have changed, and that understanding of development policy in the late 1990s is far different from what it was a quarter century or more ago.

There is no question but that experience with alternative policies and especially the contrast in success with development was influential in restoring the incentive-orientated approach to markets and the view that public policy should work with incentives, rather than against it.

But analysts and theorists contributed to that evolving consensus. There were analyses of how alternative systems had worked,[17] as well as theoretical developments illuminating the role of government.[18] Once it became clear how high the costs of the policy mistakes had been, the transfer of policy ideas both in the form of recognizing the importance of incentives and in improving the functioning of markets, became the wisdom of the day in many developing countries.

NOTES

1. There are instances where policy makers, perhaps of populist appeal, make claims that are contrary to all evidence. In Turkey, for example, then Prime Minister Tansu Ciller, an American-trained economist, attempted to force down interest rates on the ground that this would lower the rate of inflation. No theoretical argument as to why that should be so was presented.
2. Sir Alec Cairncross (1970), long an adviser to the British government, strongly took the view that most policy-relevant economics was the very simple supply-and-demand, cost–benefit story.
3. See below, for a discussion of the abuse of the infant industry argument, however.
4. This 'low-brow' application of basic theory has been tremendously important. The example of the 'human capital' literature illustrates. A 1950s' story of behaviour in developing countries had it that everyone wanted a white-collar job and frowned on working with one's hands; hence, there was an oversupply of university graduates and few skilled technicians. It took the development of the theory of human capital (and with it, the concepts of the private and social rates of return to education and other investments in man) to show that people were responding rationally to the opportunities created by educational systems in which secondary school tuition was relatively high while university education was greatly subsidized. In Turkey, for example, the private rate of return on university education was estimated to be about 25 per cent while the social rate of return was about 2 per cent. See Krueger (1972).
5. There is an irony here: observers of political behaviour generally believe that politicians have a shorter time horizon than do individuals while economists believing that there is irrationality in private intertemporal optimization believe that the social discount rate is below the private rate. These two beliefs continue to coexist in different parts of the development literature. This is a case in which theory is clear and it is beliefs regarding the underlying premises that drive policy analysis.

6. Lal and Myint do recognize the existence of benevolent social guardian states. They note that aspects of the behaviour of South Korea's government during the 1960s and 1970s seem to fit the model.
7. See Tinbergen (1984) for a statement as recently as 15 years ago to the effect that the nature of ownership does not matter.
8. See Stolper (1966) for an illuminating account of his experience in Nigeria.
9. In what follows, I draw heavily on Krueger (1997).
10. Another set of examples of misapplication of theory was the early defences, such as that of Hagen (1958), of protection because of a domestic distortion. But it took the development of a theory of domestic distortions before that was understood.
11. Some of Harry Johnson's (1958) research on trade and growth went some way towards refuting this proposition, but still in a 2 × 2 framework. Moreover, Johnson's work implied that labour-abundant countries would, while accumulating capital, undergo 'ultra antitrade biassed' growth, which seemed to support import substitution.
12. The same is true of the optimum tariff argument. In the presence of many goods with varying degrees of monopoly power, the formula becomes hopelessly complex. It is certainly true that many tariff structures would lead to lower, rather than higher, welfare in the presence of monopoly power in trade. Yet, in practice, many policy makers have been misled into thinking that they could defend very high tariffs (sometimes even on goods that their countries imported in small quantities or, even more counter to theory, prohibited importation of) on optimum tariff grounds.
13. The 'optimum tariff' argument, which certainly does not warrant different rates of protection for different imports when the supply curves facing the country are all perfectly elastic, as is true for most manufactured imports for most developing countries, was similarly abused.
14. Another example of the 'negative results' research arises from early findings (see Bhagwati and Srinivasan 1973 and Jones 1971) that the resource pulls associated with raising an effective rate of protection did not necessarily accord with those associated with increasing a nominal rate of protection. These findings did not significantly affect research efforts, in part because the authors made clear the relatively extreme conditions necessary to generate the 'perverse' resource pull and partly because other researchers were able to demonstrate that there seemed to be few, if any, empirical counterparts to the perverse pull cases.
15. See Bardhan (1996), tracing how the presumed 'efficiency–equity' trade-off has been shown to be false in considerable measure.
16. In this regard, the discussions of optimal timing and sequencing of reforms gave and still gives support to those opposing reforms on grounds that either the order is wrong or the speed is too fast.
17. See, for example, Krueger, Schiff and Valdes (1988), Little, Scitovksy and Scott (1970), and Michaely, Papageorgiou and Choksi (1991) for three examples of this sort of analysis.
18. See, for example, Findlay and Wilson (1987).

REFERENCES

Anand, S. and V. Joshi (1979), 'Domestic distortions, income distribution and the theory of optimum subsidy', *Economic Journal*, **89** (354), pp. 336–52.
Baldwin, R.E. (1969), 'The case against infant-industry protection', *Journal of Political Economy*, **77** (3), pp. 295–305.
Bardhan, P. (1996), 'Efficiency, equity and poverty alleviation: policy issues in less developed countries', *Economic Journal*, **106** (438), pp. 1344–56.
Bhagwati, J. and T.N. Srinivasan (1973), 'The general equilibrium theory of effective protection and resource allocation', *Journal of International Economics*, **3** (3), pp. 259–81.
Cairncross, A. (1970), 'Economists in government', *Lloyd's Bank Review*, **95**, pp. 1–18.

Findlay, R. and J. Wilson (1987), 'The political economy of Leviathan', in A. Razin and E. Sadka (eds), *Economic Policy in Theory and Practice*, London: Macmillan, pp. 289–304.

Fretz, D., T.N. Srinivasan and J. Whalley (1986), 'Introduction', in T.N. Srinivasan and J. Whalley (eds), *General Equilibrium Trade Policy Modeling*, Cambridge, MA: MIT Press, pp. 1–29.

Hagen, E.E. (1958), 'An economic justification of protectionism', *Quarterly Journal of Economics*, **72**, pp. 496–514.

Johnson, H.G. (1958), *International Trade and Economic Growth*, Cambridge, MA: Harvard University Press.

Johnson, H.G. (1970), 'The efficiency and welfare implications of the international corporation', in I.A. McDougall and R.H. Snape (eds), *Studies in International Economics*, Amsterdam: North-Holland, pp. 83–103.

Jones, R.W. (1971), 'Effective protection and substitution', *Journal of International Economics*, **1** (1), pp. 59–82.

Krueger, A.O. (1972), 'Rates of return to Turkish higher education', *Journal of Human Resources*, **7** (4), pp. 482–99.

Krueger, A.O. (1977), *Growth, Factor Market Distortions, and Patterns of Trade among Many Countries*, Princeton: Princeton University Press (Princeton Studies in International Finance, No. 40).

Krueger, A.O. (1997), 'Trade policy and economic development: how we learn', *American Economic Review*, **87** (1), pp. 1–22.

Krueger, A.O., M. Schiff and A. Valdes (1988), 'Agricultural incentives in developing countries: measuring the effect of sectoral and economywide policies', *World Bank Economic Review*, **2** (3), pp. 255–71.

Lal, D. and H. Myint (1996), *Poverty, Equity and Growth: A Comparative Study*, Oxford: Clarendon Press.

Little, I.M.D., T. Scitovsky and M. Scott (1970), *Industry and Trade in Some Developing Countries*, Oxford: Oxford University Press.

Michaely, M., D. Papageorgiou and A. Choksi (1991), *Liberalizing Foreign Trade: Lessons of Experience in the Developing World*, Cambridge: Basil Blackwell.

Stolper, W. (1966), *Planning without Facts, Lessons in Resource Allocation from Nigeria's Development*, Cambridge, MA: Harvard University Press.

Tinbergen, J. (1984), 'Development cooperation as a learning process', in G.M. Meier and D. Seers (eds), *Pioneers in Development*, Oxford: Oxford University Press, pp. 314–32.

PART II

Aspects of Institutional Policy Advice

4. The culture of economic policy advice: an international comparison with special emphasis on Europe

Charles Wyplosz*

INTRODUCTION

Many of those who choose to become economists do so because of a deep interest in politics and policy. Economics offers a fascinating blend of rigour and action. Economists can engage in complex and highly structured reasoning and empirical investigation and then develop competent views of relevance to burning political issues. One can hope to be useful to society and, at the same time, to pursue scientific aims. Few professions share that appeal. It is normal therefore that many economists seek to become policy advisers, when they do not become politicians.

When I was a graduate student in Cambridge (US) in the mid-1970s, I made a number of friends with other students at Harvard and MIT who shared this urge of using economic knowledge to improve conditions in their countries. When I reflect on our feverish discussions back then, I never fail to muse at how different are the paths that we have been able to follow in that pursuit. Mentioning some of my classmates will make my point. Larry Summers moved from the position of Chief Economist at the World Bank to be second in command at the US Treasury, arguably one of the most influential policy makers in the world. His deputy, David Lipton, is another classmate. Jeffrey Frankel serves on the US Council of Economic Advisers. Katharine Abraham is Commissioner of the Bureau of Labor Statistics. Domingo Cavallo has turned around Argentina in

*   I am very grateful to many colleagues who provided the raw material used in the tables: Torben Andersen, Philippe Bacchetta, Charlie Bean, David Begg, Samuel Bentolila, Juanjo Dolado, Antonio Fatas, Francesco Giavazzi, Paul De Grauwe, Jakob de Haan, Seppo Honkapohja, Patrick Honohan, Takatoshi Ito, Pierre Jacquet, Lars Jonung, Kai Konrad, Erkki Koskela, Philip Lane, Jacques Mélitz, Torsten Persson, Richard Portes, Ronald Schettkat, Lars Svensson, Guido Tabellini and Harald Uhlig. I have received useful comments and suggestions from Francesco Giavazzi, Lars Jonung and Richard Portes, as well as detailed advice from the organizers of the St. Gallen Colloquium. I am alone responsible for the interpretation of the advice generously provided.

his years as Finance Minister, much as Pedro Aspe did in Mexico. Both may return to very high office. Eduardo Aninat is now running Chile's economy with great prudence and success. Francesco Giavazzi worked for several crucial years at the Italian Treasury. José Viñals is the influential Chief Economist at the Bank of Spain. And Jeffrey Sachs, who could not be a prophet in his own country, has become the world's most travelled and arguably most influential economist, the adviser called upon for all difficult missions from Bolivia to Poland, Russia and the Philippines, now preparing the next African miracle. Many others are prominent academics who spend a significant time giving policy advice at the highest level.

Some of us have found it easy, indeed natural, to move between academia and policy advice. Others, while strongly motivated as well, have not had the same opportunities. This is my case, a source of considerable frustration, which explains why I have been so delighted to contribute to this book. This chapter is an attempt to reflect, twenty years to the day after my graduation, on the opportunities and pitfalls of moving from economics as a scientific field to economic policy making.

A few caveats are clearly in order. The literature on economic policy advice is quite limited and tends to focus mostly on the US experience. This chapter takes the US as a background and looks into Europe. Hard data are nowhere to be found. An informal polling of colleagues is used as background for this chapter, which relies mostly on personal experience and casual observation. It makes no claim at scientific rigour and seeks more to feed a debate than to provide a reliable guide. It also starts from the view that it is desirable for the profession to be involved in policy making, a view unsavoury to most other contributors to this book who adhere to the public choice school of thought. The next section describes the scene briefly. The section to follow draws the portrait of the perfect adviser. Afterwards this requirement is contrasted with what is on offer and on demand interpreting the current situation in Europe. The last section concludes by summarizing the main points.

INSTITUTIONS OF POLICY ADVICE

To start with, it is important to distinguish clearly between policy making, policy advice and policy influence. In this chapter, I define a policy adviser as an academic economist who has direct access to policy makers but who is not in a position to make decisions, and who does not hold a permanent position in an institution which makes policy decisions, be it a government agency or an international organization. I do not consider indirect advice through the media or influential books not only because this is a very diffuse activity, but mainly because direct advice imposes some degree of commitment to practical decisions, that is, the acceptance of unsavoury trade-offs and the willingness to move some way from our cherished safe turf of theoretical purity. Policy advice can be a full- or part-time activity, it can be carried out independently or within a policy-advice organization which, in turn, can be public or private. To be sure, the frontiers are not always clear-cut: academic economists and advisers sometimes become policy makers and vice versa.

Countries differ considerably in terms of the institutions that offer advice. The US is clearly the country where advice is the most directly integrated within the policy-making process. The Council of Economic Advisers (CEA) is a unique institution explicitly designed to subject all policy decisions which have economic effects to the scrutiny of professional economists. The three Council members do not make decisions, nor do they see themselves necessarily as advocates of government policies. Yet they are part of the President's administration and the Chair is seen as equal to cabinet members. Official but free from direct politicking:

> Unlike almost all other top-level appointees, their primary responsibility is not to promote and advance the platform and program of the incumbent president. Seldom cheerfully, sometimes grudgingly and possibly only after several demurrals by a CEA chair, presidents do come to recognize that fact and expect, if not zero outright cheerleading, less of it from their CEA appointees than from others. (Schultze 1996, p. 26)

The CEA is staffed mostly by academics who take leave from their universities. As they expect to return to teaching and research, their professional outlook is not one of a politician. They must preserve some degree of academic respectability even though they spend most of their time dealing with political appointees and politicians. This is not an easy exercise, as experience has shown.

In Europe, only four countries (Denmark, Germany, the Netherlands and Sweden) have had similar institutions for some time. The Swedish council works for the Ministry of Finance. It is also considered as high quality, but it is mostly producing reports. Its influence is therefore more limited. The Danish council is seen as quite influential. The same applies to the Dutch Social Economic Council, whose brief is wider and which includes both economists and sociologists. As in Sweden, the German *Sachverständigenrat* (Council of Wisemen) is composed mostly of academic economists who are not expected to be politically active. It is not part of the government decision-making process and during their tenure its members retain their academic positions, so they devote only part of their time to the task. They have no (or a very small) professional staff. They do not routinely comment on decisions, certainly not before they are taken. Their main responsibility is to publish an annual report, the *Gutachten*, which is available in bookstores. Their recommendations are widely quoted by the media but rarely influence policy.

The US CEA is widely seen as a model, at least in theory. Several countries (see Table 4.2, below) have recently moved to establish their own version of the CEA, but in fact they rather have implicitly adopted the German model or arm's-length involvement. France since 1997, Finland, Italy and the UK have each set up a council in 1998. The Finnish council resembles the Swedish one, with five members of high calibre. The French and Italian councils report to the Prime Ministry. They are too large (32 in France, 11 in Italy) to be coherent, and indeed they seem to have been designed to encompass a wide spectrum of views. They both meet once a month and may look at issues before a decision is made. The French *Conseil de l'analyse économique* tables specially commissioned reports followed by diverging comments. Like their European predecessors, the new councils are likely to be more sounding boards than policy-advice bodies. The British version is even less glamorous, made up of two relatively unknown economists seconded to the Treasury and expected to approve most policy decisions. Clearly, European policy makers would rather have professional economists outside than inside the decision-making apparatus, a fact that is revealing of the chasm between the two sides of the Atlantic.

Central banks are traditionally closer to academic economists, maybe because they are less obviously political. Indeed, a number of governors are former academics and do not owe their positions to a career in politics (for example Israel, the Netherlands, Spain, the US, or the Deputy Governor in Ireland and the UK). As they have evolved towards greater independence, some central banks have set up formal committees. The monetary policy committee of the Bank of England is now the decision-making body for interest rates. It includes several academics, all of whom carry high respect in the profession. The German *Bundesbank* has a similar structure, but academics rarely sit on its Board. The *Banque de France* also has a monetary policy committee. It includes few professional economists and they command little professional clout; the committee is seen as weak and dominated by the Governor and his Deputy.

Summarizing so far, in contrast to the US, in Europe formal channels do not seem to exist for the academic profession to affect policy decisions seriously. Cynical observers argue that where they exist, economic councils often have been designed to deflect academic criticism. This does not mean that academics do not advise the authorities: some do, but through other channels. The active links are varied. Some are formal, such as bringing academics to serve in the Treasury, government agencies or the central bank for a period of time. In these cases, however, they become part of the hierarchy, policy makers themselves, and are not considered here as advisers.

Other links are informal. A natural practice is for a policy maker to appoint one or more personal advisers who work part- or full-time in that capacity. This is occasionally the case in the UK, at various levels: the Prime Minister, the

Chancellor, the Treasury and other cabinet members.[1] There is some Rasputin flavour to such appointments and this is discussed below.

Central banks sometimes use part-time academic advisers, for example in Sweden, Finland and the local Feds in the US.[2] Most often they have a research department which regularly hires academics for limited periods of time. During their stay they may be involved with policy issues, much as other staff members. The same applies to international organizations such as the International Monetary Fund (IMF) or the World Bank, but this is closer to policy making than to policy advice. Policy advice to central banks seems to occur mainly through informal contacts. Central banks are frequent organizers of meetings, conferences and so on, where the senior staff and governors mingle with academics and debate issues of direct relevance to policy. This is mostly the case in countries where the central bank has a strong research department, which is often the case in countries which, until recently, had weak university economics departments (as, for example, in Italy and Spain).

Governments and central banks occasionally commission special studies on particular issues. Recently this has been the case in Sweden and Finland in preparing the groundwork for the decisions regarding European Monetary Union: in both cases the conclusions reached by the academic panels were accepted by the governments.

Parliaments often seek the views of academic economists. This is routine in the US where hearings on all issues are held by both chambers and involve a large number of economists. The practice exists in most European countries (France and Spain are among the exceptions) although it is usually not as elaborate as in the US or in the UK. US courts draw heavily on academic expertise: the IBM and Baby Bell cases are legendary. This reflects the wider development of the field of law and economics in the US than in Europe.

Think-tanks may be seen as the ideal opportunity for influencing policy. This is not policy advice proper, since views are not being directly solicited by policy makers. Yet think-tanks may be very close to policy makers, so that the issues that they work on may be heavily influenced by the policy agenda and tailored to prepare decisions. The links may even become formal when think-tanks do commissioned studies. In the US, the Brookings Institution and the American Enterprise Institute are traditionally close to, respectively, Democrat and Republican administrations, and both house former CEA members.

Think-tanks are especially developed in Germany where six institutes, largely publicly financed, produce a vast amount of applied research on both domestic and international issues. The quality of the institutes is variable, ranging from international level down to poor. They all naturally attempt to differentiate themselves. Part of that is achieved through the range of topics in which they specialize, but also through ideological orientation. Several countries have think-tanks openly associated with political parties (Spain) or politically motivated (Sweden, France) or supported by interest groups (as in Finland or Sweden).

Some academic economists invest in longer-term goals by being active within political parties. As economics traditionally plays an important role in election outcomes, all parties have to elaborate platforms. Policy advice to political parties can be tricky because it may involve a good deal of partisanship and ingenuity, an issue discussed below. It is also a gamble, as the association is often with individuals within each party. In all countries, though, there seems to be a large pool of economists ready to gamble and, sometimes, to compromise their academic respectability.

Finally, the need for policy advice in developing countries is considerable. In many countries there are very few economists with an advanced training in economics. International organizations provide some of the needed support. A large number of countries which offer bilateral aid occasionally send experts.

In general, as can be seen, there is a wide spectrum of activities that can be thought of as policy advice. The situation varies considerably from country to country, even among the most-developed ones. The next sections examine some of the national features which may explain these differences.

WHAT DOES IT TAKE TO BE A GOOD ADVISER?

The first quality required from a policy adviser is clarity in reasoning and presentation of ideas. The training of economists is increasingly technical, and status in the profession seems to require the systematic use of jargon, acronyms (SVAR, NAIRU and so on) and obscure references (Walrasian auctioneer, Lucas critique, Ricardian equivalence and so on). Not only must a policy adviser make him- or herself understood, he or she must also compete with other advisers who represent other concerns than economics. It is not enough that he or she speaks well and clearly, he or she must also be rapid, convincing and politically astute, which may require some sense of psychology and strategy.

The second quality is to recognize the policy maker's need for solutions. The old joke of President Truman asking for a one-handed economist is a classic. Policy makers understand that economics is complex and that there often does not exist a single answer to a simple question. What they need is to be presented with a clear description of the stakes that they face. They usually accept uncertainty if they see the reason. For instance, a tax cut may or may not lead to an increase in private spending. It depends on whether the tax cut is perceived as temporary or permanent, on how the resulting budget deficit will be financed, on whether the public trusts that the measure will not be rescinded by the present or next government and so on.

This brings us to the third quality, honesty. An adviser may have his or her own policy agenda, but he or she should let his or her customer's agenda prevail, limiting him- or herself to be faithful to his or her trade. A politician may have a vision, not an adviser; if the adviser has one, he or she should sell it privately to his or her advisee, or go into politics openly. Admitting ignorance and recognizing controversies is essential for poor advice leads to policy mistakes. Sooner or later the advisee will see through advocacy and the adviser will lose the essential trust that he or she needs to be efficient. 'An economist who wants to contribute to the policy-making process needs to be a good salesman – but not a snake-oil salesman' notes US Representative Hamilton (Hamilton 1992, p. 63).

The fourth quality is to recognize the limits of economics as a rationale for society. The economist is first and foremost a lobbyist for efficiency. But public opinion and policy makers value other collective goals, including fairness. Economists reason in terms of Pareto optimality, often ignoring that a policy action will hurt some citizens. Pareto transfers are the solution, but they are usually impossible to organize. Again Hamilton: 'I sometimes think that I should take economists with me on a trip to my district to try to impress on them the human side of the issues they analyze, often, it seems to me, with too little compassion' (ibid.).

Finally comes the question of competence. All advisers know that first-year textbook economics is the most that is needed in nearly all instances. Does it mean that any moderately trained person can act as a policy adviser? Quite the contrary. Good textbooks delineate the limits of our knowledge and that is precisely why advisers should limit themselves to what is in textbooks. Equally important is to know what is not in textbooks: what are the controversies, what previously popular idea has been proved wrong and why, which ideas are currently under study and whom to ask to know where to stand. The closer are advisers to frontline research, the more they know these things.

ECONOMIC ADVISERS: SUPPLY AND DEMAND

This section starts from the profile of the ideal adviser and examines how policy advice is supplied and demanded. It explores the production of advisers through education. It then looks at how national authorities and international organizations fill their needs. The resulting equilibrium is then interpreted, bringing demand and supply together and arguing that controversies among economists ultimately weaken the social role of the profession.

There exists no source of factual information on these questions and in general a limited amount of research. Apart from extensive research by sociologist Bob Coats comparing the US and Britain, Jonung (1991, 1998) describes the prominent role played by noted Swedish economists (Knut Wicksell, Gustav Cassel, Eli F. Hecksher, David Davidson, Bertil Ohlin) in the interwar period, a role reminiscent of the influence of John Maynard Keynes in the UK.

The information provided below is based partly on a questionnaire. Evaluating the production of economists and the way policy-making bodies seek advice involves a good deal of subjective judgement. One approach would have been to seek the views of a very large sample. This is not the route followed here for two reasons. First, a large canvass of the profession lies beyond the aim of this chapter. Second, the field of policy advice draws some of the best, but also some of the worst, academic economists. It includes strongly opinionated Rasputins with no professional clout. Detecting such situations requires value judgement. For this reason, I decided to poll internationally-renowned economists, initially approaching two per country to limit personal biases. A questionnaire (shown in Appendix 4A) was sent to 32 policy-orientated economists throughout Europe, drawing 27 responses. I have interpreted their responses to build up the three tables now presented and discussed.

Supply: Training

What is needed to prepare advisers

When looking at differences across countries, a natural question is whether the education of professional economists at the graduate level is geared towards producing individuals who will step easily into the role of advisers. The preceding section claims that an economist will become an effective adviser if he or she has a clear view of what his or her knowledge can bring in practice, if he or she can extricate him- or herself from the technicalities which bring rewards in academia and if he or she is ready to take on board the broader political picture, all of that while remaining truthful to his or her field.

Training must therefore emphasize a general knowledge of economics, at a time when the discipline is becoming increasingly specialized, breaking into fields and subfields with few people able to straddle borders. It is also important that future economic advisers learn both theories and facts, the latter including both quantitative knowledge and a good understanding of institutions and the role that they play in shaping policies and outcomes. Students should be exposed to teachers who are also advisers. This allows them to see how scholarly knowledge can be simplified, synthesized and made practical.

The trend towards formalism may seem to stand in the way of the production of economic advisers. This is not necessarily so as long as teachers remember that mathematics is a tool for rigorous and disciplined reasoning, not an end in itself. This is better achieved in departments where there is a diversity of teachers, with 'high brow' theorists mixing well with applied (but rigorous) colleagues. Similarly, balkanization of the profession will not hurt policy-orientated training in large departments where many fields are taught. Students will have a chance of being exposed to the variety of approaches and results that make up modern economics. This will be reinforced if students are required to take comprehensive exams where all of economics is considered as part of common knowledge. Departments which have decided to compete by building up niches may succeed in producing top scholars in one field or two, but the cost will be the absence of general practitioners.

More complex is the question of mainstream.[3] It is a cliché, in my view, that economics suffers from conventional thinking. The Popperian approach rightly emphasizes the need to confront theories and empirical validation. Mainstream means the accepting of results from formal testing. Theories accepted today can be proved wrong in the future, of course. In research, iconoclasts play a useful role in devoting their energies towards destroying accepted wisdom. For the training of future advisers, it is important though to emphasize what is known today, where question marks exist and to start from there. Departments which emphasize econometrics as an everyday tool are those that contribute most to the intelligent mainstreaming that advisers need when they confront difficult problems and have to feel reasonably secure about their theoretical background.

Formal courses and integrating exams
The largest departments in the top US universities come closest to the requirements set forth above. This is partly due to their size, which usually translates into diversity. It is also due to the structure of graduate curricula which emphasize formal education and exams before students are allowed to embark on their doctoral dissertations. In some cases, there may have been some overshooting when instruments and formalism displace intuition. The situation throughout Europe is documented in Table 4.1. The US approach is gradually spreading to Europe where more and more graduate programmes routinely require students to complete one or two years of course work. France, Denmark, Germany and Switzerland seem to be slower in adopting this approach, although some evolution is clearly under way. Comprehensive exams where students are quizzed on a wide range of issues drawn from all fields represent the best way to produce well-rounded economists. Having a clear view of economics as one domain of knowledge helps to distinguish the trees from the forest when faced with policy makers whose needs ignore the profession's fine subdivisions. Apparently, outside the US, only the UK and Spain have adopted this practice, with numerous exceptions but the trend is clear.

Yet, despite that evolution, the dominating model in Europe remains a form of osmosis between a teacher and his or her student, with an emphasis on in-depth inquiries in one area at the expense of breadth and awareness of developments elsewhere. This model remains clearly in place in Germany,

Table 4.1 Supply of policy advisers

	Austria	Belgium	Denmark	Finland	France	Germany	Ireland	Italy	Japan	Netherlands	Spain	Sweden	Switzerland	UK	US
Do PhD programmes in economics start with compulsory formal courses?	No	Yes	No[1]	Yes, 2 years	Yes	Few	No[2]	No[2]	Yes	Yes	Yes	Yes	Some	Yes	Yes
Do PhD programmes in economics include a comprehensive exam that covers many fields?	No	No	No	No	No	Fewer	No	No	No	Variable	Yes	No	Some	Yes	Yes
Do PhD students work part time as TA or RA, or in administrations?[3]	TA	RA (50%)	TA	TA. Admin.	No	TA, RA	TA	TA, RA	No	TA, RA	TA, RA	TA, RA	TA	TA, RA, Admin.	TA, RA, Admin.
In top universities, is applied economics (policy-orientated) seen as inferior?	2 top: yes next: no	No	No	No, the opposite	Yes	No, but…	No	No	Yes	No, the opposite	Unclear	No (or decreasing)	No	Yes	Yes
Is the national economic association run by internationally-recognized economists?	Yes	Occasionally	No	No	No	Yes	Often	No, changing	Yes	Variable	No association	No	Yes	Yes	Yes
If the national economic association publishes a review, is it of international quality?	Yes	Books uneven	No	Poor	No	Uneven		No	Yes	Yes		OK	No	Yes	Yes
Does it publish articles in English?	Yes	No	Yes	No	Rarely	Occasionally	Occasionally	Yes	Yes	Yes	Yes	No	Yes	Yes	Yes
Are there economic think-tanks?	2 institutes	1	Yes	Research Institutes	Yes	5 big institutes	1	2	Yes	Yes	Yes	Yes	No	Yes	Yes
If so, are they competent or politically motivated?	Variable	Political	Weak	Corporatist	Variable	Variable	Competent	Competent	Weak	Competent	Political	Political and competent	Variable	Variable	Yes

Notes

1. With one exception.
2. In Ireland and Italy the best students are encouraged to study abroad, typically the US or the UK.
3. 'RA means 'Research Assistant', TA means 'Teaching Assistant'.

with exceptions of course. Italy has escaped this situation by eschewing PhD programmes; it sends its best graduates abroad, traditionally to the UK and now to the US.

Extra-curricular activities: out of the ivory tower?
An important aspect of graduate education is how students earn their living. Where they need to work, some will be engaged in the university as research or teaching assistants. This may reinforce the ivory tower syndrome and the osmotic link with their mentors. This seems to be the most frequent case, as documented in Table 4.1, largely because European students often receive scholarships which imply assistantship. Outside of the US, only in Finland and the UK do students find part-time jobs in economic administrations where they can see how economics is used and where they can establish contacts useful once they have graduated. In France, graduate students rarely take up paid positions at all. The existence of a European scholarship programme, by encouraging student mobility, helps to broaden students' understanding.

A related concern is the tradition of scholarship and the vision that academics harbour of the real world. Is scholarship still seen as a life dedicated to the pursuit of the higher purpose of seeking truths? Is the real world considered as a source of corruption, including easy money, the readiness to compromise with convenient but wrong views, or at least a distraction from true scholarship? Are the Oxbridge dons still running the profession?[4] The 'ivory tower' syndrome is largely a myth, but not entirely. Table 4.1 approaches this question indirectly. Questionnaire respondents were asked whether policy-orientated economics is seen as a lesser endeavour than theory. This seems to be the case in about half the countries surveyed

Professional structures
The way national professional associations operate can be revealing. In the UK, the Royal Economic Society is a highly structured body where norms of quality and pecking order are clearly established. Those who carry weight in the profession enjoy international recognition, as do the reviews sponsored by the Society (the *Economic Journal* and the *Econometrics Journal*). A similar situation prevails in the Scandinavian countries (the *Scandinavian Journal of Economics*) and in the US (the *American Economic Review*, the *Journal of Economic Literature* and the *Journal of Economic Perspectives*). Table 4.1 shows that the situation is more muddled in Germany, France, Belgium and Italy for example, although major progress is under way in most countries as there is a tendency towards a more pan-European, more competitive, outlook.[5]

A related issue is the language of publication: non-English language reviews clearly do not enjoy the same professional status as English reviews for the obvious reason that their readership is automatically more limited. Table 4.1

shows that in most of the smaller countries such reviews now publish systematically in English, with exceptions (Belgium, Finland and Sweden). This clearly affects the quality of the review. As Table 4.1 shows, publishing in English is a necessary but not a sufficient condition for good quality, the only exception being Sweden which is an outlier on other dimensions too, as discussed below. The situation is changing, though. National reviews increasingly accept and publish papers in English or, at least, they publish summaries in English. The often-mentioned trade-off between the quality of publications and the need to serve national members who do not master English is increasingly less valid and more akin to protectionism.

Demand

Why should economic administrations (ministries, central banks, special agencies) ever ask for advice from academics? There must be a perceived need, the recognition that the staff is not necessarily providing the best analysis for all the issues that it deals with. Much depends on how the top echelons of economic administrations have been trained. It turns out that the better trained is the staff the more it calls upon academic economists. This may seem paradoxical but is not: the more one knows about the field, the more one is sensitive to one's own ignorance and aware of new knowledge.

Who are the civil servants?
Table 4.2 shows that in a number of countries economists are just a minority at the top of economic administrations. This is the case in France and in Japan, as explained in more detail below. It is also the case in Italy (the central bank is an exception), in Belgium, in Switzerland and, to a lesser extent, in Germany where lawyers have long reigned over government and industry. In Spain, civil servants are recruited through competition irrespective of their training, but economists are doing well. At the other end of the spectrum, it seems natural in the US and the Netherlands to hire economists in economic administrations. In the other cases surveyed, trained economists were a rarity until recently, but the situation is fast changing in Denmark, Finland and Sweden. The situation is also changing in the UK, through both hiring and re-training.[6]

There seems to be a close link between how top bureaucrats are educated and the use of policy advisers. Where economists are a minority (for example Finland, France, Italy, Belgium and Switzerland), the permanent staff of economic administrations see themselves as competent and able to deal with whatever issue comes up. In the US and the Netherlands, where civil servants are economists, policy advice is routinely sought from academics. This is also the case in several international organizations such as the IMF, the World Bank, the European Commission, and sometimes the Organization for Economic

Table 4.2 Demand for policy advice

	Austria	Belgium	Denmark	Finland	France	Germany	Ireland	Italy	Japan	Netherlands	Spain	Sweden	Switzerland	UK	US
Are positions at top levels of economic administrations mostly filled with people with graduate level training in economics?	Exceptionally	Few	Increasingly	No, but changing	No[1]	No[2]	PhD: Few; MA: Some	No[3]	No	Yes	Half	Few, but changing	Few	Yes, increasingly	Yes
Do economic administrations routinely ask academic economists for advice?	No	No	No	No	No	Yes	Yes	Yes	No	Yes	No	Yes	No	Often	Yes
If advice is sought only occasionally, on what issues?	Rarely	Rarely	Rarely	Big issues	No		Crises etc.		Rarely	Exceptionally					
Do politicians ask academic economists for advice?	No	Occasionally	No	Occasionally	Some	Yes	Yes	Yes	Variable	Yes	Rarely	Yes	Occasionally	Yes	Yes
Does Parliament hold hearings on economic issues?	Exceptionally	Yes	Occasionally	Yes	No	Yes	Yes[4]	Yes	Yes	Yes	No	Yes	Yes	Yes	Yes
Is there a council of economic advisers?	No	No	Yes	Since '98	Since '97	Yes	No	Since '98	Yes[5]	Yes	No	Yes	Business Cycle	Since '98	Yes
If so, does it include some of the best qualified economists?			Yes	Yes	Yes	Variable		Variable	Yes	Yes		Yes	No	No	Yes
Is there a policy-making council at the central bank? Is it influential?	No	No	Yes	No	Yes No	Yes Yes	No	No	Yes	No	No	Yes	No	Yes Yes	Yes Yes
If so, does it include some of the best qualified economists?			Yes		No	Occasionally			1 out of 9			No[6]		Yes	Yes
Do legal/supervisory institutions employ academic economists as committee members or advisers?	One case	Antitrust	Yes	Antitrust	One case	Occasionally	One case	Yes	No	Yes	No	Rarely	No	Yes	Yes

Notes

1. Top levels almost systematically filled with ENA graduates with poor training in economics. Some positions occupied by graduates in economics.
2. Federal Ministry of Economics: Economics: 37%, Law: 36%, Other: 27%; Federal Ministry of Finance: Economics: 28%, Law: 58%, Other: 24%; Other ministries: few economists.
3. Banca d'Italia: mostly PhDs in economics. Treasury: recently hired few PhDs. Elsewhere: almost none.
4. Regular hearings started recently but tend to be confined to interviewing civil servants and other public officials, not academic economists.
5. There exist deliberation councils in ministries, with top economists but weak impact.
6. The Riksbank has a formal policy-making council which does not include academic economists. The Bank also has a group of 3–4 respected academic professors who serve as advisers but who are not directly involved in the policy-making process.

Cooperation and Development (OECD), which employ trained economists (see section on 'International organizations').

One interpretation is that noneconomists do not realize how useful a support they could get. The other interpretation is that noneconomist officials have long discovered that economists are not useful, while civil servants trained as economists seek advice mainly for corporatist reasons. Yet another possibility is that noneconomists act defensively, fearing that their incompetence be exposed.

To shed light on this issue, the following section looks at two extreme cases. Some information can be gleaned from countries where policy advice is sought by administrations where economists are a minority: Germany, Sweden and Spain, with a rapid evolution in Finland. In the Nordic countries, cultural factors may play an important role: the importance of consensus implies that all concerned segments of society have to be involved in policy making. In Spain too, the civil society has displayed considerable openness in the post-Franco era. This may also apply to Germany which has built up a strong economist establishment since World War II.

Extreme cases
It is illuminating to contrast extreme cases. In the US, there is no sharp distinction between the academic and administrative worlds (and not only in economics). Not only do economic administrations hire economists but career shifts work both ways. Academics move to the administration to take up permanent or temporary positions while top civil servants may lecture in universities and even join academia permanently after a distinguished career in government. Policy advice comes naturally in such an environment, both formally and informally. The profession knows few formal barriers, a situation which also extends to business and banking.

France and Japan represent the other extreme. Economic administrations fill their top positions with a very homogeneous group of people recruited from just one school: the ENA in France and the University of Tokyo in Japan. Homogeneity leads to *esprit de corps* and the practice of avoiding as much as possible opening up to outsiders.[7] In both countries resorting to outside advisers is seen as sending a bad signal, an admission of lack of competence.

The economic successes of France and Japan seem to indicate that economic policy can be carried out perfectly well without economists. One justification would be that the less the government meddles in economic affairs, and therefore the less it needs economists, the better off is the economy. That justification does not apply to France and Japan, however, which both have a strong tradition of deep state intervention. Another interpretation, then, is that state interventions cannot be made by economists who would be too critical. That is not the case either, since in both countries the profession is strongly divided along ideological lines, with many economists steeped in the tradition of interventionism. In fact, there is an important link: where the profession is ideologically divided, it is unable to produce mainstream thought and loses its credibility. As a result its views are seen as useless and the students that it produces are not valued for decision-making positions.

Powerful administrations can be highly efficient if they are close-knit and self-sufficient.[8] All that is needed is that they attract superb minds that have gone through the toughest education selection. Technicalities, at the top, do not matter, after all. Can advanced countries do well by adopting the kind of interventionist policies that most mainstream economists reject, and by sidelining professional economists? The challenge posed by the French and Japanese cases is serious.

Surprisingly, there is no answer to this question. Economics in general, and public choice theory in particular, ought to explain the apparent paradox. Recent crises in both the Ministry of Finance and the central bank in Japan may lead to a rethink. Occasional evidence of grave mistakes by the French economic administration (for example the *Credit Lyonnais* or *Air France*), was usually followed by short-lived public criticism, but so far has posed no challenge. The French case is further examined below.

International organizations
The IMF is a policy-making institution. Its professional staff consists mostly of PhDs and it is permeated by a strong academic influence. It routinely uses academic advisers and its Research Department attracts a significant number of visitors who often contribute significantly to the Fund's work. In fact, there is some mobility between academics and the IMF, in both directions. The situation is similar at the Bank for International Settlements (BIS), the World Bank and at some regional development banks. The European Commission also routinely seeks reports from academics, even though its staff has few PhDs. The OECD is less keen to seek outside advice, except for occasional large studies (as, for example, the *Job Study*). The situation is similar at the World Trade Organization (WTO). Most of the UN agencies (International Labour Office: ILO; UN Conference on Trade and Development: UNCTAD; UN Development Programme: UNDP and so on) are relatively isolated and seem to make limited use of external advice.

There obviously exist many explanations for the situation, including traditions, but politics seems to play a key role. At the OECD political interference is widespread, since all documents must be approved by all member countries. Good analysis clearly comes second to getting the politics right and outside economists are unlikely to be of much help. In contrast, the IMF and World Bank staff work with a significant degree of protection from political pressure. UN organizations fall in between. The European Commission is more surprising in this respect.

Its output is closely scrutinized by politicians, including Commissioners and member governments. One possibility is that the staff protects itself from its political masters by enlisting academic support: even if the staff does not always like the views that it gets from its consultants, it is intellectually closer to academic economists than to politicians and can play one group against the other to occupy the 'reasonable middle ground'. The same could apply to the IMF and the World Bank.

Politicians and political parties

Policy advice may be sought directly by political leaders. Ministers surround themselves with policy advisers. Long-time political partners or well-known party insiders offer a guarantee of loyalty. What about competence? It is rare for the best economists to spend considerable amounts of time in the hope of becoming advisers to ministers. Table 4.3 shows that, in Europe, few academic economists adopt this strategy. Ministers may turn to members of the administration for private advice. Civil servants have the advantage of knowing their way around. More importantly, politicians typically have a tendency to seek advice from people who will confirm their prejudices. Finding kinship in advice is easier the less structured is the profession. Where there is a clear hierarchy in terms of professional competence, escaping mainstream views is difficult, but not impossible, even in the US as noted by the Chairman of the Federal Reserve Board, Alan Greenspan, formerly a university professor himself:

> Ministers are very reluctant to take on costs which they themselves do not perceive as absolutely necessary. And with the exceptional degree of difference among economists' views about how a particular problem is evolving, it is very easy for any government to find the appropriate economist to utter the appropriate reassurance to demonstrate that no action is required. (Greenspan 1997)

Parliaments often seek professional advice as they prepare themselves to vote on legislation. Table 4.2 shows that most parliaments have economic committees which routinely conduct hearings, the exceptions being France and Spain. The situation resembles that of politicians. Lobbies will always try to feed parliaments with 'house' economists and this is easier the less settled is the profession. With the exception of the US, and maybe the UK, the impression is that hearings play little or no role in shaping policy decisions.

Controversies, Ideologies and Culture

Economics: science or party line?

So far I have interpreted the practice of policy advice by looking at the way economists are produced (supply) and how policy makers operate (demand). These

Table 4.3 The public side of economics

	Austria	Belgium	Denmark	Finland	France	Germany	Ireland	Italy	Japan	Netherlands	Spain	Sweden	Switzerland	UK	US
Is economics considered as 'neutral', i.e. scientific and not ideologically driven?	No	No, captured	Biased	Yes	No, ideologically driven	Yes	Yes, but narrow	Yes	Yes	Yes	Biased	Yes, mostly	No	Prejudiced	Yes
Do academics regularly take up permanent or temporary official positions?	No	Yes	Occasionally	Occasionally	No	Rarely	Rarely	Occasionally	No	Yes	Rarely	Occasionally	No	Occasionally	Yes
Is policy advice seen as a source of income, research ideas or influence?	Income	Income	All 3	Influence	All 3	Influence	All 3	All 3	Research	Income, Influence Research	Income, Influence	All 3	Income	All 3	All 3
Do newspapers publish articles by academic economists?	Rarely	Occasionally	Yes	Yes (recent)	Yes	Rarely	Yes	Yes	Yes	Yes	Yes	Yes	On some issues	Occasionally	Yes
If so, are these economists the best qualified?	Sometimes			Yes	Often		Best and worst	Yes	Yes	Yes	Yes	Yes, mostly[1]	Yes	Yes, mostly	Yes
Do there exist economic programmes on TV?	Yes	No	No	Occasionally	No	Yes	Yes	Yes	Yes	Yes	Few	Yes	No	No	Yes
If so do reputable academics contribute?	No			Both, good and bad	No	No	Yes	Rarely	Occasionally	Occasionally[2]	No	Yes	Yes	No	Yes
Does TV interview academic economists? Are they the most reputable ones?	No	Occasionally; No	Occasionally; Occasionally	Sometimes; Yes	Rarely; Variable	Rarely	Yes	Yes; Yes	Yes; Yes	Yes; Yes[2]	No	Yes[1]	Yes	Yes; Variable	Yes; Yes

Notes

1. Organized groups (financial institutions, trade unions, employers' associations) employ 'media economists' in Sweden who tend to dominate.
2. 'City economists' tend to dominate debates in the UK.

63

features are partly the result of institutions and traditions. Moreover, they also relate to deeper perceptions of economics as a science. In particular, it seems that policy advice is more prevalent and more influential where the profession is more homogeneous and better structured around 'objective' standards of quality.

Obviously, there is no objective way of defining quality. It is unavoidable, therefore, that some economists argue that 'mainstream' is a code word for 'currently dominating orthodoxy'. Here is an extreme statement of the critique: 'Economic research in most of Europe is carried out along lines which the state planning institution, Gosplan, in the old Soviet Union could only envy' (Ormerod 1997, p. vi).

When Professor A says that Professor B's work is all wrong and Professor B obligingly reciprocates, how do we know which one of the two is right? The central committee will meet and support the Party member, it is argued. But where is the Committee? Peer pressure and the need to rise through the ranks, it is said. This view cannot be dismissed easily. Indeed, in economics as in all other fields, there are fashions, clubs and pecking orders (medals, professional elections and top university appointments). The important question, however, is whether unorthodox but serious research programmes systematically fail, or face unusual odds.

As usual, disgruntled researchers claim that their lack of recognition is due to censorship exercised by the central committee bent on protecting its turf from new innovative paradigms. We can never know for sure whether gems have been lost for this reason. Yet a look at the last hundred years of research does not suggest that great innovators have failed to gain recognition. The list of winners of the Nobel Prize includes a number of researchers who have spent time on the fringes, but whose views were eventually recognized. The list includes such politically and methodologically different economists as Kenneth Arrow, James M. Buchanan, Wassily W. Leontief, William Lewis, James E. Meade, Douglass C. North, Herbert A. Simon, James Tobin or William S. Vickrey.

In the end, the research community is engaged in a ferocious and open competition. Everyone can produce ideas and present them to countless reviews which compete hard against each other's. The prevailing orthodoxy is not about ideas and theories, but about the Popperian methodology of scientific research, enshrined in economics by Friedman's (1953) celebrated essay: theories must be falsifiable and judged on their predictive power. Within this orthodoxy, ideas clash. Those who reject the Popperian approach in fact develop ideologies, that is theories which are nonfalsifiable. Ideologues feel censored by the central committee, because their method of reasoning is not recognized as scientifically valid.

The French case: the impact of ideology
In every country there exist economists who reject the 'scientific method'. In most countries, they are in small numbers, in some countries without followers

in the public opinion and among politicians. But there are countries where fringe economists have substantial support in the public opinion and, therefore, among politicians. The case of France, where Marxism has exerted – and still exerts – a strong influence, is clearly special but some of its aspects are present elsewhere in Europe.

Until the early 1980s, the Communist Party, unreformed and staunchly aligned on Moscow in the Kominform tradition, garnered 20 per cent of votes in general elections. In the 1950s, and until the invasion of Czechoslovakia in 1968, a large proportion of the intelligentsia was Marxist. Most French citizens who reached maturity after World War II tended to see the world as divided into two equally extreme views of the world, capitalism and Marxism. From their early formative school years, they were trained to look for a 'third way' that was to be invented in France. The noncommunist left and the Gaullists considered themselves closer to Marxism than to capitalism. The Gaullists had adopted the Colbertist view that markets cannot be trusted and that the state must play the leading role. It was Charles de Gaulle who nationalized industries and banks after the war and François Mitterrand completed the task in 1981. The Communist Party has now declined but the far right, which receives 15 per cent of the votes, shares the fascist enthusiasm for state controls. A wide majority of the French population, and its elites, views the state as a benevolent protection against 'market excesses'. In the post-Soviet era, formerly Marxist economists have retooled themselves into 'regulationists' who recycle older views by replacing the word 'intervention' with the word 'regulation'. Liberalism, the French name for free markets, is a definite insult.

When ideological reasoning is acceptable, economics as practised by the international profession is seen as just one view of the world, biased and insensitive. In such an environment, both demand for and supply of policy advice are profoundly affected. The notion that students must learn a coherent body of knowledge cannot be defended any more: students of economics must be taught how to balance the pros and the cons of free market economics and of the regulationist approach. They are not exposed to rigorous testing methods, rather they are trained into thinking that any assumption is as good as another one. Politicians studiously avoid being cornered into one box and will want to listen to all advice. Given their inherent desire not to be told unpleasant news, there is no need to listen to advisers since all advice is partial and economists always disagree. Supply is nearly infinite and demand nil.

Table 4.3 shows that ideology remains powerful in Europe. France is the most spectacular case, but to variable degrees markets are seen as the source of evil in Italy, Spain, Portugal, Greece, Belgium and the French-speaking part of Switzerland. Trade unions in Germany, Sweden and the UK also share a deep-seated suspicion against markets as the organizing factor in an economy. German economists, on the other end, are steeped in Hayekian and social choice theories, emphasizing the role of institutions and political motives over market mechanisms. Even in the US, the Mecca of mainstream economics, fringe economists often achieve positions of influence. Describing the rise of the supply-siders in the Reagan administration or the dominance of the anti-free-trade movement in the early years of the Clinton years, Krugman notes:

> The role of the economist who cares about policy can be dispiriting: one may spend years designing sophisticated theories and carefully testing ideas against the evidence, then find politicians turn again and again to ideas you thought had been discredited decades or even centuries ago, or make statements that are flatly contradicted by the facts. (Krugman 1994, p. 292)

Controversies
Policy advisers typically think hard and long about their immediate task. What is the situation? What is the best policy response? Dealing with these two questions often represents massive work effort: collecting exhaustive quantitative evidence, using best practice and best theories to choose among possible diagnoses, digging into the toolbox to explore the best-adapted policy response, present it in a way that is understandable and convincing, and yet warn the policy makers of the risks involved and of the timing of the results.

It is, then, particularly painful to be undermined by fellow economists who, shooting from the hip, bring into the picture one of our fine controversies to criticize the policy recommendation. We all know that economics remains a fragile field as far as certitude is concerned. Academics earn a reputation by destroying previously established results and there are very few results that are not open to challenge. Any piece of advice is open to rapid attack. How to deal with that?

It requires careful thinking by advisers and nonadvisers alike. Advisers must stick to principles which command significant support in the profession – hence the view that textbook economics is all that can be used. This is what Schultze, the ultimate Washington adviser, states when describing the way the CEA operates:

> The primary task of the CEA has become one of providing the president with advice on issues with economic content that reflects the analytic approach and the views of the mainstream of the economics profession. This view . . . implies that there exists among economists a working consensus applicable to a broad range of issues. (Schultze 1996, p. 26)

Mainstream does not mean unanimity, however, nor is consensus often found on most important issues. One of Schultze's predecessors, Stein, gives his recipe: 'The CEA maintained a reputation for being willing to present all the "respectable" points of view, including those with which it disagreed' (Stein 1996, p. 12).

Put differently, policy advisers must warn policy makers of what critics will say and present them in advance with counterarguments. This significantly complicates the task. It is not enough to have the analysis and prescription right, one must also anticipate all counter arguments and find a way of presenting the policy makers with a complex package: one recommendation, why it is good, why it may be seen as bad and why it is still the best. One-handed advice with all of Vishnu's hands in handcuffs.

That is not enough. Outside nonadvisers must also play the game in a responsible way. On every issue, therefore, there will always be some reputed economists who hold opposite views. If they want to push hard (for whatever reason, not always the best), they will always be able to instil doubt in the mind of policy makers. Since economic advice almost always implies trade-offs, it is easy to exaggerate the risks and minimize the probability of achieving the results. This may be fun to do. It is bound to attract media attention. Eventually, it may even open the doors of policy advice, but the impact on the collective credibility of the profession can be disastrous.

Policy makers soon find that they cannot be given unanimous advice by economists. Either economists are not consulted at all, or they are played one against each other, or noneconomist snake-oil dealers command more attention because they play the fashionable tune of the day. Policy makers feel free to do what they see as politically expedient and, if it fails, they can blame the economists for failing to warn them.

This is where the training of economists and the structure of the profession may play a crucial role. A comparison of Tables 4.1, 4.2 and 4.3 reveals that top civil servants are more often economists and policy advice is more systematically sought, where there is a coherent training and where the ideological divide is less prevalent. It is also where national professional associations tend to be run by reputed people and publish good-quality journals. Policy advisers can call upon a mainstream. Snipers are seen as pursuing goals dangerous to the profession and then censured.[9] The opposite tends to happen either where training is less rigorous, or where policy-orientated economics is seen as disreputable. Of course, where ideology reigns, the situation is close to desperate.

Influence and the media
Policy advice can be direct, face to face. It can also be indirect, via the media. A number of economists use this channel to influence policy makers. This is a time-honoured activity. It has many advantages: it reduces the risk of compromising; it is less time-consuming; it limits accountability; it offers more visibility. It may also be efficient, given the weight of media in modern open societies.

Table 4.3 shows that this is a widespread phenomenon, including in European countries where policy advice is less frequently sought by policy makers. In almost every country, the most reputable economists routinely publish in newspapers. The situation is less favourable with television. One reason could be that articles published in newspapers are read by the most educated part of the public, while television is much more a medium that aims at a very broad public.

There are risks with indirect advice, though. First, it is not always considered as disinterested advice: politicians can see it as just one more pressure in a sea of lobbying. Second, not all advice is fit to print. For example, one would not normally propose a devaluation in public, for fear of contributing to a run on the currency.[10] Third, given the diversity of opinions likely to exist on any single issue, the media typically love to promote debates. Serious debaters will be careful not to play into the hands of the media, but not all of them will be disciplined and far-sighted enough to realize the effect on the broad public and on policy makers. The result is two-handed advice, or worse two one-handed contradictory pieces of advice. Finally, quality control can be poor. Again, the problem is less serious where the profession is well structured. Elsewhere, as in Belgium, France, Spain or Italy, many of those considered as economists by the media and the political and intellectual establishments, are in fact dilettantes with no formal training.

CONCLUSION

The culture of policy advice varies considerably from country to country. There is diversity on the demand side, whether policy advice is actually sought. In some countries it is done routinely, in others demand is nonexistent. Diversity also characterizes the channels through which policy advice is provided, from formal and highly integrated in the policy-making process to once-off at low level. There is also diversity on the supply side. On offer are all shades of the profession, from Nobel Prize winners to self-promoting, self-taught dilettantes. This chapter has attempted to document the situation and to explore some possible interpretations. Both the descriptions and the interpretations are highly exploratory and the results ought to be considered as speculative. A brief summary and appraisal follows.

Europe differs from the US, where academic advice is provided and sought at all stages of policy making: preliminary studies, elaboration within government, assessment by the Congress and debate in the media. In Europe, academic advice is used at some of these stages, never for all of them and in some cases hardly at all. Yet, even in the US, policy is often influenced by fringe ideas peddled by dubious experts.

Graduate education may explain some of the differences. Students are better prepared for policy advice where they are exposed to a wide range of the fields that make up modern economics and where they are encouraged to go back and forth between theories and facts. This stands in contrast with the scholarly tradition that emphasizes the teacher–student relation.

The kind of training received by the top echelons in economic administrations, ministries and central banks is also a matter of importance. Where economics graduates are well represented, policy advice comes more naturally. The training required for civil servants may depend on whether graduate programmes develop the skills needed for policy making. Since the skills which are needed for policy advice are similar, it is easy to see how virtuous or vicious circles can develop. Alternatively, it may be a matter of tradition, or both education and tradition.

Economics is perceived very differently from country to country. In some countries, it is seen as a useful technical field which provides the understanding of events and useful precepts for policy action. In other countries, economics is seen as lacking a core of knowledge; it is perceived as a collection of schools (Keynesians, Classicals, Marxists and so on) which profess convictions but hold no truths. Where economics is given credit for being a relevant body of knowledge, economists are sometimes perceived as co-opted by political parties or interest groups and generally not caring about the common good, and therefore not to be trusted.

The status of economics as a science, and of economists as defenders of the common good, is usually associated with the way national economic associations are structured and operate. Causality probably runs in both directions between social trust and professional structure, and between both of these and graduate training. An important component is the extent to which international standards apply. Given the dominance of English as lingua franca, the UK and the US are not able to use language barriers to protect the profession from the creative pressure of international competition.

Finally, policy advice is easily undercut when academic debates are translated into policy debates. This is probably unavoidable and certainly an old tradition, as witnessed by thousands of economists' jokes. Still, it contributes to the profession's bad press. Some progress could be made if the protagonists could agree on whether disagreements are about issues of the first order of magnitude, or about smaller points better kept for university seminars.

NOTES

1. Sir Alan Walters was influential with Margaret Thatcher, as is Ed Balls currently with Chancellor Gordon Brown.
2. Local Feds do not have direct policy-making responsibilities except when their Chair is, by rotation, part of the Open-Market Policy Committee. Academic advisers to the local Feds therefore act more in the traditional vein of producing policy-relevant research which, they hope,

may influence decisions. Presumably they benefit from the insights and data available within the Feds.
3. For a fascinating debate on this issue see the opposite views of Frey and Eichenberger (1997) and Portes (1997). See also the Symposium on 'Economists as policy advocates', *Journal of Economic Perspectives*, **6** (3), Summer 1992.
4. Both Oxford and Cambridge have refused, until very recently, to accept business schools on their campuses. Part of the reason is that business studies are seen as lacking academic rigour, a view that is not totally unfounded. But part of the reason is the perceived threat that ready money and the profit motive might exert on academic aims. A similar situation still prevails in Germany. In the US, Harvard Business School was established early in the century (not on the campus but 'across the river', but still as part of the university).
5. Two important institutions, clearly inspired by the US situation, were created in the mid-1980s. The European Economic Association, modelled on the American Economic Association, holds an annual congress and has its own journal, the *European Economic Review*. The Center for Economic Policy Research (CEPR) is a network which operates like the National Bureau of Economic Research (NBER). Both strive to establish international standards of excellence and challenge the national associations, bringing competition in terms of quality standards.
6. For some years now, the UK Treasury has sent all its staff who have no formal training in economics for MSc-level training, after they have had a few years' experience.
7. The French ENA (*Ecole Nationale d'Administration*) boasts of training its students in the belief that they can deal with any issue, be it economic, legal, political or administrative.
8. Rodrik (1995) argues strongly that reliance on market forces can slow down growth. His views are highly controversial.
9. A recent example is the exchange rate policy in Indonesia following the collapse at the end of 1997. A US economist, Steve Hanke, managed to win the trust of President Suharto and to convince him to adopt a currency board, against the IMF's advice. Within a few days, a large number of influential economists publicly criticized Hanke, both his views and his standing in the profession. While it may have looked like a witch-hunt, it was important that potentially dangerous advice be exposed as outside the mainstream.
10. I personally plead guilty of this cardinal sin, although I had long thought about the issue when I published an article calling for a depreciation (within unchanged bands of fluctuation) in an article published by *Le Monde* in September 1996 (Wyplosz 1996).

REFERENCES

Frey, B. and R. Eichenberger (1997), 'Economists: first semester, high flyers and UFOs', in P.A.G. van Bergejk et al. (eds), *Economic Science and Practice*, Cheltenham, UK and Lyme, US: Edward Elgar, pp. 15–48.
Friedman, M. (1953), *Essays in Positive Economics*, Chicago: University of Chicago Press.
Greenspan, A. (1997), 'Comments on Crockett', in Federal Reserve of Kansas City (ed.), *Maintaining Financial Stability in a Global Economy*, Kansas City: Federal Reserve of Kansas City, pp. 47–54.
Hamilton, L.H. (1992), 'Economists as public policy advisers', *Journal of Economic Perspectives*, **6** (3), pp. 61–4.
Jonung, L. (1991), 'Introduction and Summary', in L. Jonung (ed.), *The Stockholm School of Economics*, Cambridge: Cambridge University Press, pp. 1–37.
Jonung, L. (1998), 'Pioneering price level targeting: the Swedish experience', Paper presented at the Conference on Monetary Policy Rules, Stockholm, 12–13 June.
Krugman, P. (1994), *Peddling Prosperity*, New York and London: W.W. Norton.
Ormerod, P. (1997), *The Death of Economics*, New York: John Wiley.

Portes, R. (1997), 'Users and abusers of economic research', in P.A.G. van Bergejk et al. (eds), *Economic Science and Practice*, Cheltenham, UK and Lyme, US: Edward Elgar, pp. 49–59.

Rodrik, D. (1995), 'Getting interventions right: how South Korea and Taiwan grew rich', *Economic Policy*, **10** (20), pp. 53–108.

Schultze, C.L. (1996), 'The CEA: an inside voice for mainstream economics', *Journal of Economic Perspectives*, **10** (3), pp. 23–40.

Stein, H. (1996), 'A successful accident: recollections and speculations about the CEA', *Journal of Economic Perspectives*, **10** (3), pp. 3–22.

Wyplosz, C. (1996), 'Un mark à 3.75F pour sauver l'Union monétaire', *Le Monde*, **4**, September, p. 13.

APPENDIX 4A   QUESTIONNAIRE

1.   Policy advice

1.1 Are top civil servants in ministries with economic competence (Finance, economics, industry, labour, trade, etc) and central banks recruited with PhDs or serious economic training?

1.2 Do these administrations routinely ask experts to provide advice? If so, are the experts academics or others? (Please specify)

1.3 If not, do they ask for advice for special issues, and if so which ones?

1.4 Do individual politicians seek economic advice from experts? How about political parties? If so, are these advisers sticking to 'pure economics' or do they accept to take 'unorthodox' views?

1.5 Does the parliament routinely hold hearings on economic issues? Exceptionally?

1.6 Is there a council of economic advisers working for the government? Is it influential? Are its members considered as among the best qualified in the country?

1.7 Is there a policy-making council at the central bank? Does it include academics? If so, are its members considered as among the best qualified in the country? Is it influential?

1.8 Do legal/supervisory institutions (antitrust, securities commission, banking supervision) employ academic economists as committee members or advisers? (Please describe if you have time.)

2.   Training of students

2.1 Do PhD curricula start with compulsory formal courses?

2.2 Do PhD curricula include a comprehensive exam which covers a wide number of fields?

2.3 Do PhD students often earn their living as research assistants (RA) or teaching assistants (TA)? Working in economic administrations?

3.   The economic profession

3.1 Do academics regularly take up top positions in the administration or in government?

3.2 Do economic think-tanks exist? If so, are they influential? Do you consider that those who work there are competent?

3.3 Is economics generally seen as a field with little ideological prejudice or is it generally considered that there is no objective view on most policy issues?

3.4 In top universities, is applied economics seen as an inferior field?

3.5 Among academics, is policy advice seen as just a way of earning money or as a way of learning about good research areas?

3.6 Is the national economic association mainly run by internationally recognized economists?

3.7 Does the national economic association publish reviews? If so are they of international quality? Does it accept articles in English?

4. The media

4.1 Do newspapers routinely carry opinions by academic economists? If so, would you say that those who shape the debate are among the best qualified on the issue?

4.2 Does TV carry economics programmes? If so, do they use internationally reputable academics?

4.3 Is TV routinely interviewing reputable academics?

5. Economic policy advice: opportunities and limitations

A.W. Bob Coats

INTRODUCTION

On the celebratory occasion of the centenary of the University of St. Gallen, there could hardly be a more appropriate topic than economic policy advice, given the historical link between St. Gallen and the classic study of *The Role of the Economist as Official Adviser* by W.A. Jöhr and H.W. Singer (1955).[1]

In the intervening period the world has changed dramatically. The number of economists has increased enormously, and so too has their employment as economic policy advisers in many countries. Limitations of time and space makes it impossible to consider here more than a few salient aspects of this vast subject. The following treatment is inevitably influenced by the limitations of my knowledge and the nature of my special interest in the professionalization of economics, both academic and nonacademic. This has involved looking at the development of the discipline from an unconventional standpoint; one that de-emphasizes the history of economic theory (analysis, 'science') and focuses instead on what economists 'do', both in academia and – more relevant here – in the so-called 'real' world. Most of my work has dealt with British and American experiences. But while initiating and editing a series of collaborative international comparative studies I have been able to enlist the support and draw upon the knowledge and efforts of many other scholars and practising economists (Coats 1981, 1986, 1997 and 1999). Needless to say, as with most worthwhile social science research undertakings, the work has revealed how much of the relevant territory still remains to be explored.

In their pioneering study,[2] Jöhr and Singer deliberately concentrated on the role of the official economic policy adviser, but their approach was unduly restrictive, for there are usually also various unofficial contributors to economic policy decision processes, both within and outside the machinery of government. Moreover, many of these persons cannot properly be regarded as economists *proprement dites*, even on the most elastic definition of that species. In this connection it is useful to recall Sir Alec Cairncross's memorable comment that any economist who believes that he and his professional peers can successfully take over the management of economic policy

> has never been present at the kind of discussion between economists, administrators, and ministers, at which it is by no means uncommon for the economists to talk politics, the administrators to talk economics, and the ministers to discuss administrative problems. (Cairncross 1971, p. 203)

Of course, this makes it difficult to gauge the influence of economists, or indeed any particular individual or group, on many decisions. For as Cairncross elsewhere remarked:

> It is often very hard even for those at close quarters with policy making to know what does in the end shape the decisions that ministers take – or, still more, do not take. When the issue is in dispute, who except the minister (or even including the minister) knows what clinched the matter? It is very rarely that one can say with confidence that the decision would have been different if x had not been there. The people who think they know and say so may, in fact, be ill qualified to judge. (Cairncross 1971, p. 210)

In these passages Cairncross, one of the most experienced and wisest economists working in British government in the post-1945 period, was deliberately stressing the messy, even chaotic character of economic policy making, contrary to the economists' tendency to view it as an essentially orderly and rational process. In practice there are often numerous participants with differing aims, interests, knowledge and skills; and in a large government organization there will probably be significant insiders, sometimes including rival professional groups as well as ministers and bureaucrats.[3] Moreover, the borderline between amateurs and experts depends largely on the subject under consideration. In the voluminous (and often fascinating) literature on the British Civil Service a distinction has frequently been drawn between generalists – which means the more senior members of the administrative class – and specialists. Some of the latter are specialists within economics (for example agricultural or transport economists, or econometricians), whereas others are specialists in different disciplines, such as politics, sociology, mathematics, operations research, law or one of the natural sciences. Defenders of the traditional (pre-professional?) administrative class sometimes claim that the distinction between generalists and specialists is misleading because the former are in fact experts in managing administrative processes, and are therefore essential both to the formulation and the implementation of policy. The more arcane and complex these processes, the more indispensable their expertise!

*　　*　　*

The Cairncross quotations suggest two questions:

- Who are the people engaged in policy making?
- How are their activities constrained or facilitated by the institutional settings in which they work?

Both questions are dealt with in the following.

ASPECTS OF ECONOMIC ADVICE

Official or Unofficial?

Official advice emanates from, or is expressed within, the 'official' context – that is, the government. It may be for purely internal purposes, since governments 'not only power, they also puzzle' (Heclo 1974, p. 305) – or put more scientifically, they try to work out the implications of alternative policy strategies. Unfortunately, time is usually short, hence the dictum that 'the important has to give way to the urgent'. By contrast, business enterprises are, broadly speaking, single target-orientated (towards profit-making), whereas governments have a variety of objectives – political, financial, social, ethical – and multiple constituencies and commitments, both at home and abroad. Governments, especially in democracies, tend to be more concerned with the short term, whereas businesses – especially large-scale organizations – may have longer time horizons and can therefore engage in multiple-scenario planning.[4]

Officials engaged in economic advice-giving may not be trained in economics, even when the term 'economic' or 'economist' appears in the individual's job title. This situation is unusual nowadays, but it was commonplace in British government in the early post-World War II decades (see Coats 1993, pp. 519–55). The subsequent growth in the number of economic administrators, and the spread of economic literacy in the civil service, has reduced the frequency of the former anomaly.

The Sources and Quality of Economic Advice

The giving of advice, whether in economic or other affairs, is as likely to be the subject of suspicion as of serious analysis. In the economic sphere it often provokes wit, even ridicule, for example in the caustic newspaper comment on the supposed correlation between the number of economists in government and the increase in inflation, airline hijackings and terrorist outrages (see *The Guardian*, 25 July 1974). If, the commentator continues, 'it can be shown that the value of money varies inversely with the quantity of advice received, an important watershed in the field of economic theory will have been passed'. According to the Bible: 'In the multitude of counsellors there is safety' (Proverbs 11:14 and 24:6) – a principle supposedly followed by the British Prime Minister Harold Wilson in the later 1960s; and yet a German proverb warns that 'Everybody knows good counsel except him that hath need of it'.

Conventional market tests do not suffice, for much economic advice is given freely and there is no reliable correlation, either positive or negative, between price and quality. Yet one pair of political analysts recently maintained that a willingness to receive advice helps a government to seem more open and democratic, whereas it looks bad if government is not seen to be receiving, processing and acting on as much advice as possible (Peters and Barker 1993, p. 3). Such catholicity can, however, be costly, if it means that government bureaucrats or experts are forced to spend a significant part of their time examining information and recommendations from cranks and crazies. Nevertheless, in the contemporary period 'the multiplication of interest groups produces multiple sources of information that have become increasingly difficult to exclude from policy-making. . . . Moreover, the legitimacy of the process of receiving advice may be the subject of political controversy, irrespective of its quality or authoritativeness' (ibid., p. 9). The nature of the controversy will vary, among other things, according to the degree of openness of government – and here we may contrast the British persistent preference for secrecy with the United States or Scandinavian governments' accessibility to the public.

Institutional Factors in Advice Giving

The ideal image of the economic advisory process held by many economists who lack experience in government is that of a one-to-one relationship between the adviser and an influential minister or senior decision maker. More often than not, in practice, there are several (perhaps many) advisers with differing ideas, status and experience, and disagreements among advisers and decision makers are commonplace, so that somebody needs to choose among the available range of views. An economic adviser who fails to gain the ear of a significant decision maker will be impotent, whereas one who invariably agrees with his or her superiors will be neuter, rather than simply neutral. Compromise will probably be unavoidable at times, and an adviser who repeatedly submits proposals in direct contradiction to the minister's known views, or the government's publicly announced policies, is likely to be ignored, dismissed or put into a position where he or she cannot be heard.

Most economists in government are not policy advisers in the strict sense of the term. Their tasks are operational rather than advisory; although it is not uncommon for policy recommendations to originate some way below the topmost levels of government, and to percolate through the hierarchy if the supporting arguments, evidence, timely and persuasive presentation attract the attention of influential decision makers. The likelihood of such an occurrence depends on the structure of government (or nongovernmental organization) and the effectiveness of the channels of communication within the system. In an emergency, for example, the organization may be much more receptive to novel ideas than under more normal conditions (see Peacock 1979).

Economists in government rarely work in isolation unless they have been specially recruited as personal confidants of ministers. (Isolation would usually be a serious disadvantage since it would limit access to relevant information and discussion bearing on policy issues.) Some economists are employed in research units that have no direct contacts with policy makers; yet there are also specialist units that have been created in order to ensure a supply of independent analysis and commentary on policy problems. At the higher levels of the organization, political considerations become increasingly important, and the economic adviser must be sensitive to the political implications of any proposal he or she is asked to evaluate. In some continental European governments, ministers have personal staffs or 'Cabinets' to sift through and evaluate advice from permanent civil servants. In Belgium, for example, where there has long been hostility and/or mutual suspicion between the French- and Flemish-speaking communities, an incoming minister may find that most of his or her senior civil servants are members of the 'other' community. He or she may then feel uncomfortable with, or suspicious of, the advice received from such personnel and in need of more congenial and trustworthy advisers as protection against the permanent bureaucrats.

Of particular interest in studies of economic policy reform processes are the 'economic teams' that have played an influential role in a number of Latin American, Asian and East European countries. According to Stephan Haggard and John Williamson, who have analysed the reform programmes of thirteen countries between 1980 and 1990 in terms of thirteen hypotheses 'about the circumstances under which policy reform is possible and the ways in which reform can be promoted', among the most important factors contributing to successful economic policy are 'the need for a strong political base, for visionary leadership, and for a coherent team' (Haggard and Williamson 1994, pp. 562 and 478). Williamson (1994) maintains that in every successful episode there was 'strong support' for the hypothesis concerning the role of economic teams, while another highly qualified observer, Joan Nelson, has argued that: 'The cases of clear failure all traced collapse in large part to divided economic teams' (Nelson 1990, p. 347).

These teams are not entirely composed of economists; they comprise a mixture of specialists and generalists with a variety of professional backgrounds, for example technocrats (engineers) – who may be given decision-making authority by politicians – and 'technopols'. That means individuals who have some political standing in their own right (ibid., p. 345). However, these personnel categories are not clear-cut: they overlap and individuals may change their status, especially in the direction of increased political involvement.

The influence of institutional factors on the changing sources and character of economic policy advice is clearly revealed in a recent comparative study of the United States, the United Kingdom and Germany during the post-1945 period (Singer 1993). The relative decline of the influence of Keynesianism and the rise of monetarism occurred in all three countries, but with differing effects. Nevertheless, in all three cases the author argues that changing intellectual traditions among economists were less important than 'the structure of policy-making systems and the policy networks which shape how economic expertise enters into the political sphere' (ibid., p. 85). In the US, where the President's Council of Economic Advisers is located in the Executive Office, a key role in policy making has been played by the Washington think-tanks. Although the rise of conservative think-tanks shifted the intellectual focus of policy making, it did not displace mainstream economics' dominant position in the policy realm. By contrast, in Germany Keynesian economics was weaker during the early post-war decade than in the US and the UK and there were no significant professional networks acting within or outside the policy-making machinery. As a result, there was a greater degree of incoherence between economics and policy making, and the Council of Economic Experts, the so-called *Sachverständigenrat*, and the other major research institutes and policy bodies have been subject more to academic standards than to political objectives.

Until very recently Britain has had no counterpart to the American and German councils. Keynesian ideas dominated the Government Economic Service and the success of monetarism was limited, due more to political ideology than to economics *per se*. The rise of partisan right-wing think-tanks 'has been challenged only slightly by mainstream economists, revealing the professional weakness and incoherence' of that doctrinal tradition (ibid., p. 86).

It is appropriate to conclude this section by referring to the role of economists in international organizations because comments on this topic occur throughout the Jöhr and Singer volume. They reflect the experience and expertise of the latter author and the warranted belief that the international viewpoint is often neglected.

According to Singer, research in international agencies involves more general and open questions than are usually encountered in national governments, and special problems arise because of semantic difficulties stemming from the use of multiple languages and the tendency for problems to be posed by political representatives with limited command of the economists' vocabulary. Reliance on generalities is a particular danger, because specific applications of research usually lie within the internal jurisdictions of the participating countries. Much of the research consists of analysis of existing situations in terms of the organization's charter or agreements, and there is a risk of being taken in by these idealistic documents. The international economist's work is usually considered to be of a purely technical nature, originating in resolutions passed by councils and conferences – pronouncements which are themselves compromises. Often the objectives of the research are vague or inconsistent, so that the investigator is obliged to define the terms of his or her investigation. Given the teleological element in any examination of the existing situation, analysis cannot be divorced from ultimate policy objectives. Even if policy originates in the international staff it is the directing policy officials, not the professional economists, who shape it. The economist has to put the alternatives clearly and rely on the inherent logic of the argument once he or she has decided on the desirability of certain actions. (See for this Jöhr and Singer 1955, especially pp. 16, 18, 22, 33, 36–7, 40, 47 and 72–3.)

Advice or Advocacy?

In their brief chapter, 'Advice on policy', Jöhr and Singer observe that the economist dealing with policy makers cannot 'take refuge in the argument that science makes no value judgments' (ibid., p. 71).[5] The adviser not only has a right to evaluate the situation or proposal under consideration, but also a duty to do so. Of course there are difficult problems involved in weighing up the various factors to be taken into account in reaching a decision, including the degree of certainty with which the economists can deliver a judgement. But while Jöhr and Singer's account is reasonable, by comparison with some of the recent literature on these matters, it now appears far too abstract – even innocent. For example, in a recent American symposium on 'Economists as Policy Advocates' (Aaron 1992, pp. 59–77), a legislator, a former presidential adviser and a journalist reflect on their experiences in a far more frank, realistic and historically contextualized manner. The situation is, of course, vastly different nowadays given the tremendous increase in the number of economists and would-be economic advisers in and around Washington, DC, an expansion that has provoked Herbert Stein, a former Chairman of the President's Council of Economic Advisers, to speak of the 'Washington Economics Industry' (Stein 1986, pp. 1–9).

Under present circumstances both the opportunities and the temptations encountered by economic policy advisers far exceed anything dreamed of in Jöhr and Singer's philosophy. The most outspoken contributor to the American symposium, Michael Weinstein, a financial journalist and former academic economist, was deeply troubled by the 'concentration of consultants-for-hire' in first-rate American graduate schools and the number of economists employed in high-profile legal cases, who are:

writing one-sided accounts, purposely side-stepping counter claims and arguments. . . . For lawyers to write tendentious briefs in an adversarial environment presents few problems; no one expects or demands the truth from only one side. But for academics to twist facts, no matter how brilliantly, to fit the preconceived interest of their clients is disturbing. . . . More is at stake than a mere loss of innocence if the profession's leading lights can no longer be, well, trusted to tell all. Where once scholars served as reliable authorities, they now serve as advocates. (Weinstein 1992, pp. 75–6)[6]

Weinstein's comments are unusually frank and explicit, but they reflect a concern that is widely held in the American economics profession, though rarely expressed so publicly. Obviously the kind of advocacy he describes is both dishonest and incompatible with professional ethics. But unfortunately there is no widely accepted or enforceable code of ethics for economists, though there is a generally recognized professional ideology according to which the academic concept of the pure research truth-seeker, the detached nonpartisan expert, is combined in the nonacademic context with the partisan advocacy of market methods in the interests of efficiency. Although it is rarely recognized as such, efficiency is a value, albeit one among several, and economists have often been accused of giving efficiency considerations priority over the concern for equity – what has been termed 'the big trade-off' (Okun 1975; see also Nelson 1987).

The Economic Adviser–Client Relationship

As noted earlier, the one-to-one adviser–client relationship is not typical, but it can be of vital importance in certain cases depending both on the organization structures and on the personalities involved. An outstanding example is the relationship between the President and the Chairman of the President's Council of Economic Advisers in the USA. The Chairman is usually acknowledged to be a leading economist – not necessarily an academic – but the office is not strictly speaking apolitical, for the nominee has to be approved by a leading Senator (of the President's party, if there is one) in his home state. Thus the Chairman and his three colleagues are not pure professional economists.

As Gardner Ackley, a former CEA Chairman has observed, 'the effective transmission of economic understanding depends not only on the attributes of the transmitter but also on the intellect and desire to learn of the intended recipient'. Unfortunately, 'public officials are mostly just our students grown older; many of them still can't or won't learn' (Ackley 1982, p. 208).[7] The importance of the President's views and capacity in this respect has been emphasized by Herbert Stein, CEA Chairman under President Richard Nixon. The President, he says, should be seen as 'the dominant decision-maker in economic policy, as the judge of economics and economists, and as the major figure attempting to set the psychological tone of the economy. . . . In those senses he is the nation's chief economist' (Stein 1981, p. 57; see also Stein 1984).

In a fascinating comparative study of the history of the CEA the authors have shown how varied have been the relationships between successive Presidents and their economic advisers (Hargrove and Morley 1984). John F. Kennedy and Gerald Ford seem to have been the most willing consumers of economic analysis and expertise. Lyndon B. Johnson responded positively only when clear political issues were at stake, whereas Nixon, who certainly had the requisite intellectual capacity was bored by economic discussion. Hence it may not be entirely coincidental that two of the worst examples of policies undertaken against the weight of economic advice – Johnson's refusal to recommend higher taxes to pay for the Vietnam war and Nixon's insistence on imposing the first ever peacetime wage and price controls – occurred in those administrations.[8] Ronald Reagan's lack of concern about the enormous deficit and his wilful refusal to support a tax increase, led to the most serious deterioration in the relations between a President and a CEA Chairman (Martin Feldstein) in the council's history, raising the question whether that body would survive. This is in contrast to a financial crisis during the Eisenhower period, when the CEA was effectively saved by the President after Congress had (temporarily, as it proved) cut off its appropriation (see Hargrove and Morley 1984, pp. 95 ff.; also Flash 1965).

It is difficult to resist quoting a couple of the more eccentric Presidential reactions to the situations posed by their economists. So, Warren Harding, after listening to his advisers arguing over a tax issue, is said to have protested:

> I can't make a damn thing out of this tax problem. I listen to one side and they seem right, and then – God! – I talk to the other side and they seem just as right, and here I am where I started. I know somewhere there is a book that will give me the truth, but, hell, I couldn't read the book. I know somewhere there is an economist who knows the truth, but I don't know where to find him and haven't the sense to know him and trust him when I find him. God! What a job. (Orlans 1986, p. 174)

Another quite different reaction to economic advice was Reagan's, for he chose to endorse

> a rather eccentric school of economics and economists. . . . In relations with Congress he has been unusually insistent that only the precise program he has adopted will solve the nation's problems. He has been unusually explicit in public advice and directions to the Federal Reserve. And he has vigorously played the role of public salesman and salesman for the economic program. (Stein 1984, p. 57)

Yet Reagan's performance as Chairman of Cabinet discussions of economic and financial policy was lamentable. According to the memoirs of David Stockman, for a time Reagan's Budget Director, the President displayed an extraordinary inability to grasp issues or appreciate arguments, often leading him to draw conclusions opposite than intended by the persuaders (Stockman 1997). Even after discounting for Stockman's background (in theology) and his youth and inexperience, he tells a remarkable tale of Cabinet confusion, contradiction, dishonesty, deception and self-deception, incompetence and incomprehension leading to unprecedentedly irresponsible fiscal indiscipline. The budgetary forecast – directly dependent on the expert economic assessment – was in one period so wild that it became referred to as 'Rosy Scenario'. Nevertheless, once agreed, it became the basis for later negotiations over proposed budget cuts, most of which proved to be abortive. Indeed, what Stockman calls ironically a 'magic asterisk' was put against items, included as expenditure cuts, which were to be decided in the future. In practice, of course, they were subsequently treated as though they had actually been achieved. It is not clear why the economic advisers did not oppose such manipulation more vigorously.

These American examples are obviously extreme cases. But they indicate the wide range of circumstances with which economic advisers may have to contend.

THE MARKET FOR ECONOMIC ADVICE

The concept of 'the market' is so familiar and so deeply enshrined in economic discourse that it is easy to forget that it means very different things to different people, and at different times. To some dictionary authors it is defined simply as a medium of exchange between buyers and sellers. But as it can refer to a specific location and/or a geographically scattered and constantly changing set of relationships, it embraces a complex combination of concrete and abstract elements. And although mainstream neoclassical economists recognize and analyse a variety of market types – perfectly competitive, monopolistic, oligopolistic and so on – they often tend to treat the market as a singular ideal type, thereby obscuring the essential differences between markets – social, political, psychological as well as economic. The breadth and flexibility of the term and its vagueness – unless carefully defined – is even more obvious when the concept of a 'market society' is considered, for it carries massive ideological connotations.[9]

The market for economic advice (if, indeed, there is such an ongoing relationship between sellers and buyers of this service such as to justify the use of the term) is undoubtedly a peculiar case.[10] The service provided is inherently heterogeneous and there is great difficulty in judging its quality. Much economic advice is offered freely, whether on a regular (for example in magazines and newspapers[11]) or an occasional basis, so that there cannot be a stable equilibrium price. Moreover, where there is a price, it has no clear relationship to quality.

The market for economic advice is most obvious in the dealings of brokers, financial advisers and economic forecasters with their clients. On the organization level, however, there is 'contracting for knowledge', a situation in which public or private bodies employ outside consultants or agencies, rather than their own staff, to conduct investigations or to collect information considered necessary for the achievement of their objectives. Such arrangements are especially likely to occur in conditions of uncertainty – for example where knowledge and technology are changing too rapidly, and in complex ways, for the possibilities to be adequately explored by the organization's regular research staff. The growth in the number of specialist knowledge suppliers is one of the striking phenomena of advanced industrial societies, although its direct relevance to the present subject is dependent on a broadening of the concept of advice to include information or analysis.

Given the problem of quality, advice seekers are likely to turn to 'experts' for assistance, but there are often difficult questions of 'Who are the experts?' and 'What is the nature of their expertise?' The answers will, of course, vary according to circumstances, and general observations are not very helpful. Nevertheless, the myth of the neutral nonpolitical character of the experts' expertise is nowadays largely discredited, and it is necessary to select among the experts – insiders, within the organization, as well as outsiders. This often provokes strong disagreements – over professional as well as political rivalries. With many issues in economic and social policy there is less agreement among experts about the nature of reality and the role of theories, than with science or technology issues. There are also disputes about the relevance of data – as is the case, for example, with the measures of money supply in the pro- and anti-monetarist literature. As two students of policy making have observed:

> Governments are always working in a politicized environment in which opinions matter, perhaps even more than objective reality . . . so that even at the most basic level, there is no escaping the influence of opinion on the information that is being presented to government decision-makers, with the fundamental demand then being the existence and nature of that opinion. (Peters and Barker 1993, pp. 4 and 10)

Hence it is easy to understand why ministers so often want personal advisers as well as their regular and service staff. Indeed, it is arguable that 'the most common use of advice is to legitimate a decision that an organization [or an individual] wanted to make anyway' (ibid., p. 10). This type of advice is, of course, almost indistinguishable from advocacy and may put the adviser (or 'hired gun') under pressure to compromise his or her integrity. Moreover, under these circumstances the adviser may be helping the advisee to win his or her case within the Cabinet, rather than with the general public.

THE SOCIOLOGY OF ECONOMIC POLICY ADVICE

Relatively few professional economists are engaged in giving policy advice, and even those few usually for a limited part of their time. However, although this function is not readily separable from the economist's other tasks it is both important and highly visible. Indeed, the presumed success or failure of the economics profession as a whole, and the status of economics as a science, is often gauged in terms of successful or unsuccessful policy advice or economic forecasting.[12] Unfortunately there are no unambiguous criteria of success in policy making, hence judgements on this matter are likely to be based on popular impressions or misunderstandings of the complexities of the policy process. One definite consideration is the reduction of expectations of what the profession can reasonably be expected to achieve.

Public controversy among economists – whether on methodological, doctrinal, empirical or ideological grounds (or some mixture of the four) – necessarily undermines the profession's reputation as a 'science' and its usefulness in public affairs. With the discrediting of positivism and other simplistic conceptions of the nature of science, there has in the past two or three decades been a marked increase in the contest for economic ideas and disciplinary hegemony. Neoclassical economics, monetarism and Keynesianism have all met with damaging criticism, and no other single paradigm has arisen to take their place. (The possibility that this is a sign of intellectual maturity in the subject does not have wide public appeal.) On the other hand, when the British economics profession, or a significant proportion of it, endeavoured to use its collective authority to influence policy, the failure was conspicuous and embarrassing.[13]

AN ADDENDUM ON ECONOMIC EDUCATION

The provision of economic policy advice may be a small part of most economists' work, but it is of vital importance to the profession, and can be of immense value to the public. As presently constituted, advanced economic education greatly undervalues this activity, treating economics as an essentially theoretical and technical discipline rather than a key component in public policy. Of course, knowledge and understanding of economics, and especially its limitations, is a *conditio sine qua non* of an economic policy adviser.[14] But while this is a necessary condition, it is by no means sufficient. Indeed, an overconfident and narrow reliance on theoretical or technical expertise may well product a sceptical or hostile reaction, for laypeople do not generally regard economics as having the authority of a hard science. Economic advisory work requires serious consideration of the relationship between economic and noneconomic factors and calls for some attention to the personal qualities required in academic work.[15] Indeed, it has been said that young trained economists require 'at least a three-to-four-year cleansing experience to neutralize the brainwashing that takes place in these graduate programmes' (quoted by Middleton 1998, p. 359). This unhappy state of affairs has often been discussed in recent literature. But however familiar, it is a matter that should be raised whenever two or three serious-minded economists are gathered together.

As an 'economist-watcher' and historian of economic thought for several decades, I would like to end by throwing down a gauntlet – a challenge – to those of you who still have the intellectual responsibility and the opportunity to train students for the tasks that await them. We can, and must, do better than the complacency of the COGEE (Committee on Graduate Education in Economics) report (Krueger 1991) in offering them an intellectually demanding course of studies which defies the narrow constraints of the discipline and allows them to dialogue with political scientists and others, in tackling the massive economic problems that will be around for them in the twenty-first century – which the World Bank and other international agencies may have compounded rather than helped.

NOTES

1. The link is Jöhr's essay on 'The problem of the economic order', which was originally published in 1949 in a symposium volume *Individuum und Gemeinschaft* as part of the fiftieth anniversary celebrations of the Handels-Hochschule St. Gallen. Three years later, in 1952, Singer's review of Jöhr's *Die Beurteilung konkreter wirtschaftspolitischer Probleme* (1949) in the *Economic Journal* so interested the editor, E.A.G. Robinson – who had had considerable personal experience of government employment – that he suggested Jöhr's book should be expanded to take account of the special problems encountered by economists working in international agencies. The resulting joint volume by Jöhr and Singer (1955) included numerous passages by Singer on this dimension of the economic advisory process, as well as a reprint of Jöhr's 'The problem of the economic order'.
2. This is at least true with respect to the English language literature.
3. To quote Cairncross yet again, it must be remembered that 'the atmosphere of a large government department is frequently almost indistinguishable from that of the loony bin [that is a mad house]. I use this term in no pejorative sense; it is simply one of the facts of official life' (Cairncross 1970). An Australian economist has compared the economic adviser's role to that of a veterinarian charged with the task of mating elephants: 'First everything is done at a great height; secondly, a whole lot of roaring and screaming goes on; and third, you have to wait at least two years to see any results' (Hewson 1981, p. 46).
4. See the discussion in Jefferson (1983).
5. This was the position taken by Edwin G. Nourse, the first Chairman of the Council of Economic Advisers, who was only prepared to list the arguments for and against any policy under consideration. His purist restraint provoked Harry Truman's exasperated appeal for a one-armed economist.
6. Some of Weinstein's comments on the briefs submitted were scathing: 'Several big names had no special expertise in the matter before the court. Some – not all – of the submissions were pedestrian, undeserving of the names that graced their covers. They could have been – perhaps were – written by first year graduate students, leaving the impression that the submissions were commissioned for no better purpose than to keep a superstar from testifying for the other side' (Weinstein 1992, p. 75).
7. For a general treatment of the problems of dealing with ministers see, for example, the two revealing studies by Weller and Grattan (1981) and Walter (1986).

8. Harold Wilson's refusal to devalue the pound after Labour's election in October 1964, against the advice of his economists, is another example of a disastrous decision. For an excellent account of this episode, see Middleton (1998, pp. 253–7).
9. See, for example, the very different though equally valid approaches in Hirschman (1982, pp. 1463–84), and in Middleton (1996, pp. 46 ff.).
10. It is not, of course, the same thing as the market for economists. Much economic advice comes from noneconomists, whereas most economists in government, business, or international organizations are not engaged in advice giving.
11. This recalls the comment of a leading British economist that, after a long and fruitless effort to convince a minister of the wisdom of his views, his time would have been better employed in writing an article for *The Economist*, as the minister's officials kept him informed of such publications. Perhaps he had already used the argument of a pre-war Permanent Secretary in the civil service: 'Well, Minister, if you must do such a silly thing, must you do it in such a silly way?'
12. As economists' collective reputation as forecasters has fallen so markedly in the past decade or two it seems that success in this respect is nowadays less likely to be viewed as a general measure of the profession's success or failure. Fortunately, the reasons for this failure are now more widely recognized by the cognoscenti.
13. This occurred in 1981, when 364 British economists signed a letter to *The Times* attacking the Thatcherite economic policies. It had no apparent effect on the government's ideas or actions (see Middleton 1998, p. 275). This volume contains a masterly survey of the changing relationship between British economic thought, the professionalization of economics, economic history and public policy, from the 1890s to the 1980s.
14. To claim that economic theory is 'an organized way of going wrong with confidence' (Cairncross 1985, p. 6) is doubtless an overstatement, but it may serve as a warning to the overenthusiastic neophyte.
15. The desirable qualities, not often found in a single individual, include: tact; patience; adaptability; the capacity to work under pressure; the ability to communicate with nonspecialists in a variety of circumstances and at different levels of audience comprehension; skill in the arts of persuasion; a sense of timing; grasp of bureaucratic procedures and conventions – that is, the capacity to 'play the machine'; appreciation of the problems of administrative feasibility and political practicality; recognition of the limitations of one's professional expertise; and sheer stamina. For discussion, see Coats (1993, p. 620).

REFERENCES

Aaron, H.J. (1992), 'Symposium on Economists as Policy Advocates', *Journal of Economic Perspectives*, **6** (3), pp. 59–77.

Ackley, G. (1982), 'Providing economic advice to government', in J.A. Pechman and N.J. Simmler (eds), *Economics in the Public Service. Papers in Honor of Walter W. Heller*, New York: Norton.

Cairncross, Sir Alec (1970), 'Writing the history of economic policy', unpublished paper.

Cairncross, Sir Alec (1971), *Essays in Economic Management*, London: George Allen & Unwin.

Cairncross, Sir Alec (1985), 'Economics in theory and practice', *American Economic Review (Papers and Proceedings)*, **75** (1), pp. 1–14.

Coats, A.W. (ed.) (1981), *Economists in Government. An International Comparative Study*, Durham, NC: Duke University Press.

Coats, A.W. (ed.) (1986), *Economists in International Agencies. An Exploratory Study*, New York: Praeger International.

Coats, A.W. (1993), *The Sociology and Professionalization of Economics. British and American Economic Essays*, London: Routledge.

Coats, A.W. (ed.) (1997), *The Post-1945 Internationalization of Economics. (Annual Supplement to Volume 28, History of Political Economy)*, Durham, NC: Duke University Press.

Coats, A.W. (ed.) (1999), *The Development of Economics in Western Europe Since 1945*, London: Routledge.

Flash, E.S. (1965), *Economic Advice and Presidential Leadership*, New York: Columbia University Press.

Haggard, S. and J. Williamson (1994), 'The political conditions for economic reform', in J. Williamson (ed.), *The Political Economy of Policy Reform*, Washington, DC: Institute for International Economics, pp. 527–96.

Hargrove, E.C. and S.A. Morley (1984), *The President and the Council of Economic Advisers*, London: Westview Press.

Heclo, H. (1974), *Modern Social Politics in Britain and Sweden*, New Haven, CT: Yale University Press.

Hewson, J. (1981), 'The role of the adviser', in J.W. Neville (ed.), *Economics, Economists and Policy Formulation*, Australian Centre for Applied Economic Research (CAER), paper no. 13, pp. 46–67.

Hirschman, A.O. (1982), 'Rival interpretations of market society: civilizing, destructive, or feeble?', *Journal of Economic Literature*, **20** (4), pp. 1463–84.

Jefferson, M. (1983), 'Economic uncertainty and business decision-making', in J. Wiseman (ed.), *Beyond Positive Economics? Proceedings of Section F (Economics) of the British Association for the Advancement of Science, York 1981*, London: Macmillan, pp. 122–59.

Jöhr, W.A. and H.W. Singer (1955), *The Role of the Economist as Official Adviser*, London: Allen & Unwin.

Krueger, A.O. (1991), 'Report of the Committee on Graduate Education in Economics', *Journal of Economic Literature*, **29** (3), pp. 1035–53.

Middleton, R. (1996), *Government versus the Market. The Growth of the Public Sector, Economic Management and British Economic Performance. 1890–1979*, Cheltenham, UK and Brookfield, US: Edward Elgar.

Middelton, R. (1998), *Charlatans or Saviours? Economists and the British Economy from Marshall to Meade*, Cheltenham, UK and Lyme, US: Edward Elgar.

Nelson, J.M. (ed.) (1990), *Economic Crisis and Policy Choice: The Politics of Adjustment in the Third World*, Princeton, NJ: Princeton University Press.

Nelson, R.H. (1987), 'The economics profession and the making of public policy', *Journal of Economic Literature*, **25** (1), pp. 49–91.

Okun, A.M. (1975), *Equality and Efficiency: The Big Tradeoff*, Washington, DC: Brookings Institution.

Orlans, H. (1986), 'Academic social scientists and the presidency: from Wilson to Nixon', *Minerva*, **24**, pp.172–204.

Peacock, A.T. (1979), 'Giving economic advice in difficult times', in A.T. Peacock (ed.), *The Economic Analysis of Government and Related Themes*, Oxford: Martin Robertson, pp. 221–34.

Peters, B.G. and A. Barker (eds) (1993), *Advising West European Governments. Inquiries, Expertise and Public Policy*, Edinburgh: Edinburgh University Press.

Singer, Otto (1993), 'Knowledge and politics in economic policy-making. Official economic advisers in the USA, Great Britain and Germany', in B.G. Peters and A.

Barker (eds), *Advising West European Governments. Inquiries, Expertise and Public Policy*, Edinburgh: Edinburgh University Press, pp. 72–86.

Stein, H. (1981), 'The Chief Executive as Chief Economist', in W. Fellner (ed.), *Essays in Contemporary Economic Problems: Demand, Productivity, Population*, Washington, DC: American Enterprise Institute, pp. 53–78.

Stein, H. (1984), *Presidential Economics. The Making of Economic Policy from Roosevelt to Reagan and Beyond*, New York: Simon & Schuster.

Stein, H. (1986), 'The Washington Economics Industry', *American Economic Review (Papers and Proceedings)*, **76** (1), pp. 1–9.

Stockman, D.A. (1997), *The Triumph of Politics. The Inside Story of the Reagan Revolution*, New York: Avon.

Walter, J. (1986), *The Minister's Minders: Personal Advisers in National Governments*, Melbourne: Oxford University Press.

Weinstein, M. (1992), 'Economists and the media', *Journal of Economic Perspectives*, **6** (3), pp. 73–6.

Weller, P. and M. Grattan (1981), *Can Ministers Cope? Australian Federal Ministers at Work*, Richmond, VA: Hutchison.

Williamson, J. (ed.) (1994), *The Political Economy of Policy Reform*, Washington, DC: Institute for International Economics.

6. Economic knowledge transfer by research institutes in Germany: some reflections

Heinz König

INTRODUCTION

For this chapter, I was asked to present my views on institutional aspects and, in particular, the design of research institutes and their role in the transfer of economic knowledge. Given the fact that there exist more than 100 economic research institutes in Germany, all different with respect to their legal setup, their size and their goals regarding policy consulting, this would be a tremendous work. Therefore, I shall focus on some aspects especially related to proposals made by the German *Wissenschaftsrat* (Science Council) in the context of an evaluation of five research institutes cofinanced by the Federal and respective state governments.

The subject is neither new nor specific to economics. It has been discussed by Max Weber in his famous *Science as Profession* (1919), who concluded very cautiously that generally science may offer some advice if the question is properly addressed. More specifically, the subject is treated in numerous contributions about the role of economists as government advisers, for instance by Walter Adolf Jöhr, former professor of economics at the University of St. Gallen, and Hans Singer, at that time official economic adviser at the United Nations, who carefully discussed the adequate approach to policy questions, the methodological framework and the problem of advisers' neutrality concerning value judgements (*Werturteilsfreiheit*) (Jöhr and Singer 1969). In Germany, in the 1960s and 1970s the role of economic advisers drew special attention to the establishment of the so-called *Sachverständigenrat* (Council of Economic Experts) (see, for example, Härtel 1980, Molitor 1973, Schmidt 1985 or Schlecht 1963). More recently the theory and practice of economic policy consultation by independent experts and/or research institutes were the subject of papers by various authors in J.A. Pechman, *The Role of the Economist in Government* (1989). For Germany, N. Kloten gives an excellent overview about the historical development of policy consultation since World War II and the problems economists are facing with respect to the transfer of expert knowledge to government and the general public. He concludes that 'although there are features within the given structure of independent expert consultation which should be improved in West Germany, change will be difficult' (Kloten 1989, p. 64). A broadening of the spectrum of views by the members of consultative bodies to achieve a more radical approach is seen to be necessary as well as a greater variety in topics and more efficient methods in the preparation and presentation of reports. In principle, these arguments are similar to those of Nelson (1987) who suggests that economists have 'to invest greater efforts in improving writing skills, command of institutional detail, knowledge of legal processes and reasoning and to tailor their policy proposals in such a way that they will be publicly perceived' (Nelson 1987, p. 86). In the following I shall address briefly the proposals of the German *Wissenschaftsrat*, based upon the evaluation of five economic research institutes, which was commissioned in order to improve empirical research and policy consultation. Then I shall discuss some institutional aspects of consultation, focusing especially on the question of why consultation is offered mainly by research institutes rather than by individuals. The design of research institutes will be the subject of the next section, taking into account some of the suggestions of the *Wissenschaftsrat*. The final section will contain some considerations about the state of empirical economics in Germany. Needless to stress, these are my personal views, partly based upon my experience as a member of the *Wissenschaftsrat*, and partly due to my position as scientific director of a newly founded research institute participating in policy consultation.

EVALUATION BY THE GERMAN SCIENCE COUNCIL: CRITERIA AND PROPOSALS

In 1990, the German *Wissenschaftsrat* was asked by both the government of the Federal Republic of Germany and that of the former German Democratic Republic to evaluate the institutes of the Academy of Sciences of East Germany in terms of scientific quality and to make proposals for integrating them into the German research system. Subsequently, since the number of research institutes increased considerably after reunification, for example the so-called *Blaue Liste* (Blue List) institutes from 50 in 1989 to more than 80, it was decided to evaluate all institutes regularly at a four- to five-year interval. During 1995 to 1997 five economic research institutes, employing together more than 400 scientists, were evaluated. The evaluation was based upon 14 general criteria applied to all research institutes. The main criteria were

- the integration into the scientific community;
- the quality of research and quality control by scientific advisory boards, peer-referee systems and so on;
- cooperation with universities and other research institutes;
- participation in national or international networks;
- the qualifications of researchers; and
- flexibility in workforce planning.

In view of the quite different result of the evaluations in January 1997, a working group was installed by the *Wissenschaftsrat* in order to analyse

- the general situation of empirical economics in Germany;
- the goals, approaches and competition in empirical economics between universities and institutes outside universities;
- the institutional structures guaranteeing scientific quality and policy consultation; and
- international cooperation of economic research institutes.

Since, in contrast to research institutes in natural sciences, policy consultation plays a prominent role in economic research institutes and research programmes have to be adjusted permanently to actual policy problems – not necessarily interesting from a pure academic point of view – the working group interviewed experts from the United States, Great Britain, France, the Netherlands and Belgium about the institutional framework of policy consulting in their countries, the interactions between empirical research at universities and university-related research institutes, and about channels of transfer of economic knowledge.

In principle, it was found that in modern industrial economies the complexity of economic and political processes requires a science-based consultation which uses actual information and sophisticated methods, but in a way such that politicians, administrators and laypeople understand reasoning and results. For this purpose, quality of research, independence of researchers and transparency of the consulting procedure are regarded as *conditio sine qua non*. Quality of the scientific approach, and qualification in empirical research via publication in refereed journals are considered to be an essential requisite for efficient consulting. Quality depends not on the size of an institute but on the scientific competence of the individual researcher. In order to improve quality, participation in networks is seen to be necessary.

In general, the *Wissenschaftsrat* emphasizes that

- cooperation between universities and institutes has to be intensified by exchange of researchers and joint research projects;

- international cooperation should be improved in order to secure high scientific standards and attractiveness for foreign researchers;
- a coordinated research programme, which distinguishes institutes from another, should be developed; and
- quality control should to a greater extent be based on scientific principles, especially by peer-review.

Organizational arrangements for the production of economic advice differ widely among nations reflecting their political systems and culture. Economic advice to governments may be located in special advisory boards, chartered and funded, but still outside the government dealt with, by advisory staff within the government that is, but separate from the agencies directly responsible for administering governmental activity, or it might be given by administrative agencies themselves (see Nelson 1987).

In the face of different institutional approaches – free market orientation as in Great Britain, government centralization as in France or reliance on research institutes as in Germany – the *Wissenschaftsrat* concluded that, in principle, no superiority of a system of policy consultation with respect to efficiency emerges. Differences are caused mainly by tradition, political culture and economic paradigms. However, according to the *Wissenschaftsrat*, empirical economics exhibits some deficiencies in Germany, partly caused by the lack of interest at universities in policy consultation interests, partly due to a less rigorous scientific approach pursued by research institutes.

INSTITUTIONAL ASPECTS OF POLICY CONSULTATION

It is not my task to comment on all suggestions made by the *Wissenschaftsrat*. Most arguments speak for themselves, for example the request for a stronger cooperation with universities in order to increase scientific quality of consulting and to improve chances for recruiting young researchers, the request to participate in international networks or the request to coordinate research programmes, yet ones which allow for competition between institutes.

In this section I shall draw attention to only two issues: (i) what are the institutional arrangements which ensure independence of the researcher (and the research institute) and (ii) what should (and could) be the role of a scientific advisory board, favoured by the *Wissenschaftsrat*, as an instrument to guarantee scientific quality of consultation? In addressing the first problem, I do not take up the issue of 'neutrality concerning value judgements' (*Werturteilsfreiheit*). There exists enough literature on this aspect already. From my point of view, each economic research is im- or explicitly based upon some paradigm – be it Neoliberal, Keynesian, Socialist or whatsoever. Scientific consulting presupposes that assumptions are formulated in such a way that the decision maker in politics can evaluate alternative results of actions.

In the early days of the Federal Republic of Germany, scientific advisory councils, which were independent of governmental directive, were set up at the Ministry of Finance and the Ministry of Economic Affairs (subsequently followed by others). The final decisions on topics to be chosen were up to the advisory council, whose members did not receive remuneration. In 1950, because of the growing volume of statistical data and the lack of staff, and particulary in order to focus on basic decisions in the field of regulatory policy, the *Wissenschaftlicher Beirat* (Scientific Council of Economic Experts) at the Ministry of Economic Affairs decided to hand over the task of reporting on the economic situation to research institutes (see Kloten 1989, pp. 40 ff.). Subsequently, the research institutes became involved not only in the advisory process on the economic situation of Germany and its prospects but increasingly in all other fields of economic affairs.

There is no doubt that only external and internal independence of the adviser can guarantee that the consequences of alternative strategies of political action can be analysed in an objective manner without jeopardizing the decisions of political authorities. In this context, the question arises whether this independence, institutionally, can be maintained by institutes funded jointly by the Federal and state governments or by state governments alone. In principle, the answer is 'Yes', although I see possible conflicts regarding *Drittmittelprojekte* (earmarked funding projects). Very often the share of earmarked funded projects in the total budget of an institute is considered an indicator of its recognition by the general public and administration. This is one side of the coin. The other one is that earmarked funding leads not only to dependency because the institute has to look for subsequent projects in order to keep research staff employed, but may also – according to the opinion of university researchers – result in political influence on the outcome of research. It may further have the consequence that basic research is more or less neglected in favour of applied work and innovative research becomes more and more exceptional. Therefore, to guarantee independence requires a high share of basic funding (*Grundausstattung*) which, by not being earmarked, allows the researcher to take up issues not belonging to the mainstream of the political debate, but which are necessary to strengthen the scientific approach. Additionally, to avoid any false impression with respect to political influence on the outcome of projects, results of consultation must be published without any delay. Insights can thus be discussed by fellow economists and the general public in an objective way, leaving the burden of the proof of an action to the politician.

I now turn to the second aspect: the role of scientific advisory boards. The *Wissenschaftsrat* increasingly stresses their importance for quality control of research projects, of research units within an institute and for the direction of the research programme in general. Certainly, any advisory board has an advantage in terms of outside control, scientific advice, increasing competence and, last but not least, of improving the integration of an institute into the scientific community as well as into the political and economic process. However, I remember discussions at the *Wissenschaftsrat* years ago indicating that the importance of such an institution should not be overemphasized. Reasons for a cautious treatment of this subject are numerous: because effective participation on an advisory board is time-consuming, and because highly qualified advisers have therefore to consider their opportunity costs, their number is very limited. Furthermore, in special fields only a few experts may be found and, given their other duties, they may not be willing to act as an adviser. In addition, with respect to the fact that research institutes are not allowed to remunerate advisers (except with a bottle of wine at Christmas) or are not able to honour them with other rewards, the incentive for participation may be low. In summary, although I am convinced that an advisory board is a necessary and fruitful instrument (and I hasten to add that my own experience was excellent), I am still somewhat sceptical about the strong emphasis given to this institution by the *Wissenschaftsrat*.

DESIGN OF RESEARCH INSTITUTES

One of the main deficiencies of German research institutes, identified by the *Wissenschaftsrat*, is the high share of tenure contracts for researchers, hindering mobility of their labour force, and consequently employment of young researchers with new ideas. As a consequence, the *Wissenschaftsrat* demanded a reduction in this share and an increase in the share of temporary contracts. Given German labour law, this requirement seems *prima vista* blue-eyed: how could it be done? I shall briefly sketch the approach pursued by the ZEW (*Zentrum für Europäische Wirtschaftsforschung*) (Centre for European Economic Research) in order to fulfil this task. First, because this research institute is obliged to pay wages in accordance with the wage scheme for civil servants and because it is competing for young researchers with universities (and industry), it has to install incentives such that career chances are at least equivalent to those at universities. That means that young researchers joining the institute with a temporary contract must have the opportunity to further qualify themselves in a postgraduate programme leading to a doctoral dissertation (or a habilitation). This makes it necessary that during his or her employment at the institute he or she must be given time for scientific work enabling him or her the pursuit of their own ideas, either in an area covered by the institute or, else, in an area of his or her choice. The realization of such a programme clearly needs a certain amount of basic funding of the institute, which implies a well-defined upper limit to earmarked funding.

One can discuss whether a ratio of 60:40 of basic to earmarked funding, as suggested by the *Wissenschaftsrat*, is appropriate. I myself consider a share in total budget of one-third of earmarked funded projects to be more adequate, because it improves the scientific basis without neglecting the task of policy consultation.

Second, qualification requires strong cooperation with universities. Without direct contacts with university teachers and researchers, an in-house programme bears the risk of being cut off not only from new developments in science but also from personal relations necessary for the promotion of young researchers. One method of cooperation followed by the *ZEW* – and being more or less equivalent to the practice of the National Bureau of Economic Research (NBER) or the Center for Economic Policy Research (CEPR) – is based upon the institution of research associates, that means university professors acting as head of project teams. The experience has been successful so far but because of the political influences and financial pressures which German universities are increasingly facing, I fear that these chances of cooperation might fade – despite the proposals of the *Wissenschaftsrat*. Increasing the teaching load and cutting (research) funds at universities according to the share of earmarked funded projects, by excluding those activities outside universities, will certainly have a negative impact on the willingness to act as a research associate.

Finally, it is still a common practice that budget policy is based upon the cameralistic principle. Positions of members of an institute have to be structured following an externally defined wage-structure system, budget items cannot be reallocated freely, and so forth. This obstructs fast decision making and adjustment to new developments.

Instead of cameralistic budget criteria – and I refer in that respect to my own positive experience – one can only stipulate that there should be more flexibility in budget planning.

EMPIRICAL ECONOMICS IN GERMANY: SOME REFLECTIONS

Since the *Wissenschaftsrat* criticized the state of empirical research in economics in Germany, some very brief remarks on the state of that art seem to be in order. The number of Nobel prizes in economics awarded to American economists, or bibliometric measures such as the Social Science Citation Index, are frequently used to demonstrate the dominance of American economists or, more exactly, of Anglo-Saxon economists. Continental Europe's main disadvantage in applied economics is seen in the lack of modernist methodology, stressing the sequence: from theory to model to econometric specification to testing and falsification (see, for example, Portes 1987). Although this belief is widespread, I doubt that it reflects the state of the art correctly, even in the German case.

First, it neglects the different profiles of university education and university career. These are the traditional German (and French) attitudes towards publication, the inclination to write books instead of articles (and a habilitation-thesis for promotion), and the long- (and still-) lasting tradition of splitting economics into pure 'theory', economic policy and public finance. As far as research institutes are concerned this negative view neglects the fact that policy consulting is directed mostly towards special problems of the national economy. Results are (and must be) purveyed in the German language to national governments, to politicians and the public. The consequences are twofold: on the one side, the language barrier prevents foreign economists from noticing such studies. On the other side, except for some fields like international trade and finance or resource and environmental economics, specific national problems are of less or no interest at all to economists in other countries The publication practice of international journals may support this view. While it is easier to publish articles with new ideas in economic theory or econometric methodology, the probability of the acceptance of empirical studies related to national issues, even along the methodological lines stated above, will be quite low.

Second, teaching of economics and research in economics has changed slowly but, ultimately, dramatically since the 1950s. While law studies in the various fields dominated 'economics' after World War II, nowadays – if at all – they play only a minor role. Economic theory and even econometric approaches in fields considered to be immune against 'modernist' methodology became increasingly important. In larger departments or faculties the tradition of splitting up economics into the three fields as stated above ceased and was increasingly replaced by specialized fields. Along with this change came a stronger integration of applied research. In addition, postgraduate programmes based upon curricula akin to those at American universities are being installed at many universities in Germany.

Third, although there still exists a need for further improvement in international cooperation, especially between research institutes, networks initiated by the Commission of the European Union, European doctoral programmes, or participation in activities of the CEPR have become more and more attractive to German economists.

It is needless to stress that still more can and has to be done to stimulate cooperation and to enforce competition between German universities themselves and with foreign institutions.

* * *

A final remark. In spite of the developments sketched in the foregoing it is increasingly argued that in Germany economists have lost their influence on policy decisions, compared to the influence economists commanded after World War II when scholars of the *Freiburger Schule* shaped the economic order (*Wirtschaftsordnung*) of the Federal Republic of Germany or were even responsible themselves for policy decisions. One reason for this loss is seen in the declining interactions between academia and government agencies, in which economists are a rare species (see volume 38 in the *Wirtschaftswoche* 1997). Almost 70 years ago, in his essay 'Economic possibilities for our grandchildren', J.M. Keynes argued that we should not overestimate the importance of the economic problem: 'It should be a matter of specialists – like dentistry. If economists could manage to get themselves thought of as humble, competent people, on a level with dentists, that would be splendid' (Keynes 1931, p. 373).

There is not much to add. If the counterpart is missing or if there exists an internal language barrier, the chances for policy advice are not high. More generally, the *Bringschuld* of science, its obligation to transfer knowledge outside academia, is one side of the coin; the other one is not to abuse scientific advice for the purpose of justifying policy actions, but instead to look for alternatives or even visions (see also von Münch 1998).

REFERENCES

Härtel, H.-H. (1980), 'Entwicklung und Leistungsfähigkeit der wirtschaftspolitischen Beratung am Beispiel des Sachverständigenrates', in D.B. Simmert (ed.), *Wirtschaftspolitik – kontrovers*, Köln: Bund-Verlag, pp. 91–108.
Jöhr, A. and H.W. Singer (1969), *Die Nationalökonomie im Dienste der Wirtschaftspolitik*, 3rd edn, Göttingen: Vandenhoeck & Ruprecht (Kleine Vandenhoeck Reihe, 175/177).
Keynes, J.M. (1931), *Essays in Persuasion*, London: Rupert Hart-Davis.
Kloten, N. (1989), 'West Germany', in J.A. Pechman (ed.), *The Role of the Economist in Government*, New York: Harvester Wheatsheaf, pp. 47–72.
Molitor, R. (ed.) (1973), *Zehn Jahre Sachverständigenrat zur Begutachtung der gesamtwirtschaftlichen Entwicklung. Eine kritische Bestandsaufnahme*, Frankfurt am Main: Athenäum Verlag.
Nelson, R.H. (1987), 'The economics profession and the making of public policy', *Journal of Economic Literature*, **25** (1), pp. 49–91.
Pechman, J.A. (ed.) (1989), *The Role of the Economist in Government*, New York: Harvester Wheatsheaf.
Portes, R. (1987), 'Economics in Europe', *European Economic Review*, **31** (2), pp. 1329–40.
Schlecht, O. (1963), *Was soll und kann der Sachverständigenrat leisten? Die Aufgabe des Sachverständigenrats zur Begutachtung der gesamtwirtschaftlichen Entwicklung*, Bonn.

Schmidt, K. (1985), *Der Sachverständigenrat zur Begutachtung der gesamt-wirtschaftlichen Entwicklung: Institution, Meßkonzepte und wirtschaftspolitische Leitlinien*, Stuttgart: Steiner Verlag-Wiesbaden-GmbH.

von Münch, I.(1998), 'Wissenschaft und Politik – Unterschiede und Gemeinsamkeiten', in H.P. Gallert and G. Wagner (eds), *Empirische Forschung und wirtschaftspolitische Beratung (Festschrift für H.-J. Krupp zum 65. Geburtstag)*, Frankfurt am Main and New York: Campus Verlag, pp. 522–34.

Weber, M. (1919), *Wissenschaft als Beruf*, München and Leipzig: Duncker & Humblot.

Wirtschaftswoche (1997), *Der Einfluß der Ökonomen auf die deutsche Wirtschafts- und Finanzpolitik wird immer geringer – mit fatalen Folgen*, **38**, pp. 36–43.

Wissenschaftsrat (1998), *Stellungnahme zu den Wirtschaftsforschungsinstituten der Blauen Liste in den alten Ländern. Allgemeine Gesichtspunkte*, Drucksache 3320, Berlin.

PART III

Teaching and Application of Economics

7. The making of applied economists: challenges for undergraduate curricula

Manfred Gärtner[*]

INTRODUCTION

Not all is well with economics – at least when we go by the number of students who flock to our lectures and seminars on a painfully decreasing scale in recent years. Granted, there have always been ups and downs in enrolment and graduation numbers. Indeed, researchers have used the turnout of academic majors in fields such as engineering or teaching as illustrations for the cobweb cycle once taught in intermediate microeconomics before the rational expectations revolution.[1] Recent experience appears to be more dramatic, though, and cannot be shrugged off by reference to cyclical swings that were always there. College- and university-level enrolment in economics has not only been losing ground to close competitors such as business administration and management sciences, but has often even declined in absolute terms. And these are not only isolated observations at a few institutions (such as the University of St. Gallen) or in individual countries, but they seem to have been at work on an international scale for quite some time.

The vanishing of economics students has implications for all of us involved in the teaching business, for the institutions that employ us and that must channel scarce resources to their most efficient use, and also for society, the course of which is not independent of the amount of economic literacy and expertise around (at least so we think).

There is some literature out there, though mostly motivated by and focused on recent trends in the United States, analysing the causes of this decline and suggesting remedies. Much of this takes the position of an interest group protecting its turf. When stepping back to look at it from a scientific viewpoint, economists appear rather ill-equipped to lament this decline and argue whether anything should be done at all. After all, unless convinced of market failure for the case at hand, economists prefer to allow supply and demand to interact to

* I would like to thank Matthias Lutz and Friederike Pohlenz for their extensive comments on an earlier draft and for help with the data.

produce an efficient result. If the market has realized that it does not need as many economists as previously thought, then that is how it should be, even if it hurts.

Of course, this has not been the position advanced in pertinent discussions, and it is not the position I am going to take here. To justify thinking about change, however, we need to argue that the market has been misled and needs to be guided back on to the right track.

The first such argument would be that we are not selling economics in the right package. Therefore, while the market may be responding rationally to what and how we have taught so far, a change in what we teach and how we teach may create a different product that appeals better to potential employers and to potential students than the old one.

A second such argument emphasizes that economics expertise generates substantial externalities which the market takes into account insufficiently, if at all. This would give economics a status similar to the arts or philosophy or maybe mathematics, calling for subsidization or specific support in one form or another.

This chapter begins with a presentation of the facts, documenting the international nature of the decline in economics majors that is causing our current concern. The subsequent section elaborates briefly on the implications of this stagnation or downturn for economics departments, for universities and for society. In the remaining two sections I discuss what we should teach and how we should teach in order to make economists better competitors in the labour market and economics a more attractive subject to study. The position taken there is that the target of our efforts must be the nonacademic labour market. The kind of economists educated for the nonacademic labour market will be referred to here as *applied economists*. The final section sums up in the form of a proposal for a reorientation of the undergraduate curriculum in economics.

CYCLES AND TRENDS IN ECONOMICS MAJORS

The number of degrees awarded in different fields of study varies substantially over time, usually showing both trends over time and cyclical fluctuations. The difference between countries is in the relative importance of trends and cyclical factors. What seems to set the 1990s apart from previous changes is that trends and cycles move in the same direction, thus adding up to a particularly dramatic picture.

Trends in Undergraduate Economics Degrees in the United States

Figure 7.1 shows Bachelor in Economics degrees awarded in the United States between 1948 and 1996, both as absolute numbers and as shares of all bachelor's degrees awarded. The steady upward trend in the number of economics bachelor's degrees awarded each year reflects population growth and the general expansion of the academic sector that is common to all industrial countries. What catches the eye are the three drops in the number of economics degrees awarded that occurred after 1950, after 1970 and again since the beginning of the 1990s. While all three run against the long-run trend, the general 'explanation' for the first two does not work for the third. In the 1950s and the 1970s, the number of degrees recessed towards their long-run trend values after previous spikes had pushed them beyond. The first spike occurred in the immediate aftermath of World War II, when the active war generation resumed and completed their formal education. After that the number plummeted, partly as a return to normal levels and partly as a consequence of the Korean war. The late 1960s saw another spike, reflecting the baby boom and above-normal rates of college attendance presumably caused by the Vietnam war. Again, the bulge disappears soon after. What sets the recent experience apart from these two earlier episodes is that no obvious factors seem to have caused abnormally high degree numbers prior to the drop. The interpretation that the recent drop is a downward departure from the long-run trend is an obvious cause for concern.

The recent decline in the number of bachelor's degrees awarded in economics might simply reflect a general decline in the number of academic degrees awarded. The percentages given in the right-hand panel refute this interpretation. First, the recent decline in the absolute number of economics majors obviously stems from a severe loss of market share, from about 2.2 per cent around 1990 to an all-time low of about 1.5 per cent in 1996. Second, the market share of economics majors seems to be coming down in cycles. Even if we ignore the initial spike in 1948, the market share is lower at the bottom of each cycle than during the previous one.[2]

Trends in Undergraduate Economics Degrees in Germany

Figure 7.2 shows enrolment in economics majors (*Volkswirtschaftslehre*) at German universities from 1970 to 1996. The left-hand panel displays absolute numbers. The right-hand panel shows enrolment in economics as a proportion of total enrolment. The left-hand panel features a striking resemblance to the US experience after 1990. While there had been a steady increase in economics enrolment for about two decades (enrolment more than doubled in a little more than twenty years), with a minor cyclical overlay, enrolment numbers have been receding substantially in recent years. This replicates what happened at American universities (as shown in the left-hand panel of Figure 7.1). What makes the German experience even more serious, however, and this is where the similarity ends, is that this recent dip adds to a downward trend that has been there all along. As the right-hand panel shows, by 1990 economics had already lost more than

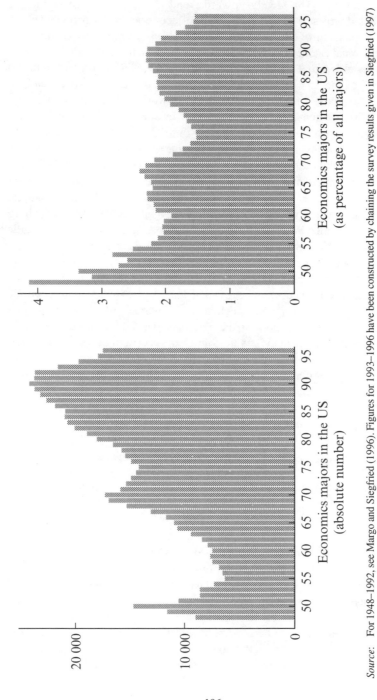

Source: For 1948–1992, see Margo and Siegfried (1996). Figures for 1993–1996 have been constructed by chaining the survey results given in Siegfried (1997) to the figures provided in Margo and Siegfried.

Figure 7.1   Economics majors in the US, 1948–1996 (in absolute numbers and as percentage of all majors)

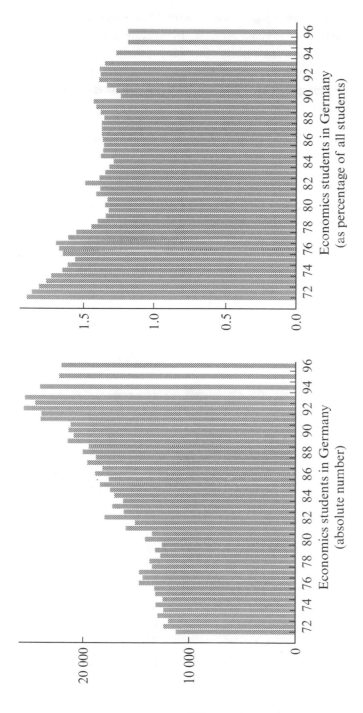

Source: Federal Office for Statistics of Germany (*Statistisches Bundesamt*), direct communication.

Figure 7.2 Students enrolled in economics in Germany, 1972–1996 (in absolute numbers and as percentage of all students)

a quarter of the market share it held in 1970. The recent downturn of absolute enrolment only adds a dramatic climax to this already unpleasant trend and is putting a lot of pressure on many economics departments.

Trends in Undergraduate Economics Degrees in Switzerland: The Case of the University of St. Gallen

Federal statistics on Swiss university education and degrees provide little information on trends and cycles in the field of economics. In fact, 1997/98 data distinguish for the first time between economics (*Volkswirtschaftslehre*) and business administration/management (*Betriebswirtschaftslehre*). Previous years subsume both categories together under the label 'economic sciences' (*Wirtschaftswissenschaften*). As Figure 7.3 shows, there is a general upward trend in joint economics/business administration majors, with their market share

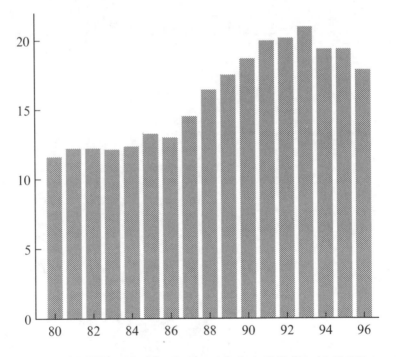

Source: Swiss Federal Office of Statistics (*Bundesamt für Statistik*), Fachbereich 15: Bildung und Wissenschaft, Reihe: Studierende an den Schweizerischen Hochschulen, various years.

Figure 7.3   Percentage of students enrolled in economic science in Switzerland, 1980–1996

almost doubling from less than 12 per cent in 1980 to 21 per cent in 1993. Since then the share has receded to some 18 per cent in 1996.

Since national statistics cannot be used to detail how economics has fared relative to close competitors and in the academic market in general, we try to gain some insights from looking at the experience of the University of St. Gallen. While St. Gallen's experience need not be representative of that of other universities, it derives its weight from the fact that St. Gallen has by far the largest enrolment in the economic sciences in Switzerland. Pertinent enrolment in St. Gallen was 3550 during the winter semester 1997/98. The University of Zurich was second with 2113 in these two fields. Total enrolment in the economic sciences at all Swiss universities was 11 009.

The number of majors annually awarded by the University of St. Gallen also reflects the general expansion of university education. Starting from 104 graduates in the academic year 1970/71, the number had tripled three years later (Figure 7.4, left-hand panel). After a decade of consolidation, numbers began to climb again after the mid-1980s, reaching a peak in 1995 at 600. Since then the number of majors has dropped to 440, but is still way above what it was ten years earlier. The number of economics majors does not reflect this upward trend. If anything, numbers are lower in the 1990s than they were in the 1970s.

Of course, the stagnating number of economics majors during a period of overall expansion of the University of St. Gallen must mean a falling share of economics in the total number of majors awarded. The right-hand panel in Figure 7.4 shows this quite drastically. Economics appears to have fallen out of favour in steps. During the 1970s the share of economics hovered around 20 per cent of all majors granted. This level could not be sustained in the 1980s, when the new resistance level appeared to be about 10 per cent. The 1990s has brought no comeback. If anything, economics seems to have had a hard time defending its 10 per cent share, having failed four years in a row and hitting an all-time low of 5 per cent in 1997/98.

To make matters worse (although this also provides opportunities), the lagging performance of economics is not part of students turning away from the economic sciences in general towards new, possibly more attractive fields of study. While business majors were on a par with economics majors in 1970, with a market share of some 40 per cent each, their share rose particularly at the beginning of the 1980s, commanding a market share consistently above 60 per cent ever since. The huge performance difference between business studies and economics is shown in that while there was one business major for every economics major in 1970 and two business majors for every economics major during the rest of the 1970s, there were 15 business majors for each economics major during the academic year 1997/98.

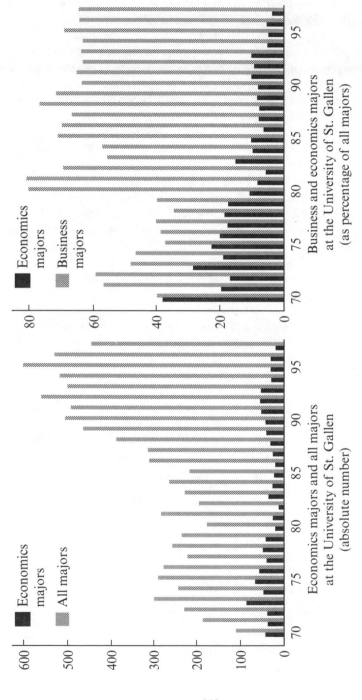

Source: University of St. Gallen, *Pressestelle*. Data for missing years were filled in using the number of students who registered for the final exam (*Prüfungsstatistik*).

Figure 7.4 Majors in business, economics and all fields at the University of St. Gallen, 1970–1997

IMPLICATIONS OF THE (RELATIVE) DECLINE OF THE NUMBER OF ECONOMICS MAJORS

There are at least three angles from which to view the implications of the relative, in some cases absolute, decline in student interest in economics as a major field of study. The first and most severely and directly affected are the economics departments with their employed faculty at all levels. Here, funding and positions are at stake. And even where tenure provides protection, infrastructure may be cut down or faculty may be forced to move to other universities to join their departments. The second angle is from the university's point of view. The third is society as represented by the government. We shall discuss these three perspectives in turn.

Implications for the Economics Departments and their Faculty

As said, the most direct impact of a declining interest of students in majoring in economics is felt by the economics departments and their faculty. In the US this is 'presumably because decreasing demand portends downward pressure on the demand for economists and may damage earnings and employment prospects for economics faculty, especially at public universities where budgets are often linked to enrollments' (Margo and Siegfried 1996, p. 326). Within the different university systems in many European, particularly German-speaking, countries, effects are likely to be less direct. Salaries are usually independent of enrolments and tenure prevails at the professorial level. What may happen nevertheless is that entire departments are closed and tenured staff is requested to relocate to some other university where their reception may at most be lukewarm. The University of Constance's economics department, one of the most renowned for research in Germany, barely escaped this fate in 1997.

Another serious threat is that economics departments are closed and staff is transferred to the business administration department which then mutates into a business school. Well-known US business schools have already chosen this structure, keeping a few economists to teach business majors whatever microeconomics and macroeconomics is considered inevitable, akin to how economics departments commonly keep a mathematician or a statistician to teach those technical skills deemed essential for economics majors. This prospect is hardly enticing for economists, even though in Switzerland, Germany and Austria the economics ration fed to business majors is spread over the entire four years of study, and therefore surpasses what is covered in a principles course and usually also what is covered in intermediate microeconomics and macroeconomics texts. Nevertheless, and understandably so, most economics faculty abhor the idea of teaching only students who have expressed that economics is not their subject of choice. While such solutions may serve as a welcome buffer in a changing academic market, they would jeopardize the sacred unity of research and teaching and be a deterrent to bright new talent in the field.

Implications for the University

From the perspective of the university, downsizing economics is a process it has most likely experienced and handled previously with other majors. Problems may arise, though, if large segments of staff on tenure track prevent the administration from resizing the economics department so as to follow student demand.

Implications for Society

Most economists subscribe to the view that economics is a superior way of understanding and analysing many of the world's issues, not only in the traditional realm of economics, but also in other areas such as politics, geography or the law. To the extent that this is true, society would be better off if economists had more of a say in such 'noneconomic' fields and, certainly, if economists were to replace noneconomists (often lawyers) in positions where explicitly economic decisions are made. However, it may be difficult to underscore this belief with facts.

There are a number of noteworthy examples of how economic reasoning has shaped institutional progress in important ways. The setup of the European Central Bank (ECB) is a very recent example. We like to believe that the ECB would be designed very differently without the discussion originated by public choice scholars and carried on in the 1980s and 1990s under the label of time inconsistency. On the other hand, the Bundesbank and the Swiss National Bank had been designed in a similar way decades earlier without these recent insights. Another example is the World Trade Organization (WTO) and globalization, which are best seen as the ultimate consequence of economists' repeated arguments in favour of competition. Few global developments have brought out as clearly how little compatibility there often is between the goals of raising income and of distributing it fairly. Only after the changes made are irreversible, do economists begin to think about what sacrifices globalization will demand from groups or countries in terms of income and cultural identity. With the first results at hand, one may question whether economists have really led and guided these changes with scientific responsibility and care, or triggered them with some simplistic arguments about how the world functions that ignored or did not care about the broader picture. A final example is the move towards a single European currency. The public attitude towards this move in different EU member states seems to reveal considerable expertise in judging the benefits a country may expect from the euro. The drawback here is that politics in a number of countries has moved ahead, unimpressed by such judgement (see Gärtner 1997).

*   *   *

To sum this up: claiming market failure due to externalities in producing economics majors will hardly sound convincing outside economists' circles. Whether economists want to do something about the economic perspective being underrepresented in the political decision-making process or believe that the market does not see the direct merits of an economist's education the way it should, the way to go is to reconsider what our product is and who buys it. More specifically, we need to put more thought into what we teach and how we teach it than we did during economics' long years of plenty.

WHAT SHOULD WE TEACH?

What we teach prospective economics majors must strike a balance between the views of teachers who supply education and those of students (and firms that eventually are to hire economics majors) who demand the product. Neither sticking uncompromisingly to what we think makes up an economist nor bowing to what students and firms want even at the cost of discarding the very core of what we believe defines an economist, would make any sense in the light of vanishing enrolment.

A crucial point to remember here is that only a small fraction of economics majors seeks and finds employment in academia. Even in the US, with its huge market of some 3300 institutions teaching economics at the academic level, only a little more than one in two new PhDs initially takes an academic position. This share must be decidedly smaller in Germany and Switzerland. One qualification level lower, Slembeck (1992, p. 140) found that only 10 per cent of prospective economics majors at the University of St. Gallen aspire to employment in academia. Fifty-four per cent do not even pursue employment as an economist. It is obvious, therefore, that the key to rebounding enrolment numbers lies with how nonacademic employers receive our product. Students trained to succeed in this market, as economists or in related positions, are referred to here as 'applied economists'. Economists destined for work in academia will have additional needs, but not completely different ones. Given that they represent the next generation to teach applied economists, it is crucial that they know what and how applied economists are being taught today.

The View of Employers

Nonacademic employers rarely formulate specific demands in terms of theories and models to be covered in the curriculum of economics majors to be employed. While they may sometimes require an emphasis on microeconomics, macroeconomics or environmental economics, or certain technical skills, say in econometrics, this is a case-by-case thing which merely suggests that we should offer options to specialize in such fields if students wish to. A more important aspect for employers appears to be that rookie economists commonly join a team, group or organization where others depend on their contribution.

Where specific demand or criticism is voiced, it is either of a more general nature or it addresses the lack of practical skills that are not directly related to economics. The first category entails the complaint that economics is too detached from the real world. While this complaint is almost as old as economics as a science, it certainly deserves more attention when the market share is shrinking. A second criticism, even voiced by nonacademic employers of new economics PhDs in the US, emphasizes the poor writing and oral skills, in other words the disability to communicate effectively. This brings us back to applied economists in nonacademia being team players: what limits their value is rarely a lack of expert know-how, but that they cannot apply their knowledge to practical issues or cannot communicate with or convince others.

The Students' View

Students' interest in economics comes partly from an intrinsic interest in the issues we address and the way we address them, and partly from an extrinsic motivation deriving from how much they believe studying economics can help them launch a satisfying and successful career.[3]

Based on questionnaires returned by 257 St. Gallen students, Slembeck (1992) finds evidence of surprisingly high intrinsic motivation. Eighty-seven per cent of respondents (most of which had not chosen to go for a major in economics) partly or completely agreed with the statement that economics deals with important issues. Fewer, but still many, agreed with the statement that economics helps solve important problems in society (71 per cent). That this basically positive attitude towards economics has both intrinsic and extrinsic foundations is shown by the fact that 89 per cent of students agreed with the proposition that economics deals with issues that interest them personally, and 71 per cent subscribe to the statement that a *basic* (my emphasis) knowledge of economics is important for their career.

Regarding job prospects, 22 per cent thought that a major in economics made it more difficult to find a job than a business major. This latent but modest concern is underscored by a German survey which found that in 1994/95

13 per cent of prospective economics majors expected difficulties in finding a job. This is lower than in many other fields, but higher than among prospective business majors (where the number is 3 per cent) and up more than 10 percentage points over the previous two years (Ramm and Bargel 1997).

When, despite the positive general picture most students have of economics, less than 10 per cent choose it as their major, there must also be critical aspects. Slembeck (1992) found the following four:

1. *The contents of economics are of little practical relevance.* Two-thirds of all respondents subscribed to this statement fully or partly.
2. *The contents of economics are too abstract.* Seventy-four per cent agree.
3. *The methods used in economics are too complicated and require too much maths and too much statistics.* Students are split right down the middle on this issue.
4. *Economics covers too much ground at the University of St. Gallen.* Sixty-four per cent agree.

The Teachers' View: Essentials for the Economist

There is surprisingly little disagreement among economists as to what makes the economist's way of looking at things unique and what the essential concepts and models are that we should teach undergraduates. Consensus on the relevant concepts and models becomes obvious after looking at the contents of intermediate micro and macro texts that dominate the market.

The classics Branson (1989), Dornbusch and Fischer (1994) and Gordon (1993) completely dominated intermediate macroeconomics teaching in Switzerland in the early 1990s (Slembeck 1992, p. 50). Baumberger (1990) had already voiced concern about a lack of diversity and new ideas, expressing some sympathy for the only 'alternative' text, Barro (1987), on the market which had adopted a completely nontraditional approach. Interestingly, the market has not changed much since then: two more US heavyweights, Blanchard (1997) and Mankiw (1997), entered the arena, following very much the same eclectic approach embracing everything from IS–LM to new classical ideas as did their seasoned predecessors, trying to carve out a segment of the market by innovative exposition rather than new content. A new mix was introduced by Burda and Wyplosz (1997), containing not only increased depth compared to their US counterparts, but also a serious effort to introduce microfoundations more cautiously than Barro had done a few years earlier, putting microfoundations alongside traditional approaches rather than replacing them. While both the Barro as well as the Burda/Wyplosz texts appear to have captured considerable shares of the market, obviously striking a chord with some instructors, both received clear signals from potential adopters that made them strengthen the more traditional features in second and later editions.

The level of consensus appears even higher in microeconomics where leading texts such as Varian (1996) set the stage for what is taught at the intermediate microeconomics level virtually around the world.

Two aspects regarding the consensus documented by current textbooks and course syllabuses are open for debate: Is this the right consensus? Is this lack of diversity good? The appropriate way to judge is by considering it from the combined perspectives of lecturers, students and nonacademic employers.

A Combined Perspective

Behind the question of whether the current consensus in economics majors syllabuses is the right one is a concern that what we teach students may not properly reflect the things we discuss and the progress we achieve in research. After all, the IS–LM model seldom concerns researchers these days. Does this mean that new insights from research enter course syllabuses too slowly, as Baumberger (1990) or Heertje (1995) have complained? This is a valid concern. What speaks in its favour is that teaching out of research, and particularly out of our own research, is a superb way of conveying the excitement to our students that many of us feel for our subject. Thus teaching from the borderline of current research certainly has a place in economics majors programmes. But how important should it be in core courses? A main point to recall here is that nonacademic employers are rarely worried that the theoretical knowledge of economics majors is not sufficiently sophisticated or advanced. Serious deficiencies are seen in the abilities to apply even the most basic concepts, to communicate one's insights and position and to convince others. Communicative interaction between age groups takes place horizontally or vertically. On the academic level, young economists communicate with fellow academics who took courses at about the same time as they did and with academics from previous academic generations. Some of these will also be economics majors. But most of them may be academic majors from related fields who enjoyed only a very basic education in economics.

Horizontal communication with economics majors is obviously a minor problem. All that is required here is some consensus on the core curriculum. If recent developments are emphasized and integrated quickly, this is fine.[4] Communicating with coworkers from other academic backgrounds, a business or a law major with only an elementary economics education, for example, may pose more of a challenge. In order to succeed and convince, the argument is preferably cast in terms of the more basic concepts they know. If more modern and advanced models suggest a different result, it is essential to point out and convince why the more traditional or simple models are not appropriate. It is hard to see how this could be achieved if these models, even if not the focus of current research, are not thoroughly covered in the economics majors curriculum.

Similar arguments apply when interacting vertically with economists (and related majors) who learned their trade earlier. Superiors or older colleagues, whose macroeconomics education may have culminated in an accelerator-enhanced version of the IS–LM model, are not going to be easily persuaded to accept a real business cycle interpretation of some current issue with the argument that the older approach lacks microfoundations and implies unrealistic covariances between this and that variable. Again, the common language to start out from would have to be the IS–LM model. One would either have to make one's point in the context of this model, maybe with a few modern refinements, or argue carefully and convincingly why this model is inappropriate in the current context and why it needs to be replaced or supplemented by a more modern approach. Again, a prerequisite for this is that even older models and approaches that are rarely employed in current research papers have a prominent place in today's economics major curriculum.

Consensus in the core curriculum is useful for establishing a communications platform horizontally, and a certain persistence of core curriculum elements over time is essential for establishing a common language vertically. Courses outside the core curriculum – called 'fields' in the Krueger (1991) report – on the one hand provide opportunities to apply the knowledge acquired in the core curriculum to real-world issues, and on the other hand provide areas where students can refine and augment the theoretical skills acquired in the core.

Reality could hardly be further from this ideal, as established by Krueger (1991) for graduate programmes at American universities and underscored by more casual evidence from our own and surrounding institutions. The sacred principle that what to teach in a given course is entirely up to the instructor is held so high that we often do not even want to know what is being taught in other courses – for fear that such knowledge might put indirect demands on what we are to teach in our course.[5] As a consequence, our core and field courses often appear to students like unrelated bits and pieces rather than a structured, well-thought-out programme. The key weakness encountered is that field courses tend to refine and expand theory rather than use core theory to explore real-world features. This gives students the strong impression that there is no empirical and applied basis to most of the economics curriculum (ibid., p. 1046). Where fields do address real-world issues, they rarely draw on theory presented in the core, but instead develop models and theories themselves as needed.

What this boils down to is that economics departments rarely succeed in making a series of courses into a coherent programme. Modest efforts to at least institutionalize a simple information system for instructors about course contents were stopped cold at the University of St. Gallen's economics department a few years ago. Evensky and Wells (1998) document a similar fate of an effort, pursued with much persistence and enthusiasm, to make Syracuse University's economics department collaborate on making a series of courses into a coherent programme that would 'provide a developmental flow from course to course, from theory to applied level'. Their noteworthy conclusion reads:

> In the culture of academe, and especially in the economics department, the bias against institutional intervention and the value placed on autonomy are very high. This culture came into conflict with the notion of a departmentally defined, administered, and assessed core curriculum . . . and autonomy won. (ibid., p. 80)

HOW SHOULD WE TEACH?

Going by the results reported by Slembeck (1992, p. 136), we must worry more about what we teach than about the way we teach (though there cannot be a clear separation between the two): only 4 per cent of respondents fully disagreed with the statement 'The quality of teaching in economics is high at the University of St. Gallen'. More, 15 per cent, partly disagreed. But also, only 13 per cent fully agreed. With reservations, 67 per cent agreed. This seems to indicate that teaching is not a serious problem, but also that there is room for improvement.

Looking beyond our own university at the more general picture, economists appear to be less concerned with sharpening and updating their teaching skills than any other profession (see Becker 1997, p. 1351). The results reported by Becker (ibid., pp. 1352–3) are striking. The typical instructor in the Becker and Watts (1996) survey spends 83 per cent of his or her classtime lecturing on the chalkboard. A few have already discovered the overhead projector, but cooperative learning techniques in which students work together in class are virtually absent from all economics courses at research universities.[6] Even computers, in spite of all the hype, appear notably only in the teaching of econometrics and statistics.

Maybe this conservative attitude of economists towards teaching is rational. After all, research based on educational production functions has not been able to identify specific methods for teaching economics that are superior to old-fashioned lecturing and writing on the chalkboard (see Becker 1997, p. 1357). As Becker (ibid., p. 1362) argues on the basis of more recent work, however, the problem may be less in the inability of methods to make a difference, but rather in the simplistic way educational studies measure teaching success. That the way we measure student performance makes a difference to what we find empirically is illustrated by recent work on the role of class attendance (see, for example, Romer 1993 or Durden and Ellis 1995). Contrary to earlier studies that measured achievement by multiple-choice test scores, when performance also assesses abilities such as written communication skills, class attendance exhibits a quantitatively important and highly significant influence.

Becker (1997, p. 1365) also reminds us that even if we accept standardized multiple-choice test results only, the reported failure of other instructional techniques to improve student learning over chalkboard lecturing at the same time means that the latter has not been significantly superior to other techniques. This leaves room for switching to or adding alternative instructional techniques for other reasons:

1. An argument often made is that teachers stick to the lecture and chalkboard tradition because other, collective, approaches to learning slow down and prevent teachers from covering as much ground as they would like to. Now if teaching method affects learning success neither positively nor negatively, we might as well experiment with techniques that, as a byproduct, sharpen writing, speaking and communication skills and group interaction in general, as desired by nonacademic employers.
2. A firmly established fact in educational research is that different students learn in different ways. There is no preferred or best instructional method for all of them. Yet, in order not to lose a sizeable segment of potential economics students by sticking to the lecture method alone, we might as well experiment with a mix of different methods, addressing a wider spectrum of learners.
3. At the University of St. Gallen (and numbers in most other institutions will be similar) more than 90 per cent of the students who take the principles course and the intermediate courses because these are mandatory, afterwards decide against pursuing the economics major. A strong result in educational research is that students are much more likely to persist in a field of study if (i) there is student/teacher interaction and (ii) there is interaction with other students taking the same course. In order to claim a larger share of those students taking the principles and intermediate courses, economists might consider weaving elements into their courses that permit such interactions.
4. Grades are a factor to consider. For reasons that do not appear straightforward, economics departments consistently show up among the low-grading departments in comparative studies. This leeway could be used to encourage enrolment through two channels. First, higher grades would lead more students into the economics major track, because students employ an effort/result calculation when choosing courses or tracks (see Sabot and Wakeman-Linn 1991). Second, the reassurance from good grades raises the likelihood that students persist in a given line of study. Becker (1997, p. 1357) notes that this mechanism could even be taken advantage of without raising average grades. What might be considered is widening the grade distribution by giving those who are good and qualify for potential economics majors

better grades than before, and lowering the grades of those who are not 'economics-major material' anyway.

5. Handing out class notes to students appears to be a practice about which instructors might want to think again, for two reasons. First, note taking and graph drawing are activities that involve students intellectually. Thus students who, for example, draw graphs on their own have been found to perform better in exams than those who do not (see Cohn and Cohn 1994). Second, in addition to this direct benefit, not handing out class notes forces students to attend class. As mentioned earlier, class attendance has a substantial and significant positive impact on student performance beyond that which is measured in multiple-choice tests.

6. The literature discusses a number of modest, simple and low-tech innovations that can augment almost any lecturing method and have consistently been shown to improve learning success and active student participation in class. The innovation most widely discussed and used is the 'one-minute paper', designed to obtain regular feedback from students. In the last few minutes of class time students are asked to respond to the following two questions:

    a.   What is the most important thing you learned today?
    b.   What is the vaguest point still remaining at the conclusion of today's class?

    On using this technique in an experimental setting, Chizmar and Ostrosky (1998, p. 8) conclude that 'the one-minute paper does enhance economic knowledge by .6 of a point on the [standardized] exam, ceteris paribus'.

7. Computerized learning has made little inroads into the economics classroom (with the mentioned exception of statistics and econometrics courses). While many publishers and authors now offer supporting material on disk or via the Internet, the one major effort to redefine teaching is the British WinEcon project. For UK universities this software is virtually free, and it is widely used. Preliminary results indicate that it is a significant factor in explaining examination marks – though with a gender gap: WinEcon usage is highly significant in explaining examination results of males, with a large positive coefficient. It does not seem to make any difference for female examination performance (see MacDonald and Shields 1998, p. 227).

SUMMARY AND A PROPOSAL

Measured by revealed student interest, economics has not fared well in the 1990s. While in the US this may be viewed as just another downturn in the cyclical development of market shares, in Germany and at the University of St. Gallen this adds to a downward trend that will put economics under pressure for quite a while.

When looking at why economics may be running out of favour, the problem seems to lie less in the way economics is taught (though there appears to be scope for innovations) than in what is being taught. The most frequently expressed criticisms from students and nonacademic employers are first that economics is too detached from real-world problems and second that basic abilities to communicate (speaking, writing, and discussing) are seriously underdeveloped.

While educational research suggests that how we teach does not significantly affect learning success, narrowly measured in the form of multiple-choice testing, it matters when we apply broader measures of accomplishment. Particularly, different modes of instruction offer different practice grounds for those skills found wanting by employers and suit different groups of students in different ways.

Based on these observations the following propositions could be the cornerstones of an economics education that is more competitive in the market than it has been in the past.

Economists need to understand the economy This comprises a theoretical understanding of how the economy works (or may be considered to work), but also a thorough knowledge of the empirical magnitudes of parameters and variables, and of the relevant institutions within which the economy operates. The theory part is undisputed and has been the focus of most economics programmes in the past. Many academic teachers, however, skim over institutions and data (often being insecure about these themselves) on the grounds that acquiring knowledge of these poses no intellectual challenge and is not really a requirement of being a trained economist. While this is probably true, it is equally true that many issues cannot be discussed, except in the abstract, without a familiarity with the relevant institutional setup in a country. Talking about unemployment without knowing how the labour market works and how wage negotiations are conducted and applied in a particular country is a case in point.

Economists need to be able to think like an economist This refers to the particular problem-solving skills based on the economic approach. It receives plenty of emphasis in current curricula. But it remains bloodless and falls short of what students and employers expect if it is not augmented by the proposition.

Economists must be able to solve real-world problems like an economist This skill is rarely taught in today's curricula, although it is the most important single skill of substance desired by the market. With the restriction that neither the total workload for students nor semester hours should be extended, space for practising the application of theoretical concepts may be provided in two ways:

1. By cutting back in the curriculum the coverage of theories and even methods. Being able to apply a basic model may be more important than working through the next level of theoretical refinement but not being able to apply it.
2. By structuring the curriculum, connecting (sometimes seemingly, sometimes actually) unrelated courses into a coherent programme. This would not only generate time for applications, but also give students the motivating impression that economics was taught with a purpose.

Economists need to be able to communicate and to convince   Agreeing with this proposition opens a Pandora's box of implications. While the most obvious implication is that economists need good writing, speaking and discussion skills, there is much more. First, it suggests that, whenever possible, we should switch to methods of instruction that provide practice opportunities for the mentioned skills. Second, it emphasizes the importance of graduating economists having a common core of knowledge, horizontally and vertically: economists should be particularly well versed in the theories taught to graduates from adjacent disciplines with much less exposure to economics, and they should also have a firm command of theories and models that constitute the core knowledge of older graduates with whom they will most likely collaborate. Of course, this does not mean that insights from current research should be omitted from the teaching of economics majors. But on this level these results should be introduced cautiously, if possible as developments and refinements of traditional views.

NOTES

1. A modern discussion and application with further references is Stein (1992).
2. There is some discussion, though, about whether a downward trend actually exists. Employing cointegration techniques, Margo and Siegfried (1996, pp. 328–9) conclude that the market share of economics majors is stationary, meaning that the percentage of economics degrees exhibits mean-reversion to a fixed share.
3. Monetary and nonmonetary aspects of life and professional careers have reversed roles since the end of flower-power. Drawing on results from a survey of nearly 350 000 students at 665 US colleges and universities, *The Economist* ('A long way from flower-power', 17 January 1998) reports that in 1997 '75% of freshmen consider financial success to be an essential or very important goal of education, compared with 41% who are seeking a meaningful philosophy of life. These answers are an almost complete reversal of those given by students in the late 1960s'.
4. Even there, however, I sometimes wonder whether we should not be more patient to wait and see what passes the test of time and scrutinize more closely before we add elements from the current debate in research to the body of knowledge we teach our students. The way the rational expectations revolution entered teaching twenty years ago with an exclusive focus on surprises for the next ten years appears to be a particularly extreme example.

5. To illustrate: students at a southern German economics department report that during their first two years of study a total of five instructors spent at least an hour each explaining graphical manipulations of the neoclassical production function, that is that its slope measures marginal productivity, the ray through the origin measures average productivity, that marginal productivity diminishes, and so on. The five courses were: the Principles course, Macroeconomics I, Macroeconomics II, Microeconomics I and Theory of Costs (*Betriebliche Kostenrechnung*).
6. The lecture and chalkboard technique refers to when instructors lecture and write during class only, no matter whether it is actually on the board, a flip chart or an overhead projector. The lecture and overhead technique refers to when instructors lecture and use prepared acetates.

REFERENCES

Barro, R. (1987), *Macroeconomics*, 2nd edn, New York: Wiley.
Baumberger, J. (1990), 'Die Makroökonomik des Wirtschaftspolitikers', in M. Haller, H. Hauser and R. Zäch (eds), *Ergänzungen. Ergebnisse der wissenschaftlichen Tagung anlässlich der Einweihung des Ergänzungsbaus der Hochschule St. Gallen*, Bern: Haupt, pp. 457–65.
Becker, W.E. (1997), 'Teaching economics to undergraduates', *Journal of Economic Literature*, **35** (3), pp. 1347–73.
Becker, W.E. and M. Watts (1996), 'Chalk and talk: a national survey on teaching undergraduate economics', *American Economic Review*, **81** (2), pp. 448–53.
Blanchard, O.J. (1997), *Macroeconomics*, Upper Saddle River: Prentice-Hall.
Branson, W.H. (1989), *Macroeconomics. Theory and Policy*, 3rd edn, New York: Harper & Row.
Burda, M. and C. Wyplosz (1997), *Macroeconomics. A European Text*, 2nd edn, Oxford: Oxford University Press.
Chizmar, J.F. and A.L Ostrosky (1998), 'The one-minute paper: some empirical findings', *Journal of Economic Education*, **29** (1), pp. 3–10.
Cohn, E. and S. Cohn (1994), 'Graphs and learning in principles of economics', *American Economic Review*, **84** (2), pp. 197–200.
Dornbusch, R. and S. Fischer (1994), *Macroeconomics*, 6th edn, New York: McGraw-Hill.
Durden, G. and L.V. Ellis (1995), 'The effects of attendance on student learning in principles of economics', *American Economic Review*, **85** (2), pp. 343–6.
Evensky, J. and M. Wells (1998), 'Making a series of courses into a program: a case study in curriculum development', *Journal of Economic Education*, **29** (1), pp. 73–80.
Gärtner, M. (1997), 'Who wants the euro – and why? Economic explanations of public attitudes toward a single European currency', *Public Choice*, **93** (3/4), pp. 487–510.
Gordon, R.J. (1993), *Macroeconomics*, 6th edn, New York: Harper Collins.
Heertje, A. (1995), 'Teaching new ideas in economics', *Economia*, Summer, p. 13.
Krueger, A.O. (1991), 'Report of the Commission on Graduate Education in Economics', *Journal of Economic Literature*, **29** (3), pp. 1035–53.
MacDonald, Z. and M.A. Shields (1998), 'WinEcon: an evaluation', *Journal of Economic Surveys*, **12** (2), pp. 221–31.
Mankiw, G.N. (1997), *Macroeconomics*, 3rd edn, New York: Worth.
Margo, R.A. and J.J. Siegfried (1996), 'Long-run trends in economics bachelor's degrees', *Journal of Economic Education*, **27** (4), pp. 326–36.
Ramm, M. and T. Bargel (1997), *Berufs- und Arbeitsmarktorientierungen der Studierenden. Entwicklungen in der ersten Hälfte der 90er Jahre. (Beiträge zur*

Arbeitsmarkt- und Berufsforschung Nr. 212), Nürnberg: Institut für Arbeitsmarkt- und Berufsforschung der Bundesanstalt für Arbeit.

Romer, D. (1993), 'Do students go to class? Should they?', *Journal of Economic Perspectives*, **7** (3), pp. 167–74.

Sabot, R. and J. Wakeman-Linn (1991), 'Grade inflation and course choice', *Journal of Economic Perspectives*, **5** (1), pp. 159–70.

Siegfried, J.J. (1997), 'Trends in undergraduate economics degrees: an update', *Journal of Economic Education*, **28** (3), pp. 279–82.

Slembeck, T. (1992), *Hochschuldidaktik der Volkswirtschaftslehre: Analyse, Probleme, Ziele und ein Konzept*, Dissertation No. 1343, University of St. Gallen.

Stein, J.L. (1992), 'Cobwebs, rational expectations and futures markets', *Review of Economics and Statistics*, **74** (1), pp. 127–34.

Varian, H. (1996), *Intermediate Microeconomics*, New York: Norton.

8. Financial innovation, the transfer of knowledge, and implications for postgraduate education

Heinz Zimmermann[*]

INTRODUCTION

Capital markets are known to be highly efficient in processing information. New information is transmitted almost instantly between market participants, stock exchanges and electronic networks, such that trading strategies based on exploiting publicly available information do not offer abnormally high returns. This is the well-known market efficiency hypothesis, and it constitutes a well-accepted hypothesis about the role and transmission of information in capital markets.[1]

However, this chapter is not about the transmission of information, but about a related topic, namely the diffusion of knowledge in the finance sector. What distinguishes knowledge from information is learning, or to put it in more neutral terms, adaptation. The question addressed in this chapter is: are capital markets also efficient in adapting new technologies, new products, new procedures, new analytical tools? This immediately raises the question about the role, the determinants and the speed of innovation in capital markets. At a first glance, one has the impression that capital markets are extremely innovative in terms of technology, know-how, products and structural adjustments to a changing regulatory or economic environment. There are hundreds of examples to illustrate this – however, some critical remarks will be discussed in this chapter.

The financial services industry in Switzerland is a particularly interesting case for analysing the relation between innovation and the transfer of knowledge, and thus for studying the role of postgraduate education as a major driving force of this development.[2] 'Finance' did not exist as a scientific discipline at any of the Swiss universities twenty years ago, and well-established financial models such as portfolio optimization tools, the CAPM (capital asset pricing model), or the Black–Scholes option pricing model were not used in any of the banks

* I would like to thank the editor, Ernst Mohr, for helpful comments, and Elion Chin and Christian Pirkner for assistance.

or insurance companies known to me. This is a surprising fact, given the international reputation, size and importance of the Swiss financial marketplace at this time. Today, Switzerland has one of the most integrated, computerized trading systems for securities and derivatives; it hosts three of the biggest ten asset management firms worldwide; and a quick look at a daily business newspaper shows a variety and volume of derivative and structured financial products which is unique. This chapter tries to identify the driving forces behind this transformation process, particularly the role of know-how.

The rest of the chapter is structured as follows. In the next section, I try to characterize the state of finance in Switzerland in the early eighties, as I perceived it as a student. I think that this is a useful starting-point in a study where the knowledge transfer in a fast-growing and innovative field is studied. In the following section, I characterize the major driving forces behind the innovation process in financial markets, again with special emphasis on Switzerland. In the fourth section I argue that the market of derivatives can be regarded as the single most influential driving force for the innovation and educational process in this country. I try to characterize the innovative power of knowledge in the process of building up a derivative market and in implementing risk management procedures. Today, risk management functions determine the structure of most modern finance curricula, particularly those in postgraduate education. In the final section of the chapter, I suggest a series of features of postgraduate curricula which should have the potential to accelerate the knowledge transfer between 'theory' and 'practice'.

Here I would like to stress that this study is *descriptive*, and its content is not related to my research in finance, but rather to my personal experience over twelve years in designing derivative instruments, consulting, establishing curricula for financial analysts and teaching many courses. I hope that the academically more sophisticated readers will not get too frustrated with this approach.

FINANCE IN SWITZERLAND – THE STATE OF THE ART IN THE EARLY EIGHTIES

Finance – as a scientific discipline and as a part of an academic and executive curriculum – did not exist in Switzerland twenty years ago. In 1980 when I was a student in economics there was not one single class on modern finance – this was 28 years after the path-breaking portfolio paper by Markowitz (1952) or 7 years after the publication of the famous Black–Scholes paper on option pricing (Black and Scholes 1973). Finance lectures were given mostly by part-time practitioners and covered, at best, institutional details about the structure of the financial system and business practices. But none of this was related to a specific theoretical background or to empirical research. At the same time there were excellent lectures on microeconomics, uncertainty economics, incomplete information and statistics – but they bore hardly any relation to financial markets or investments. An exception was econometrics taught by Karl Brunner and Walter Wasserfallen and a 'money and banking' class taught by Bruno Gehrig, which were the only opportunities to gather some ideas about modern finance. But the situation was no better in the banks. The typical executive training of practitioners did not cover topics such as asset allocation, capital budgeting, equity valuation or option pricing.

Let me illustrate this by a few examples. In 1981 I had to write a seminar paper in applied econometrics about time-series characteristics of exchange rates (Zimmermann 1981). Compared to my colleagues who investigated the temporal behaviour of inflation rates, GDP, unemployment and other macroeconomic aggregates, the results of my first empirical project were quite frustrating. Whatever time period I was investigating, whatever exchange rate I was looking at, the series were just white noise after taking first differences – no interesting ARIMA (autoregression integrated moving average) structure could be identified. I was very pessimistic about presenting such 'bad' results to my supervisor, but, contrary to my beliefs, he was very happy with these results and I learned that there is in fact a theory why the series should not be different from a random walk. It was fascinating for me to learn that a theory implies the *absence* of a systematic structure. I was then instructed to read Eugene Fama's most recent book, *Foundations of Finance* (Fama 1976), which containted the first textbook treatment of the notion of efficient markets. By reading this book I discovered many other fascinating things, for example how to calculate the variance of portfolio returns, how to diversify portfolios, how to calculate the systematic risk ('beta') of assets or how to determine expected returns on risky securities. I contacted the investment research departments of two major Swiss banks to learn about beta estimates of Swiss stocks. They did not have this information. But worse: they did not even know about betas, and even worse: they were not even interested in knowing why 'beta' may be relevant. It was not clear to me how the mutual fund department could calculate the risk-adjusted performance of the funds (the so-called 'alpha') without knowing betas. After contacting the respective departments, it was obvious that nobody made any effort to calculate alphas, and that the whole thing was regarded as highly theoretical stuff without practical relevance. This was, just to stress it again, roughly 15 years after the famous performance studies by M.C. Jensen, W. Sharpe, J. Treynor and others (for a review, see Ippolito 1993).

The next natural step was to calculate betas on my own. This required stock price data, which could be processed by computer. But there was no database which was accessible for academic purposes. At least one of the big banks had made substantial efforts in building up an electronic database, but was – and I could understand this – not willing to make these data available at this stage. So we decided to build up our own database; this was joint work with Thomas Vock. Fortunately we received much handwritten data (month-end prices, dividends, capital-dilution adjustment factors) on a monthly basis from the stock research department of the Union Bank of Switzerland (UBS) – but a lot of missing data and information about stocks had to be collected manually from old newspapers in the Swiss National Library and the Federal Tax Authority. After several months of not very academic work we had a database of stock returns covering a time period of almost 10 years, including more than 100 stocks of all major listed firms in Switzerland (most firms had more than one stock category outstanding).

We were now able, with a time lag of twenty years, to replicate essentially all the empirical work which had formerly been done using US and other data: distributional properties; time-series characteristics; single- and multifactor models; betas; variance decomposition; some kind of CAPM test; and so on. A summary of these results was published in *Schweizerische Zeitschrift für Volkswirtschaft und Statistik* (Vock and Zimmermann 1984). The database formed the empirical basis for Thomas Vock's and my own doctoral dissertations. This article received some public attention, even in the financial press. The publisher of *Finanz und Wirtschaft*, a major financial newspaper, wrote the following comments about it:

> Would the authors believe that there is a theory of investments for stocks? . . . I consider such studies as entirely worthless because they create the impression that the ups and downs of stock market prices can be calculated. . . . [And finally:] I think that we should not apply pseudo-scientific standards to non-scientific subjects.[3]

This was the type of reaction in 1985, a little bit more than ten years ago. We survived it – although it was not a very motivating experience for young scholars. Imagine today's banking and investment business without analytical models! It is true that I shall be less obdurate about the usefulness of analytical models as the *only* device in financial decision making later in this chapter. Nevertheless, theoretical and empirical models play a crucial role in the financial decision and intermediation process, and I argue that there was not the slightest perception of this fact until the mid-eighties in one of the major financial centres in the world, neither in academia nor in practice.

It was not only the misperception of the usefulness of analytical models which characterized the thinking of the financial community in the mid-eighties, but also the misunderstanding of the economic function of financial innovations in general. Options and futures were regarded as highly speculative instruments without any economic purpose, and it is thus not surprising that the first step towards establishing an organized option exchange was to make sure that the Swiss *Gesetz über Spiel und Wette* (Gaming law) did not apply for these instruments. The following statement is characteristic of that time: 'The fashionable trend of financial innovations is likely to displace the long-term orientated banker, and to replace him with short-term orientated salesmen'.[4] This is a statement by the chairman of the biggest bank in Switzerland, UBS, at the general shareholders' meeting in 1987. The same bank earned more than 50 per cent of the overall earnings in the derivatives business ten years later. I think it is useful to keep the state and perception of modern finance in mind when we discuss the role and requirements of educational issues later in this chapter.

INNOVATION DRIVERS AND THE EVOLUTION OF KNOW-HOW IN FINANCE

In the mid-eighties, a series of fundamental changes occurred in the Swiss financial marketplace which drastically increased the pressure on banks and other market participants to increase their exposure to modern finance theory. Based on a new law, institutional investors, such as pension funds, emerged as a new investment force and established new standards in the money management industry; the new information technology started to revolutionize the financial services industry; deregulation occurred in the banking sector and increased the competition in virtually all kinds of services; derivative trading started at an organized exchange and required modern risk management functions; a tremendous growth in over-the-counter derivatives accelerated the speed of product innovation; the decentralized structure of stock exchanges was redesigned to become a fully integrated electronic trading system; a new stock exchange law was established to regulate exchanges, brokers and takeover activities; and new regulatory efforts were undertaken to control the risk of financial intermediaries and to put much more emphasis on risk measurement and risk management issues. These were drastic changes. Most of them required a substantial knowledge in modern finance – or at least a rough understanding of basic concepts – which, as mentioned, scarcely existed at that time. This implies that substantial efforts were necessary to build up the respective know-how. Before discussing the educational implications, I shall describe the driving forces of these changes in more detail (see also Zimmermann 1998 for a similar discussion). It will then become obvious that the success and speed of these innovations was directly linked to the transfer of knowledge between 'theory' and 'practice', and that this will remain true in the future.

Deregulation and Competition

Deregulation and competition are typically mentioned as the first and most important forces behind the transformation in the financial services industry in the eighties and nineties. It is true that the elimination of cartels, syndicates, interest rate controls and the liberalization of stock exchange laws drastically increased the competition in the banking and securities industry – including securities exchanges. Deregulation was instrumental for the globalization of financial markets and services, which in turn is the precondition for an efficient international specialization of services and risk allocation. Increasing competition implies lower profit margins, and enforces new and more reliable cost accounting procedures – also with respect to risk. The perception of risk changed fundamentally in banks: risk was now regarded as an explicit economic resource, which must be priced, managed and allocated to the various products and activities. This makes it possible to determine the marginal profit or loss generated by the individual products and activities on a risk-adjusted basis, that is to determine whether they are value generating or not. However, this requires a clear understanding of the determinants of the risk-adjusted cost of capital of the firm. This is a fundamental topic of capital market theory – both theoretically and empirically. Recent research addresses differences between industries' cost of capital based on the global economic risk exposure (see, for example, Oertmann and Zimmermann 1998).

A major effect of deregulation was product differentiation; the growth and variety of new financial instruments offered by competitive market participants over the past years is quite unique. Deregulation particularly enabled foreign and institutional investors to implement more sophisticated investment strategies and to use a wide range of financial products. In earlier times, many pension plans were allowed to hold only government bonds and real estate. Today, a more liberal law allows them to hold a wide range of financial instruments including derivatives, provided that some basic risk management principles (with respect to diversification, hedging and leverage) are in place.

Risk Perception

Overall, deregulation and competition require a more detailed understanding of the economic nature, diversifiability, transferability and the pricing of risk. This *ex ante* view contrasts sharply with the traditional *ex post* view of risk management. This can best be seen in credit risk management. Credit defaults were typically treated as unexpected events and they were covered by regulatory reserves. Modern credit risk management, however, takes a rather different view. It addresses the following questions: what are the determinants of the *ex ante* credit quality of loans (rating)? How must credit risk be priced across different rating categories and with respect to the overall market risk? How can specific, contractual loan characteristics with option-like payoffs be priced and hedged? How should loan portfolios be diversified across business sectors, regions, currencies? Obviously, this view requires a completely different job profile for today's credit risk manager. The implementation of up-to-date risk management systems was often enforced by new regulatory standards. This will be discussed below.

Institutionalization

Institutional investors, their investment practices and needs, have become the driving force in the asset management and securities trading business. As of 1994, mutual funds and pension plans owned 35.5 per cent of all US households' assets and 40 per cent of the US stocks outstanding (see Edwards 1996). I would guess that this figure is similar for Switzerland. Here, the implementation of the *Bundesgesetz über die berufliche Vorsorge (BVG)* (Federal pension fund law) in 1985, can be regarded as the driving force behind this process. The consequences of institutionalization are numerous and cannot be discussed in detail. However, the innovative power of institutions is manifold:

1. The investment objectives of institutional investors are different from those of private investors, which implies that there is a demand for special products and services (see Zimmermann, Arce, Jaeger and Wolter 1992). Product innovation, particularly the design of new financial products, was strongly related to the investment characteristics and the associated regulatory framework, but also to the accounting standards, under which these investors act. Stock index-related instruments, derivatives or passively managed funds are good examples of that. The emergence of certain derivative instruments – *Stillhalteroptionen* (Covered Options) – allows Swiss pension plans to reach their regulatory return targets more easily.
2. The growth of institutional investors can be regarded as the major driving force behind the structural revolution in the securities trading business. Ten years ago, Swiss stocks were traded at seven local stock exchanges with open outcry; today the Swiss Exchange is a fully computerized trading system, and it is in the process of being integrated, jointly with the *Deutsche Börse* (German Exchange), to a global trading system called Eurex. How these institutional changes affect the pricing and risk allocation of stock markets, is not yet clear.
3. The growth of institutional investors put the banks under substantial pressure to improve their investment consulting and asset management services. But notably, the implementation of risk-based performance standards has become the most important competitive factor in the institutional money management business.
4. The institutionalization of equity-holdership has dramatic consequences for corporate governance. A good example is the pressure Martin Ebner has put on the management of UBS over the past years. The implementation of

value-based business standards is thus driven substantially by the growing role of institutional investors as equity shareholders. This is particularly true in a relatively small equity market as in Switzerland.

Technology

The innovation in securities trading and asset management is to a large extent technology driven. It can even be stated that in areas such as risk management, trading and asset management there is a real technological battle between the market participants. 'Technology' includes all activities and systems related to the processing of information, data, orders and the management of risks. Given the number and variety of systems used within the same institution, the firmwide integration of risks is a task which determines more and more the competitive power of large financial institutions. The success in issuing, pricing, trading, hedging and processing derivative instruments is almost entirely determined by the efficiency, reliability and speed of electronic systems. The supply of financial online-services is directly related to the availability of electronic networks. Fraud involving credit cards, Internet shopping and the use of various forms of electronic money requires global, fast and 'intelligent' control systems with large associated data archives. 'Data mining' has become a major topic in the operational risk management of financial institutions; data mining includes procedures and algorithms devoted to 'learning' from large data sets and to identifying a 'hidden' structure underlying billions of observations. It is therefore not surprising that several big players have started to establish their own electronic networks and databases to maintain their independence and to get competitive advantage. The statement that modern banking is competition between systems and information technology is a good characterization of the situation.

It is true that technology is worthless without knowledge. But in finance, it is often true that substantial breakthroughs of knowledge require some advanced technology. Efficient portfolio diversification is impossible to implement in practice without fast computers. It is nice to have an algorithm to find efficient portfolios, but the practical use is very limited if it involves the estimation of hundreds of asset correlations and the inversion of huge matrices, and if there are no databases and computer programs to perform these computations. Not surprisingly, the success of portfolio theory was strongly related to the availability of computer systems. This is even more relevant for derivatives and risk management. It was a prestigious task for the new Swiss Options and Financial Futures Exchange (SOFFEX) in the mid-eighties to establish a trading platform and settlement procedures anticipating the possible future trends in information technology.

Derivatives

When the first standardized options were traded on the Chicago Board Options Exchange (CBOE) in 1973, the more innovative among the option traders calculated their price quotes on electronic pocket calculators using a pricing model developed by Black, Scholes and Merton a few years previously (however, the model was only published in 1973; see Black and Scholes 1973 and Merton 1973). This was innovative in several dimensions. It was the beginning of a new area in trading financial derivatives. Options were now traded as standardized contracts (instead of individual securities) at an organized exchange, where bid and ask prices were continuously quoted by market makers. Option prices vary substantially over short time intervals; this is known as the leverage effect. Hedgers must therefore adjust their hedge positions frequently, while traders must update their price quotes almost continuously over time. In both cases, a mathematical model is needed which provides the relevant parameters for constructing and adjusting the hedge portfolio, and which yields a consistent (arbitrage-free) price system across stocks, puts and calls, exercise prices and maturities. The Black–Scholes model offers such a framework. Most importantly, the model represents a simple formula for the fair value of options, but it requires some computations of cumulative standard normal densities – which cannot be performed using pencil and paper. However, programmable pocket calculators became popular at this time, so that the necessary calculations could be easily performed for a relatively large number of prices and strategies. Of course, this was only the beginning. But it illustrates how closely innovation in products, market architecture, know-how (the pricing model) and technology are linked. This is a key characteristic in the evolution of derivative markets and risk management processes. I shall argue below that the growth of derivatives, and particularly the role played by derivatives in the Swiss financial market, had the most substantial impact on the knowledge transfer in the financial community.

The innovative power of derivatives, however, emerges not only from the growing volume of instruments which are traded on organized exchanges or over the counter. It has been shown repeatedly that the basic structure of option payoffs profiles can be used to characterize a wide range of financial contracts such as loan guarantees, collateral, deposit insurance, credit lines, equity-linked life insurance, defined benefit claims in pension plans or even investment decisions with time flexibility. This implies that option pricing models can be used to price and hedge a wide range of financial contracts. A recent example in Switzerland is the valuation of *Staatsgarantien* (state guarantees): most Swiss cantons started to recognize the economic value of the guarantee they provide to the depositors of the state-owned cantonal banks and are now getting paid by the banks for providing this guarantee. Also, bank balance sheets exhibit a variety of explicit or implicit options, many of which are related to interest rate ceilings or floors compared to fluctuating market rates. Banks recognize the value of these options more and more, and charge the associated costs to the customers.

Regulatory Pressure

In the first paragraph of this section, deregulation was mentioned as a major driving force of financial innovation. In at least one area, the contrary is true: new regulatory measures in *risk management* and *capital adequacy standards* lead banks (and other financial institutions) to substantially improve their analytical skills and to adopt innovative techniques to measure and manage risks. This statement is, of course, a little bit controversial, and many observers would not agree at all. Does regulation enforce more than what market participants would do in their own interest? I think I saw a few cases where this was true. In the beginning of the nineties, almost no Swiss bank had a clear picture of the interest rate exposure of assets and liabilities – and thus, of the interest rate exposure of its stocks. It was a memorandum of the Swiss Banking Commission in 1993 that forced banks' auditors to comment on the global interest rate exposure of the balance sheet, and since 1997 the banks' capital must cover the market risks on the trading book. These regulatory measures have drastically accelerated the efforts to implement reliable asset-liability management procedures and to formulate explicit benchmark risk exposures, which also created a huge market for interest rate hedging products, such as swaps, swaption, caps, floors and so on. For the first time, the bank law also explicitly stipulates senior management and board responsibility for risk management topics.

A significant regulatory innovation is the 'model approach' in bank capital regulation as proposed by the Basel Committee. It stipulates two basic options for calculating market risk-adjusted bank capital: the 'standard' approach is valid for all banks which do not use individual models for calculating the global market risk on their balance sheet, while the 'model' approach gives banks the opportunity to use more sophisticated models, provided that they satisfy certain minimum requirements. The models are approved by a special committee within the Swiss Banking Commission. Of course, the model approach allows a more differentiated calculation of the risks and is thus much more attractive in terms of the required capital. This is a surprising deviation from the old practice of bank supervision and had the effect that banks currently undertake substantial efforts to improve their risk measurement systems and to adjust them to the best industry standards.

Knowledge

Obviously, the innovation process described in the previous paragraphs contrasts sharply with – or even contradicts – the state of knowledge described earlier in this chapter. Deregulation, a different perception and role of risk management, institutionalization, the revolution in information technology, the growth of derivatives and new regulatory standards in risk management are definitively the key factors in explaining the financial innovation process, but they require a substantial amount of know-how in order to lead to successful innovations. The acceleration and transfer of knowledge thus became a major success factor in the process of financial innovation. This can be explained best in the context of derivative markets and risk management procedures, which will be done in the next section.

KNOWLEDGE AS AN INNOVATIVE FORCE: THE CASE OF DERIVATIVES AND RISK MANAGEMENT PROCEDURES

The role of knowledge in the transformation process of financial markets can be best illustrated by looking at the market for derivatives. I am not aware of a single area in finance where the interaction between know-how, systems and management processes is equally important as in derivatives. Or to put it differently: there is probably no other area in finance where institutions can capitalize their investments in education and systems equally well as in derivatives. I argue that those institutions which have built up a long experience in derivatives get a comparative advantage in many other fields such as

- risk management;
- product design;
- pricing and hedging implicit options in traditional financial contracts; and
- asset management and performance measurement.

The interested reader is referred to Merton (1995) to find a detailed analysis of the impact of financial innovation on the structure and performance of the financial system, and on the management of financial intermediaries.

In this section, I shall address the question of why systems and knowledge are more important in the derivatives business than in other fields of financial services.

Characteristics of Derivatives

Why are information systems and knowledge so important for derivatives? First, pricing derivatives is often a much more analytical task than pricing the underlying cash securities. This has a long tradition; it started with the early work of Bachelier (1900) at the turn of the century. He laid the foundation of modern option pricing theory by developing a valuation approach based on continuous time stochastic processes and differential equations. The models developed in the sixties by Paul Samuelson (who rediscovered Bachelier's work), Merton and Black and Scholes are extensions to that work. Today, option pricing requires even more advanced mathematics and, more and more, heavy programming and computer simulation. It is thus not surprising that this task is performed by people with a strong background in mathematics or physics. The competition among market participants to improve pricing models and calibration techniques is strong nowadays. Better models decrease hedging costs, enable a more attractive pricing of products or imply arbitrage profits. A crucial feature in this development is that a substantial part of the associated research is no longer done at universities, but in the research departments of banks, brokers, insurance companies, funds and so on. The level of sophistication of these departments is often outstanding, but the research results are, for obvious reasons, typically not available in detail to the public. In many areas it has even become quite difficult for university researchers to keep up with state-of-art research, which explains – besides monetary reasons – the 'exodus' of many highly esteemed university professors from academia to work for these institutions. This is particularly true for areas which require a lot of computational resources, or data, which are not publicly available (real-time price quotes, data on credit default and so forth). This shows that the transfer of knowledge is a *mutual* process between 'theory' and 'practice'.

Second, derivative instruments represent heavily levered positions in the underlying cash security and are, therefore, substantially more risky than the underlying cash securities. A one per cent move in the underlying market can well lead to a 20 or 30 per cent price move in a corresponding derivative asset. It is therefore essential that the market value of all available option contracts can be continuously recalculated over time and that the corresponding hedges can be adjusted sufficiently quickly. This requires not only extensive computational resources for the individual banks, but also a trading structure which allows for trades to be implemented almost instantaneously. A fully integrated, computerized trading, clearing and settlement system for both the derivatives and the underlying cash market seems to be the only way to minimize the risk of a market failure.

Third, valuation models are used not only to price derivatives, but also to hedge the associated risk exposures. This was one of the earliest insights from modern option pricing theory: tell me how to hedge the risk which results from selling a call option, and the capital I need for establishing the replicating portfolio (the hedge) determines the price which I ask for the call option. Pricing models thus play a crucial role in risk management. Using an inadequate model implies not only noncompetitive price quotes, but also inadequate hedging strategies and the potential to suffer substantial losses. An example: the Black–Scholes–Merton option pricing model assumes a constant variance of the underlying asset price (which is modelled as a Wiener-process). However, the variance of securities is often and substantially changing over time. A hedge strategy based on the Black–Scholes–Merton model is only 'safe' and reliable if the reality does not deviate 'too much' from the model's assumptions. If this happens, substantial losses may occur, as the October 1987 crash has demonstrated. Similarly, the German *Metallgesellschaft* used a model for hedging crude oil futures commitments, where futures prices are below the expected spot price (this is called 'backwardation'). As soon as this changed (and the reaction of the *Metallgesellschaft* amplified the reversal), the firm had substantial problems in implementing the required hedge strategy, and finally went bankrupt. 'Model risk' has become a major concern in the business. It means not only that inadequate models are being used, but also that the parametrization of the models – the specification of the input variables and the estimation of model parameters – may be inadequate. In the 1997 annual report, the UBS explicitly states that part of the substantial equity derivative loss amounting to half a billion Swiss francs was caused by the misspecification of parameters in an option pricing model. This shows that the parametrization and calibration of a given model is at least equally important as the choice between different models.

Fourth, product design is an extremely value-generating activity in derivatives compared to cash instruments. There are not too many ways to design stocks or bonds (except by adding option components!), but there is an almost infinite number of ways to design derivative contracts. There are basically two types of derivatives. First, there are standardized, exchange-traded contracts, where the product design is simple and straightforward, spreads are low and profits arc volumc-drivcn. Hcrc, the required know-how is in the first place related to trading and arbitrage strategies. As opposed to that, over-the-counter (OTC) derivatives and exotic instruments require stronger analytical skills for valuation and hedging, and a strong marketing and sales force – because many of these products are specially designed to the customers' needs. This naturally implies that product design plays by far a more important role in the OTC segment. Since the beginning of derivative trading in the mid-eighties, Swiss banks have been equally strong in both market segments – which is different from the US, where the growth in the OTC business started later. One of the reasons is that, as opposed to exchange-traded options, counterparty risk plays a crucial role in the OTC markets, and Swiss banks are able to capitalize their typically good rating here. This implies that Swiss banks need a particularly strong know-how in areas such as product design, pricing of nonstandard derivatives and marketing.

Fifth, it is easier to make mistakes with derivatives than with 'traditional' instruments – and moreover, public attention is more sensitive with respect to derivative losses and disasters. Which banks suffered big credit losses in the past ten years? Nobody outside the business will remember the names. Where did the big derivatives losses occur? Everybody remembers the Barings, *Metallgesellschaft*, Orange County and perhaps other cases which received wide public attention. Misusing derivatives has a higher potential to ruin well-known banks and institutions than other instruments. This means that banks with a substantial exposure in derivatives must invest much more of their resources in risk management procedures than do other banks. To put it differently: surviving in the derivatives business requires a higher level of sophistication with respect to valuation and hedging models, risk control and settlement procedures. It is therefore likely that extensive derivative trading has positive spillover effects on many other activities outside derivatives, particularly to credit risk management and transfer pricing. This point will be discussed further below.

The Innovative Power of Derivatives

The previous discussion clearly shows that knowledge plays an important role in derivatives, probably much more than with 'traditional' financial assets. I claim that the growth of derivatives in Switzerland since the mid-eighties was instrumental in the transformation of the financial marketplace, both with respect to the financial market structure as well as to the know-how gap relative to other financial centres. The institutional setting of the Swiss stock (and bond) market made it virtually impossible to identify a large number of stocks where options could be traded on. Trading was fragmented among several exchanges, the equity of most firms was subdivided into several stock categories, many stocks were traded only a few times during a day, there was no information about trading volumes or liquidity, about the ownership structure of the firms (in order to estimate the free float) or about many other things.[5] The risk of producing a disaster with a new derivative market was substantial under these circumstances.[6] I do not want to describe the structural adjustment which had to be implemented, but rather stress that after only two years of work, in 1988, SOFFEX started operating as the first options exchange in the world where trading and clearing were fully integrated and computerized. It constituted a landmark in the architecture of exchanges and was instrumental in the redesign of the underlying spot markets.

The innovative pressure from SOFFEX on the underlying markets, on education, on risk management procedures and on regulation was considerable. For instance, the fact that SOFFEX was completely unregulated due to the old-fashioned *Börsengesetz* (Securities Law) of the canton Zurich (which did not cover derivative exchanges), meant there was substantial pressure to work on an adequate federal regulation, the *Eidgenössisches Börsengesetz* (Federal Securities Law), which enables potential competition among exchanges and systems performing similar functions, and stipulates the notion of self-regulation of exchanges, among other important things.[7] I shall now restrict the discussion of the innovative power of derivatives to an area which is instrumental for the evolution of know-how, namely the role of option pricing models, and how they changed the perception of old issues in financial contracting.

The Innovative Power of Option Pricing Models

Option pricing models represent a landmark in the evolution of financial modelling; the models developed by Black and Scholes and Merton were instrumental in this development. Combined with the insight that virtually any financial contract can be decomposed into a portfolio of cash securities and derivatives, these models represent the analytical framework which allows for a consistent analysis of the generic structure, the risks and the economic value of a wide range of financial instruments and contracts. In this context, it is not so relevant whether these models are right or wrong, or whether the assumptions are too restrictive or not. The point is that they fundamentally changed the perception of value and risk in the entire field of financial contracting. For example, recognizing that loan guarantees, collateral, counterparty default, credit lines and so on have the basic structure of options, and that these options can be priced and hedged, will have dramatic implications for the design, pricing and hedging of credit risk and thus, on the pricing of loans. An option pricing perspective fundamentally changes the valuation of financial contracts and, based on the stochastic nature of the underlying processes, adds a dynamic perspective, which is essential for risk management purposes (an excellent contribution in this field is the recent doctoral dissertation by Ziegler 1998). My guess is that the adaptation of option pricing models in commercial services will have an even larger effect on the banking business in the future than the use of derivatives in asset management in the past.

The interesting observation about derivatives is that knowledge, which was originally concentrated in rather specialized option trading departments, became more and more disseminated to other areas in the banking business. I have already mentioned commercial banking. Today, option pricing is used almost everywhere: for determining performance fees in asset management, for pricing reinsurance risks, for capital budgeting decisions in industrial firms, for determining fair premiums for pension plan insurance, and many other areas. The question is just why is there so much progress in a specific area, but not in others? For instance, most big asset management banks are still not yet able to provide performance reports which take into account the research of the past 25 years; mutual fund alphas and investment-style characteristics are still not available, as in the early eighties. Why did the capital asset pricing model not get the same practical attention and quick dissemination as option pricing models? The textbooks and finance curricula cannot be blamed: they cover both issues equally well. Two potential answers are as follows: first, there was simply no (or no sufficient) external *pressure* to use certain models such as the CAPM, and second, the immediate *benefit* of using certain models is not very obvious. More on this in the next paragraph.

Recognizing the Performance and Benefit of Models

The nice thing about an option pricing model is that it was *not just* a methodological framework, but it was *also* related to specific instruments (namely options). There was a concrete playing field to learn a lot about finance. But there was also, unlike the CAPM, a competitive pressure from institutional investors, as well as from senior management and regulators, to use these models. There was pressure, because the perception was that options are dangerous, and option pricing was perceived to be difficult. Ignoring the models and the research in option pricing would have had serious consequences. This is definitely not true for the CAPM: surviving in the asset management business did not – at least until today – depend on using analytical models. I cannot remember a single legal case where an asset manager was regarded as liable for damages because he or she underperformed the risk-adjusted benchmark in a rising stock market. And who knows how to specify the relevant 'market portfolio' in the CAPM in an international setting? There is simply no academic agreement on many important issues here. And even if there were to be agreement on the appropriateness of the model, our statistical standards would not allow a practically relevant conclusion about the *performance* of the model. This can be illustrated as follows.

Consider the case of CAPM-based performance measurement. Performance is defined as return differential between a specific fund and a prespecified benchmark portfolio. Performance of mutual funds typically does not exceed 1 per cent per annum. The annual standard deviation of the portfolio (or its tracking error with respect to the benchmark) is assumed to be 5 per cent, which implies a *t*-statistic of 0.2. These are annualized values; it is assumed, however, that performance can be observed monthly. Increasing the time horizon, while leaving the previous parameters constant, also increases the *t*-statistic. This can be interpreted as follows: if a certain (constant) performance can be maintained over a longer time-horizon, then the 'confidence' increases that the performance is not random, but 'systematic'. A natural question to ask is how long the time horizon must be such that the *t*-statistic implies statistical significance on conventional confidence levels. Modelling asset values as geometric Brownian motions, the implied continuously compounded asset returns grow linearly with the length of the underlying time interval, while the respective standard deviation grows with the square root of time. Assuming a *t*-statistic of 1.64 (which corresponds to a one-sided 95 per cent confidence) implies a time horizon of eight years, which is substantial – much longer than the typical investor is willing to wait for being convinced that the performance is not random. If the excess return is only 0.5 per cent, however, the time horizon increases to 22 years! If a confidence of 99 per cent was required instead, then a performance of 0.5 per cent would imply a time horizon of 45 years.

Models Versus Procedures

The previous example indicates a fundamental problem in using quantitative tools in financial decision making: the time horizon of decisions is typically much shorter than investors would actually need to feel confident, based on conventional significance levels and textbook models. This also explains why many practitioners are extremely reluctant to base decisions on analytical or statistical models. In the context of performance measurement it might help to explain why – in spite of dozens of equilibrium models and hundreds of empirical papers on the performance of actively managed portfolios – *qualitative* factors such as reputation, customer relations, awards, marketing efforts and so on still play a crucial role in explaining success in asset management.

But this insight is, to a large extent, also true for evaluating risk management procedures. The exclusive use of formal models is more and more complemented by analysing risk management *processes*. I get elected to the board of directors of a bank; this is a part-time job. How much effort should I put into analysing the risks of the trading department, the customers' accounts, the asset-liability management and so on? In order to have 99 per cent confidence to comment on the state of risk management at the next board meeting, it would require so much time and effort that no homo oeconomicus would do this job for 25 000 Swiss francs a year. The only solution is for the board to define the basic structure of the risk management process, which includes, for instance

- the schedule and time priority of the various steps in risk management;
- the various steps leading from the current situation to what is being considered as a reasonable 'target';
- the allocation of resources for different tasks in risk management;
- the definition of responsibilities for the different management levels;
- the structure of risk reporting within the organization.

Of course, quantitative information on an aggregate basis (such as value-at-risk figures) is very useful, but it does not tell me everything about the firm-wide risk. Quantitative information *must* be complemented by a *process-orientated* (or evolutionary) view of business risk. Such a model is presented in Heinzl,

Senger and Zimmermann (1998), where risk management is characterized as a maturing process evolving over six subsequent steps.

Here, model-based risk management has its limitations. First, models rely heavily on the specification and precision of input variables; the parameters must be estimated, and there is estimation risk, which can be substantial in financial markets. This is no problem in statistical testing *per se*; a low precision implies low significance of the estimated parameters – but it is an open question how economic agents *decide* under these circumstances. The additional problem we face in the context of risk management is that the model (or more generally: the system), which is used to measure risks, represents a risk itself. How should somebody wearing glasses find them in the morning after getting up? This works only if certain processes are clearly structured – but it cannot work in principle. This is the same in risk management. Since risk perception heavily relies on specific models, but the models rely on *a priori* assumptions about the risks (most importantly, about the measurability of risk *per se*), self-reflecting procedures must be implemented in the risk management process. Of course, neuronal networks or data-mining algorithms are often used, but this just shifts the problem to a different level of abstraction. In addition, the management literature suggests a series of approaches to model business risk in a dynamic perspective.

Analysing the big derivative losses suggests that the implementation of basic, organizational risk management procedures would have – at least – saved Barings bank from bankruptcy. I think that the adaptation of management procedures to an area which is typically dominated by 'quants' is fundamental, but not easy. Risk management is, after all, not a purely computational exercise but a management function delegating explicit responsibilities to specific persons or committees. As a conclusion, I believe that it is important to think more seriously about the implications of a 'process-orientated' view on regulatory issues, supervision and education. This approach would have the additional advantage of being consistent with the analysis and evaluation practice for business processes performed in external and internal auditing, as well as in total quality management (TQM). Why not extend this to risk management processes? Anyhow, risk management seems to be a field where the knowledge transfer between finance and management science should be accelerated.

IMPLICATIONS FOR POSTGRADUATE AND EXECUTIVE EDUCATION IN FINANCE

In the previous sections of this chapter, the determinants of the financial innovation process have been investigated, and the role of knowledge as an innovative force was discussed in the area of derivatives and risk management.

In the following I try to formulate some implications for postgraduate (or executive) education in finance.

Designing a Curriculum

Today, there is a tremendous supply of executive education in finance related topics. There is a whole industry offering two- or three-day courses in five-star hotels at rates exceeding 5000 Swiss francs a day. Sometimes, there are even outstanding speakers. For bankers it is an excellent forum to sell products, to demonstrate expertise and to get in touch with potential customers, and for university professors it is a good opportunity to earn some additional money.

The basic drawback of these courses is that they are not part of a curriculum. Finance is an extremely wide area with many specialized fields, but nevertheless, the various topics are strongly conceptually linked. In order to get a good understanding of modern finance, my estimate is that one needs about 80 to 100 days or 16 to 20 weeks of education including exercises and case studies. At least this was the assumption when the University of St. Gallen and the Stern School at New York University designed a master's programme in finance for executives. It also approximately corresponds to the amount of coursework in the AZEK/IFFA-programmes,[8] which prepares students for a diploma called *Eidgenössisch diplomierter Finanzanalytiker und Vermögensverwalter* (Swiss Federal Diploma for Financial Analysis and Portfolio Management), supervised by the *Bundesamt für Berufsbildung und Technologie* (*BBT*) (Federal Office for Business Education and Technology). This programme was established in the early nineties by the Swiss Financial Analysts' Association, and is, currently, the only well-defined curriculum for postgraduate education in finance in Switzerland. It is similar to the CFA (Chartered Financial Analysts') programmes in the US, but is much more concise and puts more emphasis on modern finance than on traditional financial analysis and accounting. The Swiss Federal examination already has a high reputation, and the diploma is often required as a prerequisite for certain jobs.

A typical finance curriculum should include the major areas such as portfolio theory, asset pricing, derivatives and risk management, capital budgeting and corporate finance and regulatory issues.

As a first step to finance, in order to get 'familiar' with the major topics and concepts, our institute, the *Schweizerisches Institut für Banken und Finanzen* (*s/bf-HSG*) (Swiss Institute of Banking and Finance), had some success in offering a series of 20 pre-evening lectures 'Fit for Finance'. There is an option to take an examination at the end of the programme to obtain a certificate issued by our institute. The continuous success of this 'mini' programme demonstrates the demand and need for programmes which *get people started* in finance and which cover a *broad* range of topics within a *well-structured* curriculum. Teaching a basic and intuitive understanding of the major topics is the first and most important step in postgraduate education for practitioners.

Recognizing the Heterogeneity of Participants

The fascinating thing about executive teaching, at every level, is the heterogeneity of participants, both with respect to their background and current employment. A typical audience always includes lawyers, officials from regulatory agencies, engineers, consultants and sometimes even head hunters. As mentioned above, finance is a particularly attractive field for mathematicians and physicists, but they typically work in very specialized fields. Many specialists are eager to get a broader view of finance, and thus find a postgraduate programme to be an adequate way to build up their knowledge or to acquire the background for a more management-orientated career. Therefore, a successful finance curriculum must be particularly designed for people with an academic background *different* from economics and management. Fortunately, my observation is that people *with* such a background typically do not complain about excessive redundancy with respect to what they are taught and to what they already know.

But there is also a huge heterogeneity among participants within the same organization. The previous sections of this chapter showed that modern finance is needed essentially everywhere in the financial sector, and therefore a curriculum should try to address accountants, lawyers, portfolio managers, controllers, treasurers, auditors, analysts, computer scientists, software engineers and many others simultaneously. This is not always easy; but getting a shared view of problems and possible solutions, and finding a common language (terminology) to talk about things is an indispensable part of an educational process.

Certification

Education needs examinations. What makes a curriculum different from an unstructured series of individual seminars is that participants are forced to work constantly and hard. Also, the quality of courses offered all over the world is extremely heterogeneous such that a diploma or a certificate issued by a well-known institution signals quality. This is particularly important in the field of finance because there are essentially no quality standards or generally accepted business principles available compared to other fields in management or technology. Such standards are now being developed in various fields such as performance measurement or risk management, but they are far from being generally accepted. Portfolio theory and option pricing can be taught in many different ways, from telling business anecdotes to highly mathematical lectures. In a field of education where quality is so difficult to recognize and explicit standards are missing, certification plays a crucial role.

Research Orientation

Finance curricula are too textbook orientated. This is important for a basic understanding of issues, but curricula offered by academic institutions must demonstrate the role of research as the single most important know-how provider in this field. I do not say that practical experience is unimportant; research results must be confronted with current business practices in order to be interesting for practitioners. But I stress that in executive curricula participants must learn about the state-of-the-art of research. This includes current theoretical and empirical work, which also means that participants must acquire a basic understanding of statistical techniques (see below) which is particularly important for people without academic degrees. It also implies that one of the objectives of executive education is that practitioners are able to read and understand the basic message of articles published in certain specially designed journals or magazines. I am always surprised at how little practitioners know about what is written in journals on their specific field; this is even true for research departments. I found out that about 80 per cent of what people would like to know is already extensively researched in the literature. There are about a dozen finance journals specially published for practitioners where articles are mostly written in a very readable nontechnical way (*Financial Analysts Journal, Journal of Portfolio Management, Journal of Investing, Journal of Derivatives, Risk, Financial Markets and Portfolio Management*, and many others). I even think that specific seminars offering a review of the most recent research results in various fields would be a perfect complement to the programmes and courses which are now available. Anyhow, practitioners *must* recognize the role of academic research as a 'cheap' and easily accessible source of knowledge.

Modularity and Continuity

Finance is an extremely dynamic field, driven by new research results and practical experience. It is indispensable that curricula are continuously updated, but it is also necessary to offer continuing education programmes. In contrast to the basic curriculum covering the broad field of finance, these programmes can be organized in a modular way where the individual modules are devoted to specific topics and can be taken separately. Typically, participants are executives with a senior management function and have severe time constraints, but on the other hand, they have rather specific interests. There are not many of these programmes right now. A good example is the Advanced Executive Program (AEP) of the Swiss Banking School, which offers a series of three-day seminars on various applied banking and finance topics, mostly based on case studies. Given the growing responsibilities of senior management for finance-related topics such as asset-liability management, firmwide integration of risk, asset allocation and performance measurement, and given the fact that most of today's senior managers typically did not have a systematic education on these issues during their career, offering such courses should have a much higher priority. Unlike in Europe, offering specialized executive courses (in finance, marketing, information systems) taught at evening classes has become an essential part of the funding of most US business schools.

Implementation Issues and Empirical Work

The finance education today, at universities and outside, takes an almost exclusive view on financial modelling. What assumptions are necessary, which are sufficient, for the CAPM to hold? How must the Black–Scholes model be adjusted in order to take stochastic volatility into account? These are important questions, but for practical purposes, at least two questions are equally relevant: how can the input parameters be estimated? What management framework do these models require? The second question will be addressed in the next paragraph. A good example to show the relevance of the first question are the papers by Jackson, Maude and Perraudin (1997) and Marshall and Siegel (1997). They basically address the same issue: value-at-risk (a widely used risk measure of global market risk) can be measured by different analytical models. This is particularly true for modelling interest rate risk. The regulators are, under the BIS (Bank for International Settlements) 'model approach' mentioned above, very much concerned about the appropriateness of these models. But each of these models can be parametrized (implemented) in many different ways – with respect to the underlying database, the time horizon, the econometric estimation technique and so on. The papers show that there is almost no variation in the risk figures by using different models but the same implementation technique, while the results are extremely sensitive with respect to using different implementation strategies – even for the same model. This clearly illustrates that implementation issues, estimation procedures, sampling problems or similar topics play a crucial role in financial modelling. The fact that a big bank loses several hundred million Swiss francs due to the misspecification of an option pricing model demonstrates the importance of this fact. This means that econometric methods should get a much greater emphasis in our finance curricula. Students must learn how to handle financial data and how to perform standard econometric tests with widely-used software packages. This also includes a basic understanding of data-driven modelling procedures (data mining) and stochastic simulation techniques. Of course, econometrics is not the right thing to teach to executives. But it would be appropriate to make the 'quants' (that is mathematically orientated people) more aware about the implementation issues of the models they develop. What is the practical use of a three-factor model for pricing interest rate options if the required market parameters cannot be estimated because of the illiquidity of the underlying bond market? It is a fact that a more complicated analytical or econometric structure of models substantially increases the risk of parameter misspecification.

Process-orientated View

It was mentioned in the previous section that a model-based view of risk should be complemented by a process-orientated view of risk management. This is also true for other topics than risk management. Finance has for long not recognized the role of the institutional and organizational framework within which financial decisions are taken. The only exceptions are agency theory and corporate governance. Also, behavioural finance is a growing field where the psychological and social background of the decision makers is explicitly taken into account. A substantial part of practical decisions has to do with structuring complex processes. It is not difficult for the chief investment officer of a bank to understand the meaning of Jensen's alpha; but the much more difficult part is to implement a management process such that, at the end, the alphas of several thousands clients' portfolios are available on a daily basis and, moreover, are reliable. This involves the coordination of dozens of processes, the allocation of personnel, information technology and financial resources, while keeping up with the daily business. I think that the knowledge transfer from theory to practice could be drastically accelerated in many fields if management-related issues were regarded as an explicit part of executive curricula.

Product-orientated View

A final point concerns products. Read a finance textbook or a journal article, and you will miss something without which the financial industry would simply not exist: products. A widely used textbook on derivatives includes a chapter on portfolio insurance strategies (strategies promising a minimum return while offering some upside potential), but no relation to any actual financial instrument can be found, although there was a tremendous growth of these instruments over the past years. Academic researchers should recognize much more that knowing products, their characteristics, risks, costs, tax consequences and how they are related to customers' cash flow projection ('financial planning'), is an essential and extremely value-generating part of the investment management business and the basis of active product-related marketing strategies. Unfortunately, academic research is providing little help, and at the same time, the product-related knowledge in practice is sometimes very poor. In this respect, insurance salespeople often exhibit a much better expertise and 'marketing' skills for their products. When you buy medicine the law stipulates that a short, standardized information sheet about the composition, risks and side-effects of the product is included in the package. I do not postulate that we should have a similar law for financial products. But it is true that derivatives, hedge funds and warrants can sometimes be bad for your health, and therefore, the portfolio manager or investment adviser should possess a detailed expertise about the investment characteristics of the available products in his or her field of specialization. I think that the relevance of many financial models would be understood much more easily by practitioners if they were explicitly related to existing or potential financial products – that is, if it were shown that many of the models are extremely useful for a better understanding, characterization, comparison and marketing of various products. Unfortunately, this product-orientated view is missing in most finance textbooks, articles and educational programmes.

I hope that the discussion in this last section has shown that postgraduate and executive education plays a crucial role in the knowledge transfer in the financial sector, and I would argue that improvements in the educational efforts will immediately raise the quality and safety of the financial system.

NOTES

1. A nontechnical and entertaining reference for most topics in finance is Bernstein (1992). A good, classical description of market efficiency can be found in Fama (1976, chapter 5).
2. Most of this chapter will be related to Switzerland. An extremely interesting exposition of the evolution of modern finance knowledge in the US and its relation to practical issues in the investment management business is Bernstein (1992).
3. The original German text reads as follows: 'Ja – hätte man denn annehmen wollen, es gäbe eine Theorie der Kapitalanlage im Bereich der Aktien?' ... 'Solche Untersuchungen halte ich für höchst müssig, weil sie den Eindruck erwecken können, es sei quasi berechenbar, wie Aktienkurse steigen oder fallen.' ... 'Ich meine, man sollte an eine unwissenschaftliche Materie keine pseudowissenschaftlichen Massstäbe legen.' See *Finanz und Wirtschaft*, 30 January 1985, p. 19.
4. In German the statement of Dr Robert Holzach, chairman of the board of UBS reads: 'Die Modewelle der Finanzinnovationen droht den langfristig denkenden Bankier zu verdrängen und durch den auf kurzfristigen Erfolg erpichten Verkäufer zu ersetzen'. Reference based on Schütz (1998, p. 142).
5. A critical, empirical analysis of the structure of Swiss financial markets in terms of risk allocation, information processing, liquidity, and corporate governance is provided by Zimmermann, Bill and Dubacher (1989).
6. The problems we faced in designing stock option derivatives under these adverse circumstances and the solutions which were proposed, are described in Zimmermann (1987/88). The same analysis related to derivative stock index products is published in Cordero, Dubacher and Zimmermann (1988).
7. A complete and up-to-date monograph on Swiss capital market law, its structure and historical roots, is provided by Nobel (1997).
8. AZEK is the *Ausbildungszentrum für Experten der Kapitalanlage*, IFFA is the *Institut für Finanzmarktanalyse*.

REFERENCES

Bachelier, L. (1900), *Théorie de la Spéculation*, Dissertation Ecole Normale Supérieure, Paris, reprinted in *Editions Jacques Gabay*, Paris, 1995.

Bernstein, P. (1992), *Capital Ideas. The Improbable Origins of Modern Wall Street*, New York: Free Press.

Black, F. and M. Scholes (1973), 'The pricing of options and corporate liabilities', *Journal of Political Economy*, **81** (3), pp. 637–54.

Cordero, R., R. Dubacher and H. Zimmermann (1988), 'Zur Entwicklung des neuen Swiss Market Index (SMI) als Grundlage für schweizerische Indexkontrakte: Eine Evaluation potentieller Aktienindices', *Schweizerische Zeitschrift für Volkswirtschaft und Statistik*, **124** (4), pp. 575–600.

Edwards, F. (1996), *The New Finance. Regulation and Financial Stability*, Washington: American Enterprise Institute.

Fama, E. (1976), *Foundations of Finance*, New York: Basic Books.

Heinzl, Th., C. von Senger and H. Zimmermann (1998), 'The capability–maturity approach for risk management', Working Paper, St. Gallen: Swiss Institute of Banking and Finance at the University of St. Gallen.

Ippolito, R. (1993), 'On studies of mutual fund performance', *Financial Analysts Journal*, **49** (1), pp. 42–50.

Jackson, P., D.J. Maude and W. Perraudin (1997), 'Bank capital and value at risk', *Journal of Derivatives*, **4** (3), pp. 73–89.

Markowitz, H.M. (1952), 'Portfolio selection', *Journal of Finance*, **7**, pp. 77–92.

Marshall, Ch. and M. Siegel (1997), 'Value at risk: implementing a risk measurement standard', *Journal of Derivatives*, **4** (3), pp. 91–111.

Merton, R.C. (1973), 'Theory of rational option pricing', *Bell Journal of Economics and Management Science*, **4**, pp. 141–83.

Merton, R.C. (1995), 'Financial innovation and the financial system', *Cases in Financial Engineering*, chapter 1, Englewood Cliffs, NJ: Prentice-Hall.

Nobel, P. (1997), *Schweizerisches Kapitalmarktrecht. Einführung und Überblick*, Bern: Stämpfli.

Oertmann, P. and H. Zimmermann (1998), 'Global economic risk profile', *Schweizer Bank*, no. 4, pp. 24–7.

Schütz, D. (1998), *Der Fall der UBS – warum die Schweizerische Bankgesellschaft unterging*, Zürich: Bilanz Weltwoche-ABC-Verlag.

Vock, Th. and H. Zimmermann (1984), 'Renditen und Risiken schweizerischer Aktien', *Schweizerische Zeitschrift für Volkswirtschaft und Statistik*, **120** (4), pp. 547–76.

Ziegler, A. (1998), *A Game Theory Analysis of Options. Contributions to the Theory of Financial Intermediation in Continuous Time*, Dissertation No. 2188, University of St. Gallen, forthcoming.

Zimmermann, H. (1981), *Rationale Erwartungen und kurzfristiges Wechselkursverhalten*, Diploma thesis, Universität Bern: mimeo.

Zimmermann, H. (1987/88), 'Der schweizerische Options- und Financial Futures-Markt: Die geplanten Instrumente', *Journal of Financial Markets and Portfolio Management*, **1** (2), pp. 33–46; update 1988 in *Journal of Financial Markets and Portfolio Management*, **2** (1), pp. 67–72.

Teaching and application of economics

Zimmermann, H. (1998), 'Innovationsprozesse im Finanz- und Risikomanagement', in
W. Popp and T. Zimmermann (eds), *Strategie und Innovation in Universalbanken*,
Bern and Stuttgart: Haupt, pp. 11–32.
Zimmermann, H., C. Arce, St. Jaeger and H.-J. Wolter (1992), 'Pensionskassen Schweiz.
Neue Strategien für wachsende Leistungsansprüche', *Wirtschaft und Gesellschaft*, no. 6,
Zürcher Kantonalbank.
Zimmermann, H., M. Bill and R. Dubacher (1989), 'Finanzmarkt Schweiz. Strukturen
im Wandel', *Wirtschaft und Gesellschaft*, no. 4, Zürcher Kantonalbank.

9. The new media: chances and challenges for suppliers of economic education

Heinz Hauser and Sascha Spoun

INTRODUCTION

To introduce our topic of expected changes in the university industry, let us have a look at the market for opera music. There are theatres in almost every major city in Europe that perform operas in varying quality. Some of them, such as the houses in Vienna, Munich, London or Paris, also attract visitors from a wider area. A small number of top performers such as the Metropolitan at New York or the Scala at Milan have a worldwide reputation and are preferred places for artistes and visitors. The offer of festivals is similar and ranges from regional events to Bayreuth. Most of the artistes are on the permanent staff of a theatre, but a relatively small group of the internationally renowned can sell their performances at very high prices. Whereas tickets for the top performances are difficult to obtain, despite high prices, local theatres face more and more difficulty in selling their seats. They experience a growing competition from compact discs or videos, performed by artistes with international reputations, which enable everybody to enjoy the best music in their homes.

Replace music consumers by students, artistes by faculty members, theatres by universities, a live performance by on-campus teaching, compact discs and videos by media channels for economic education, festivals by special (summer) programmes, and you have an analogy for the future structure of the market for economic education as it might evolve as a consequence of globalization and new technology. One can already find some support for this analogy in today's environment, but we are convinced that the process of change in the university industry will accelerate quickly and lead to a substantial restructuring of the university market in the next 10 to 20 years.[1]

The upshot of this chapter is that we can no longer expect the university to be the 'natural' and exclusive locus for production, distribution and interpretation of (economic) knowledge. The accelerating change in the communication media from print to electronics can be compared with previous shifts from speech to writing and from writing to print with their consequences in creating, recording, storing, distributing and receiving information. New media will change education inside the universities and alter the environment of universities, particularly through increasing competition. Other institutions, such as software and publishing houses or in-house universities of companies, will enter the market and fulfil some of the universities' functions.[2] Furthermore, institutions from very distant places can compete against each other because distance becomes less important. The explosion of knowledge, the true driver of change, becomes accessible everywhere.

Major changes driven by new media will be outlined in the first section to show the tremendous potential.[3] The second section, 'Whither the campus university' then develops arguments confirming the continuing strength of the traditional university. After identifying core competencies and barriers to change, we highlight testing and prestige as crucial assets of a university. The chapter closes with arguments for strategic choices of universities.

NEW MEDIA AND THE LEARNING PROCESS

By new media we understand those advanced technologies which enable interactive and simultaneous transmission of voices, of moving images and of data at falling costs while increasing speed and improving quality. Virtual learning relies on different media: first of all, the Internet, e-mail, electronic bulletin boards, World Wide Web browsers and search engines, what, then, is called a university in cyberspace. Second, there is the already traditional audio and video taping and videoconferencing. But third, and most revolutionary, is the combination of these techniques with application-sharing software, synchronous group discussion software and other features. Teaching and learning will no longer be tied to a certain institution and, as a result, need not be confined to students of a certain age group pursuing full-time studies for a given period at a given location. Rather, technology enables education to be transmitted everywhere over a lifetime and as a part-time occupation. Learning develops into an individual 'just-in-time' process that also allows specialized and interdisciplinary work.

Traditional long-distance teaching providers, such as the Open University in the UK or the *Fernuniversität* Hagen in Germany, are pushing new media technologies in their courses on offer.[4] To what extent and with what speed this development will become a dominant force in traditional university teaching will very much depend on relative costs of alternative modes of education. The success of the University of Phoenix' virtual programmes relies on the fairly small tuition compared to traditional campuses (see McCartney 1996, p. 33). Through new media, universities can also become a player in fields where they were not present before. In Germany for example, the University of Münster set up the legal training forum JurLINK.[5] Based on the interactive structures of the Internet, JurLINK is designed as an online journal to facilitate students' preparation for the first state examination. Traditional universities generally fail to provide such preparation for law examinations and almost all law students take private preparatory courses. The new media-based course is said to close this gap at least to some extent. The above mentioned examples are completely new endeavours potentially replacing traditional university programmes, whereas most of the online universities are offered in addition to traditional courses and are mainly supposed to initiate international virtual collaboration.[6]

As a result of these developments, the learning process will change in some of its until now unquestioned characteristics: learning will change from a unidirectional transfer of knowledge to self-discovery and construction of knowledge. Whereas today, teachers transmit the knowledge and are at the centre of the learning process, in the future the students themselves will become the centre and the teacher will take on the role of a facilitator whose primary task is to teach the methods of learning. The possibility of organizing an individualized schedule on the basis of stored sessions (on video tape or CD-ROM for example), to repeat or to skip single topics or lessons and to extend or to explore interesting aspects through the hyperlink method will complement and partly replace the existing linear learning process based on structured sequential programmes.[7] In consequence, learning will become more individualized and customer focused.

There is a debate in the pedagogical literature as to what extent different modes of teaching influence the effectiveness of the learning process, measured by grades, test scores or job performance. Russell compared the results of more than two hundred studies and found no clear evidence for significant differences.[8] If there exists no clear pattern of learning effectiveness, relative costs of different modes of teaching become important.

New media will influence the learning process in all settings. Compared to today's situation, potential productivity gains will be strongest in interactive long-distance learning. This concerns mainly standardized learning topics in undergraduate education, but also teaching and research in specialized fields. Teaching of subjects with a relatively standardized body of knowledge, regardless of level, will be partly or totally outsourced with increasing use of new media technology providers. The production of interactive course units for standardized topics such as microeconomics, macroeconomics, international economics, statistics and econometrics, will find potentially large markets, particularly if the development and delivery of these courses is under the control of faculty members who have a significant international reputation. If the tests have credibility, universities might decide to outsource part of the teaching to reduce their cost and students may decide to choose their curriculum from preferred professors and topics at different universities. Even if such trends develop slowly and have reduced scope for many years, one should not underestimate their impact on university structures, because something like 50 to 75 per cent of our teaching refers to a relatively homogeneous standardized body of knowledge.

Interactive long-distance learning requires up-front investment, both in terms of physical infrastructure and learning how to make the best use of available technologies, for students and teachers alike. It is therefore not surprising that interactive long-distance learning has developed fastest where opportunity costs of alternatives are high. In particular in the high-cost, high-prestige arena of business education, where opportunity costs, measured in potential income from alternative career paths, are high, long-distance learning could offer the greatest advantages. Executive education with the Global Executive MBA of Duke University as a prime example of high prestige and the online MBA of Colorado State University as one of the first online offers have already started to move very strongly in this direction.[9] Distance learning is also popular in fast-growing markets where the career potential for well-educated young professionals is very high.

We are still in the experimental phase and relative costs of interactive long-distance learning are still high, but they will be substantially reduced over the next 10 years. Individual infrastructure costs will be lower as soon as the equipment for multimedia is produced on a larger scale, as experienced with computer or fax technologies. All major universities will be equipped as they are today with PCs, in particular if the prices for the use of communication facilities decrease and multimedia networks become public infrastructure comparable to phone and cable television. In consequence, the costs for an additional virtual course are marginal. In addition, computer literacy increases with each new generation of students, as does the preference for more flexibility in the allocation of time among learning, working and leisure.

With lower-cost access to new media, we shall experience strong economies of scale in the learning process. A traditional live lecture or seminar can only be duplicated at close to the cost of the original one. Textbooks also have high economies of scale, but they require decentralized delivery, interpretation and testing of acquired knowledge. With interactive forms of new media one can supply the full range of the teaching process within the network at relatively low marginal (and average) costs.[10] Suppliers of such courses might be universities with a good reputation which want to cover costs for their investment in new media teaching, or faculty members with a highly qualified support staff, or network providers which buy the support of specialized staff and renowned faculty. Most probably, we shall see a combination of these three groups of providers with innovative contractual relations. With the tendency to globalize educational markets and with English as a dominant language, there is the potential for strong market growth in virtual courses.

On a more generalized level: production, distribution and interpretation of knowledge will become separate functions of the learning process to a much stronger degree than today. Distribution costs will be reduced and the provider of the information package will take at least partial responsibility for interpretation and testing. Today, distribution and interpretation dominate the market structure for university education; tomorrow, production, together with specialized distribution firms, might become the dominant market force. As in other industries, technological developments alter the relative productivity of different modes of delivery, which will exert great pressure on existing market structures.

WHITHER THE CAMPUS UNIVERSITY?

Although interactive long-distance learning will become a strong driver for change, university systems based entirely on long-distance learning will not become the dominant form of tertiary education. On-campus learning will have a smaller share of the total learning process and will change its nature, but it will remain an important part of higher education.

Core Competence: Personal Development Beyond Knowledge Transfer

University education goes far beyond the teaching of particular subjects and the transmission of information. It includes social processes, the acquisition of intuition and habits that contribute to personal development. Mentoring, interacting, role modelling and guidance need physical presence and personal contacts. Group interaction, face-to-face discussion and learning-by-doing for the acquisition of research or problem-solving strategies cannot be replaced by new media technology. The core competencies of on-campus universities are in areas where the learning processes rely on personal interactions and on nonstandardized knowledge. On-campus education will focus on how to apply knowledge which has been acquired previously, whereas the transfer or the acquisition of knowledge can become the domain of interactive long-distance learning systems, which better exploit economies of scale.

Recruiters are looking for graduates who are willing to exercise leadership for projects, are team players, open-minded and show social responsibility, particularly in business education (see, for example, O'Reilly 1994, p. 38 and Ford 1994, p. 212). These are personal characteristics which are better developed in the social setting of a campus university.

Although everyone would agree to the description of the main functions of on-campus education, few are aware of the radical shift of university teaching that this would imply. Today, university teaching is primarily unidirectional in the transfer of information. Students are not well trained to develop their own learning strategies. Construction of knowledge and learning-by-doing are not dominant features of a university curriculum, particularly in the continental European system with its strong reliance on mass lectures.

Barriers to Change

New media teaching requires thoroughly planned courses, high motivation by the lecturer, his or her permanent accessibility for students and immediate response to questions and mail. The teacher is required to initiate and facilitate the process and to coach in technical aspects as well as in matters of content. Even if one concedes a steep learning curve for virtual classes, such courses will require more effort than traditional classes for some time. This will lead to teacher resistance against changes.

Not all students will be able to learn through the new media, because this requires a certain level of computer literacy and a high degree of motivation and self-discipline. Also, some are less involved, feel unable to ask questions, and are generally less comfortable with the new methods (see Swift, Wilson and Wayland 1997, pp. 85ff.). If a clear learning structure, determined by fixed syllabuses and schedules, turns out to be an important facilitator and motivator of learning, then virtual courses face difficulties in competing (see Kearsley and Lynch 1996, p. 191). The main disadvantage of distance learning is that students are separated from colleagues sharing the same interests and comparable goals. Informal interaction is more difficult to realize, and verbal communication is limited to simultaneous video sessions. As we indicated earlier, students will become familiar with new technologies over time, but the factors mentioned will delay change.

What has been said for the learning process applies also for physical infrastructure and operating costs. Going beyond the Internet, virtual courses require videoconferencing, which is a sophisticated and expensive infrastructure, particularly for international communication. Until now only projects sponsored by information technology and telecommunication companies such as a project within the Community of European Management Schools (CEMS),[11] or fully priced programmes such as the Duke Executive MBA, could be realized. If one considers the speed of technical development in the computer industry and the decrease of telecommunication prices in Europe during recent years, we can expect cheaper and more customized opportunities for long-distance education within a few years.

There is another structural barrier that will delay full exploitation of the potential of new media. Particularly in Europe, where public universities are dominant, alternative modes of providing academic education are discriminated against compared to in-house teaching by permanent staff. Universities cannot reallocate part of their personnel budget to outsourced teaching services. In addition, students do not pay the full cost of their education so that their choice is also biased towards traditional forms of education. Even in the more competitive American environment, the tenure system introduces inflexibility for short-term adjustment in the budget. Again, these forces might become less important with time, as financial and competitive pressure on traditional universities becomes stronger. They will most probably retard, but not prevent the underlying trend for strong structural changes in the market for tertiary education.

Universities as Franchisers of Degrees

Universities contribute to the learning process of their students, but they also confer degrees which have signalling effects for the labour market as well as for society. This will remain an important factor in explaining market changes. Signalling is based on the reputation of an institution, more precisely, on the reputation of its graduates, which has public good characteristics for the individual student. Accordingly, quality control is important and is based on three mechanisms: entry selection, interaction during the learning period and comprehensive testing at the end of the programme. Public universities in Europe rely more on end programme testing, whereas private universities have a stronger focus on selection and interaction during the learning process. But all systems have in common that they have to be concerned about the signalling properties of their degrees, if they want to provide good services to their students. The signalling effect of an institution's reputation will become even more important with the internationalization of recruitment for post-graduation job opportunities. Universities which provide a reliable pre-selection of candidates will become preferred recruitment places for international firms and international organizations.

The signalling effect of institutional reputation will most probably be one of the strongest barriers to entry for new suppliers and new modes of university education. If universities want to build up a reputation for high-quality graduates, they have to consistently produce such students with a higher probability than one would find in the overall university population. They have to stress the relation between students' performance and the learning process of the institution. For the positioning of a university this requires both high-quality students and a clear relationship to the educational programmes of the school.

These arguments speak against a flexible combination of course offers from different sources which could combine to make up a university degree. Universities will outsource certain areas, but they want to keep control by means of selective accreditation of such outside providers. These limitations might look very convincing in the present context, but we feel unable to make predictions for the future. To take an analogous case: in much the same way as Harvard case studies have been exported to many other MBA programmes, we shall see much broader reliance on educational material which has been provided by leading universities. Imagine that new technologies had been available in the 1960s and 1970s and that Paul Samuelson had established a private firm providing teaching material, interactive electronic teaching and reliable testing. Our expectation is that many universities would have accredited such a course for their home degree programme. One could certainly find names who could find a good market with such an enterprise in the next ten years.

There is another development which might threaten the monopoly of universities to certify quality standards. In an increasingly global marketplace for first job opportunities and with the great variety of university degrees with no clear correspondence between the European and the Anglo-Saxon university model, there might be growing demand for a common international standard for economists who work in different fields of policy analysis. There is broad consensus on methods and skills necessary to do empirical research. We could imagine that an organization, such as the American Economic Association, the European Economic Association or the National Bureau of Economic Research, will take the lead in developing an international standard for economists who claim to perform successfully in empirically based policy analysis. As one finds Chartered Accountants, one could find Chartered Empirical Economists, who would have a good market in international firms or organizations.

More Market Power for Suppliers and Customers

New media will alter not only the market for educational services, but also the employment market for faculty and research staff. As a result of increasing internationalization of faculty recruitment, universities face stronger competition for high-quality faculty members. We shall witness an increasing differentiation in employment contracts and remuneration, which will reflect the earnings potential in other spheres of economic education. The market for economists will never be exactly analogous to that of opera singers, but the trend will go in that direction. Today, there are strong incentives for faculty members to join institutions enjoying a high reputation. In the future, the highest earnings might be generated by an efficient intranet provider who writes project-based contracts with a group of internationally renowned economists. For universities as academic institutions it will be decisive whether high-quality faculty members retain their loyalty to the institution or whether they will follow market opportunities and will change their affiliation according to earnings potential.

Predictions on the consequences of these developments for the university market structure are difficult to define. On the one hand, decreasing loyalty of faculty members to the institution makes it more difficult to maintain its reputation. On the other hand, there could be strong tendencies to stabilize existing reputational hierarchies. Availability of (public or private) funds and attractiveness for faculty members are positively correlated, which produces vicious circles for universities. Regardless of whether the availability of new opportunities will lead to higher or lower stability in the hierarchy of educational institutions, increased market power of star faculty members will make university management more difficult, and good management an even stronger critical success factor. Particularly in Europe, we need a decisive move towards greater autonomy and flexibility if European universities are to stay competitive in an increasingly global market for qualified faculty members.

The 'customers', the students, can choose from a broader range of opportunities for studying, because a large number of universities and university programmes becomes accessible. The loyalty to one institution may decrease if students can choose their curriculum from different providers while staying at one location. Whereas in the past, rigid curricula offered professors captive markets, now the management of the learning process needs a much broader perspective including the choice between in-house teaching and accredited courses from external providers. In addition university management from the demand side becomes a much more complex task than before.

STRATEGIC CHOICES FOR UNIVERSITIES

As outlined, the university system will come under great pressure, both from the students (they have a greater choice of options available) and from the suppliers (faculty have better opportunities to become entrepreneurs in the educational market). We shall see much experimenting, and it is very difficult to make clear predictions about the evolving structure. If we take the experience of other industries, stronger competition and the globalization of the market will lead to greater specialization.

Universities have to respond proactively and with a strategic orientation if they want to avoid becoming or remaining local 'theatres' with no clear profile and very limited reach – with reference to the analogy with which we started. Such 'theatres' will have their audience, but they will not be able to attract high-quality performers. Applied to universities, they will be part of a local system for tertiary education, which includes polytechnics, universities and a great variety of vocationally orientated schools.

There will be a relatively small number of universities that differentiate successfully and gain an international reputation, be it on a regional (language) or global scale. They will have a strong research base and aim for high-quality teaching. The major topics for university management will be the restructuring of curricula, the change of employment contracts, a shift in the investment policy and the importance of alliances.

If new media alter the learning process as described in the first section, universities need to innovate with regard to existing curricula both in their format and content. Speed and depth of change will be major forces of differentiation for university programmes.

Until now, the *conditio sine qua non* for good teaching has been the quality of the permanent faculty. In the future, courses can be purchased from external suppliers. Therefore, the depth of production of a single university will decrease and the structure of employment has to change. The make or buy question will be central in university management. Only very few can profit from a life-long employment contract to enable the university to react quickly to new demand.

Investment policy of universities will have to change: the physical library, the heart of every campus, will lose importance dramatically because new media allow an almost unlimited storage of and access to information from everywhere. A future university information centre will take on this role and offer access to search engines and databases which permit a full-text download, if digitized texts replace hard copies. Until now, a fast and cheap access to knowledge needed physical presence at a library; in the future the access to databases is decisive.

New media will put in question the exclusivity of some institutions, because, first, open access to information by new media challenges the competitive edges of existing curricula and second, other institutions than the universities can compete with them. Universities themselves will face an increasing competition for alliance partners not only within the university sector, but also beyond. In the more open structure for university education, collaboration with software houses, multimedia providers, publishers and private enterprises will be decisive.[12]

Because European universities have operated in highly protected national markets, due to regulations, public financing and language barriers, they still have to adjust to increasing competition and to the growing internationalization of the university system. If they want to become members in the evolving 'global champions league', they have to opt for an explicit strategy of excellence (elitism), internationalization of students and faculty, competitive specialization, and latest advances in media technologies. Universities are no different from other industries, for which globalization and new information technologies have caused major restructuring. Because of strong protectionist barriers, restructuring will be delayed, but there are no reasons why universities should be sheltered against strong pressure from global competition and increased technological opportunities over a longer period.

We would like to conclude with a precautionary note. This chapter has been written from an industry analysis perspective, namely, what will be the likely changes in the market structure if technology has an uneven impact on different segments or different modes of delivery. We have not asked the question how we evaluate these changes from a social or political perspective. Universities have played and do still play a crucial role in the development of civil societies based on human rights, democratic institutions and social mobility between generations. New media could accelerate changes which are caused by a rising number of students, budgetary restrictions and stronger competition – changes which eventually threaten to undermine the social and cultural functions of the traditional university system. If reduced to fragmented providers of specialized educational services, universities lose their particular role of socializing and educating the next generation. Values and commitments to a civil society need to be an integral part of university life – a challenge which is at least comparable to structural changes from new technology and competition.

NOTES

1. Already in 1995, Eli Noam referred to the threats and challenges of electronics for the educational functions of universities and predicted wide-ranging shifts of existing positions. See Noam (1995).
2. See, for example, Moore (1997, p. 77) to get an idea of the growth of corporate universities: until the eighties one could perhaps find a dozen, among them Motorola, Disney and Arthur D. Little, whereas in 1994 there were as many as 400 institutions and in 1997 more than 1000 corporate universities. For functions of the university, see Altbach (1996, pp. 21 ff.) and Frijhoff (1996, p. 53).
3. Walker (1996) gives an overview of the digital revolution for higher education and what major Western governments regard as key priorities in this development.
4. Curran (1997, p. 335) gives an overview of the history and the importance of distance learning and its relation to traditional universities. For more information on the Open University and the *Fernuniversität* Hagen follow the internet links http://www.open.ac.uk and http://www.fernuni-hagen.de. The *Fernuniversität* Hagen, which is Germany's major open university, claims to run one of the most advanced 'virtual university' projects that not only sends out interactive teaching material on the net, but also offers different opportunities for informal communication among students and access to the administration and the library.
5. JurLINK (Internet link: http://www.uni-muenster.de/Jura.tkr) is an initiative supported by the Department for Science and Research of North Rhine-Westphalia.
6. Different efforts to use new media in a large state-run university in Germany are made by the Berlin Brandenburg College, a virtual university designed in cooperation by the universities in Berlin and Brandenburg in 1996, and the University of Münster (follow the Internet links http://www.tk.tu-berlin.de/tubkom/Info/virtualCollege.html, http://www.prz.tu-berlin.de/~virtualC and http://www.Universität-muenster.Multimedia/Projekte.html). Another example is the Keio Virtual University in Japan (link: http://duroc.unolab.sfc.keio.ac.jp).
7. For the case of the Center for the New Engineer at George Mason University, Denning (1996) describes what such a hyperlearning process can look like.
8. See Russell (1997), who refers to results published in journals and doctoral dissertations from 1928 until 1996. On the other hand, recent publications claim a significant difference between traditional and virtual learning. See Orr (1998).
9. More information on the Duke case can be found following the Internet link http://www.fuqua.duke.edu/programs/gemba/index.htm. See also Bartlett (1997). Phillips (1998, p. 120) refers to the case of the virtual MBA at the Colorado State University.

10. Culver estimates the costs of teaching a student online at $1000, while classroom teaching at university costs an average of $12 000. See Culver (1997, p. 40A).
11. A class in marketing offered by the Stockholm School of Economics and the University of St. Gallen in the winter semester 1997/98 was taught as a virtual course for students of both institutions. This class was able to use the Internet and videoconferencing, sponsored by Telia of Sweden and Swisscom.
12. EuroPACE 2000 (Internet link: http://www.europace.be) with its 60 member organizations, among them 45 universities, gives an example of this kind of alliance.

REFERENCES

Altbach, P.G. (1996), 'Patterns in higher education development. Towards the year 2000', in Z. Morsy and P. Altbach (eds), *Higher Education in an International Perspective*, New York and London: Garland, pp. 21 ff.

Bartlett, Th. (1997), 'The hottest campus on the Internet', *Business Week*, 20 October.

Culver, K. (1997), 'Online MBA gains attention for UCCS', *Denver Business Journal*, **48** (47), p. 40A.

Curran, C. (1997), 'ODL and traditional universities: dichotomy or convergence?', *European Journal of Education*, **32** (4), pp. 335 ff.

Denning, P.J. (1996), 'Business designs for the new university', *Educom Review*, **31** (6), Internet source at link: http://www.educom.edu/web/pubs/review/reviewArticles/31620.html.

Ford, J. (1994), 'Management education: shifting our assumptions', *Journal of Management Education*, **18** (2), p. 212 ff.

Frijhoff, W. (1996), 'Grundlagen', in W. Rüegg (ed.), *Geschichte der Universität, Bd. 2: Von der Reformation zur Französischen Revolution*, München: Beck, p. 53.

Kearsley, G. and W. Lynch (1996), 'Structural issues in distance education', *Journal of Education for Business*, **71** (4), p. 191.

McCartney, L. (1996), 'Virtual MBA. Going back to school doesn't have to mean sitting in a classroom again', *Information Week*, issue 604, 4 November, p. 33.

Moore, Th. (1997), 'The corporate university: transforming management education', *Accounting Horizons*, **11** (1), p. 77.

Noam, E. (1995), 'Electronics and the dim future of the university', *Science Magazine*, 13 October.

O'Reilly, B. (1994), 'Reengineering the MBA', *Fortune*, **129** (2), p. 38.

Orr, B. (1998), 'A significant difference', Internet source at link http://teleeducation.nb.ca/anygood/asigdiff.shtml.

Phillips, V. (1998), 'Online universities teach knowledge beyond the books', *HR Magazine*, **43** (8), p. 120.

Russell, Th. (1997), 'The "no significant difference phenomenon"', Internet source at link http://teleeducation.nb.ca/phenom/html.

Swift, C.O., J. Wilson and J.P. Wayland (1997), 'Interactive distance education in business: is the new technology right for you?', *Journal of Education for Business*, **73** (2), p. 85.

Walker, J. (1996), 'Managing the digital revolution: a strategy to maximize the use of high capacity communications services in Australian education and training', Internet source at link http://www.comm.utas.edu.au/Publications/managf.htm.

PART IV

Interdisciplinary Perspectives of
the Transfer Process

10. The relevance of psychological aspects for policy design

Bruno S. Frey[*]

INTRODUCTION

Actual economic policy is full of psychological aspects. Rarely a day passes in which a politician would not be asking citizens to behave in a 'socially' responsible way. 'Moral suasion' has been extremely popular when inflation was a pressing social issue; but it is equally used today when unemployment is considered the major social ill.

Economists tend to laugh about such pronouncements; they simply do not take them seriously. Indeed, the theory of economic policy disregards psychological aspects *in toto*. Consider the major areas of this field:

- The traditional technocratically orientated version maximizing social welfare under resource constraints has no room for any psychological effects. This applies to the quantitative theory of macroeconomic policy (Tinbergen 1956; Theil 1968) as well as to its microeconomic application in the form of optimal taxation or to optimal public pricing (see, for example, Bös 1986).
- The more recent political economy, constitutional or democratic approach to economic policy (Buchanan 1991; Brennan and Buchanan 1985; Frey 1983) is not much better. Again, psychological aspects are systematically disregarded.
- At first sight the more recent versions of the theory of economic policy, relying strongly on game theory, look more promising. The central concepts of 'reputation' and 'credibility' have a psychological ring. However, these variables have no basis in micro behaviour but are constructed to perform a function at the macro level only. Indeed, the respective literature (see Persson and Tabellini 1994 for a survey) does

* I am grateful to Lorenz Goette, Marcel Kucher, Felix Oberholzer-Gee, Alois Stutzer and Isabelle Vautravers for their helpful suggestions. This research has been supported by the Swiss National Fund (Project No. 12-42480.94).

not even think of making an effort to find a basis for reputation and credibility in psychology (or, for that matter, in sociology).

- What about those (few) economists who have tried to integrate psychological elements into economics (see Simon 1983; Akerlof 1984; Frank 1985 and 1988; Thaler 1992; or Rabin 1998). While they have provided fascinating analyses of human behaviour, they have rarely drawn any implications for economic policy.[1]

    The same holds for the movement of 'economic psychology' or 'psychological economics' (for example Furnham and Lewis 1986; Lea, Tarpy and Webley 1987; McFadyen and McFadyen 1986; van Raaij, van Veldhoven and Wärneryd 1988; Earl 1990). This work has hardly concerned itself with economic policy.

- Finally, can we expect any help from the heterodox economists who have always had a liking for psychology? Important advocates are Jöhr (1972) and Schmölders (1962), and (later) in the United States, Katona (1975), Leibenstein (1976) and Scitovsky (1976). Again, the prime interest of these scholars was not directed at policy issues. In any case, they have not developed a consistent body of theory on economic policy, and their work has not been integrated into current textbooks.

This chapter endeavours to demonstrate that psychological aspects are important for economic policy and that it is perilous to disregard them. This is shown by demonstrating that a particular psychological relationship – the 'crowding effect' linking intrinsic and extrinsic motivation – significantly influences economic affairs and should therefore be taken into account in economic policy making. The crowding effect states that under empirically identifiable conditions an external intervention, via monetary rewards or regulations, negatively affects – or crowds out – intrinsic motivation. Under other identifiable conditions, an external intervention crowds in intrinsic motivation. Thus, a systematic relationship between constraints (external interventions) and preferences (intrinsic motivation) is postulated (see Frey 1997b).

Seven propositions will be advanced and discussed:

1. Psychological factors have crucial and systematic influences on the micro and macro economy, and therefore, on economic policy.
2. It is useful to start from theoretically well-identified and empirically supported specific relationships (such as the crowding effect) rather than try to capture 'psychology' in a broad and unspecified way.
3. The crowding effect has important implications on the rules level, that is for constitutional design. This is demonstrated for market versus command and for discipline versus trust as social decision-making mechanisms.
4. The crowding effect also significantly affects the current policy level.

5. The crowding effect helps us to explain apparent paradoxes in orthodox economic theory, for example, that high-income recipients, that is people with the highest opportunity cost of time, are more active as volunteers in the social sector than those with lower opportunity cost.
6. Crowding theory, unlike traditional economics, offers alternative policy recommendations. In particular, it appreciates the benefits of nonintervention.
7. Intrinsic motivation is not good as such but must be balanced against extrinsic incentives.

The first part of the chapter considers economic policy at the *constitutional level* where the basic institutional foundations of society are determined. The following section deals with the fundamental political decision of using the market versus command. Next the role of discipline versus trust is discussed. The second part of the chapter looks at *current economic policy* within the given constitutional rules. First I analyse moral suasion on the one hand and direct intervention in environmental and regulatory policy on the other hand. Then I discuss agricultural subsidies, social policy in the form of volunteering and infrastructural policy. Finally, some conclusions are offered.

MARKET VERSUS COMMAND

The Market

The basic principle of the price system is that output produced and compensation correspond to each other. In a perfectly competitive economy the wage rate is exactly equal to the marginal product. Thus, an extreme form of 'pay-for-performance' is realized.

Such compensation may, however, provoke a substitution of intrinsic by extrinsic motivation: if individuals who (at least partly) enjoy doing their work because they are interested in it are paid in exact correspondence to how they perform their intrinsic motivation becomes superfluous. Maintaining their intrinsic motivation in this circumstance would mean that they are overmotivated for the particular task. It can therefore be expected that their intrinsic motivation is reduced. Their overall performance is thereby not necessarily reduced. Rather, using monetary incentives for work has two countervailing effects: the fundamental relative price effect (Becker 1976; Kirchgässner 1991; Frey 1992) raises work effort while the 'crowding-out effect' lowers it. Whether the employees' affected work effort increases or decreases depends on the relative size of the two opposing effects.[2]

The extent to which work is performed by intrinsic or extrinsic motivation, however, affects the value of the work to the recipient as well as how it is performed. It often makes a difference, for example, if one receives a service from people who do a particular work for intrinsic reasons such as out of love rather than because they are paid. Most people would agree that this holds for sexual services but it is also true for a much broader range of services and even for some goods. The mixture of motivations also affects innovative activity. While monetary incentives are crucial for what might be called 'institutional' creativity, intrinsic motivation is of great importance when it comes to 'personal' creativity.[3] This is particularly true for the transfer of tacit (that is noncodable) knowledge within organizations (Osterloh and Frey 1998). Principal–agent theory has extensively worked out that monetary payments are not efficient when either the necessary measurement and monitoring is costly, or when such activity differs between the various components of output. In the latter case, employees shift their work effort away from those tasks which cannot be adequately measured and compensated. This is another case in which intrinsic work motivation may be superior to monetary incentives.

Commands

When individuals are forced to work by threat of punishment, intrinsic motivation is also crowded out. If they like to do the job for its own sake, a command leads to overmotivation. Indeed, commands undermine work morale more strongly than pay because the addressees are left fewer choices. The total effect on work effort again depends on the size of the relative price effect (based on the cost of not obeying the command) relative to the crowding-out effect. But as the latter effect tends to be systematically larger than with the price system, it can be expected that the application of commands in an economy often produces low work morale and initiative. More generally, citizens' civic virtue will be low and a cynical attitude towards the state and society will be widespread.

These predictions are well borne out by the practical experiences of Soviet-type command economies. Thus, Lane (1986, p. 105) reports that the 'centralized Soviet economic system makes people lazy and immoral. . . . Labour is . . . prone to a combination of cynicism, apathy and largeness.' There was a pervasive 'middle class pessimism and cynicism' (Bushnell 1979, p. 9). Another scholar states: 'The observation that workers' efforts and morale tend to be poor in the USSR today is familiar enough. So is the perception that the economic system itself fosters shoddy work, idleness and dishonesty' (Hanson 1984, p. 85).

According to this analysis, the virtual breakdown of the Soviet political and economic system is not only due to the lack of institutions (an aspect now fully appreciated by economists, see, for example, Shleifer 1997), or to the lack of monetary incentives (which was treated extensively by economists, see Murrell 1991; Sachs and Woo 1994; or Blanchard 1996), but also to the destruction of intrinsic motivation in the form of low work morale, civic virtue, social capital and trust.[4]

Table 10.1 lists social capital measured as trust ('Generally speaking, would you say that most people can be trusted, or that you cannot be too careful in dealing with people?') or as intensity of participation in a variety of civic activities such as: social services for the elderly and deprived; education, art and cultural activities; local community affairs; activities related to conservation, environment and ecology; and work with youth. The data reported for various groups of countries were collected by the World Values Survey of 1000 people in each of the 40 countries from 1990–93 (World Values Study Group 1994).

Table 10.1   Social capital according to the World Values Survey (averages 1990–1993)

Country groups	Trust		Participation	
Group 1: Developed economies	44.5		11.4	
Group 2: Post-Soviet transition economies	29.3		3.4	
a. Where participation not stated		29.3		n.a.
b. Including countries with information about participation		26.5		3.4
c. Including also China		29.3		3.4
Group 3: Developing Countries	24.2		5.9	
a. South America		21.5		4.9
b. Asia (including Turkey)		26.5		10.6*
c. Africa		26.1		n.a.
Mean	35.3		6.9	

Notes
*   Refers to South Korea only. No data available for Turkey and India.
Group 1 comprises Sweden, Norway, Finland, Denmark, Netherlands, Canada, United States, Ireland, United Kingdom, Iceland, Switzerland, Japan, Germany, Italy, Spain, Belgium, Austria, France and Portugal.
Group 2a is formed by Poland, Czech Republic and Belorussia; 2b includes Russia, Lithuania, Bulgaria, Estonia, Hungary, Latvia and Slovak Republic; in 2c, China is included as well.
Group 3a consists of Mexico, Argentina, Chile and Brazil; 3b includes India, South Korea and Turkey; 3c includes South Africa and Nigeria.

Source: World Values Survey (1994), own calculations.

Table 10.1 compares social capital for three groups of countries. Both indicators for social capital are much lower in post-Soviet transition economies than in developed economies: the index for trust is 29.3 in the post-Soviet countries compared to 44.5 in the developed ones; the index for the intensity of civic participation is 3.4 compared to 11.4. While trust in the post-Soviet countries is slightly higher than in developing countries (29.3 compared to 24.2), the rate of participation – arguably a more suitable indicator of civic virtue – is much lower (3.4 compared to 5.9, which is only somewhat more than half as large).

This evidence is consistent with the proposition that the Soviet command system resulted in a crowding out of intrinsic motivation which still exists under present conditions as reflected in high crime and Mafia activities. Frye and Shleifer (1997) found in a survey undertaken in March and April 1996 that 39 per cent of 55 shop managers in Moscow were 'contacted by rackets in the last six months'. As a result, the transactions cost of doing business is high. Seventy-six per cent of the shop managers said that 'one needs a roof (that is, a paid private security agency) to operate'. The situation may be better in some of the other post-Soviet economies (Shleifer 1997, pp. 392–3) which may reflect the less stringent command systems (as for example in Hungary).

We can observe a basic asymmetry. The price system can be, and has been, introduced by a 'sudden jump' (Sachs 1993; Goldman 1994) to which individuals quickly adjust. In contrast, the civic virtue crowded out by the preceding command system is difficult to build up again. As a consequence, the price systems do not work better because of the high transaction costs entailed.

Comparative Evaluation

The relationship sketched between intrinsic and extrinsic motivation is based on a well-established socio-psychological theory known as 'hidden cost of reward' (see, for example, Lepper and Greene 1978, Deci and Ryan 1985, or Lane 1991; see Deci and Flaste 1995, for the theoretical background and the extensive experimental support). The crowding effect (Frey 1997b) is a generalization of this psychological theory: it applies to external interventions via both payments and commands. Critical meta-analyses of the great number of experimental findings of the negative relationship between intrinsic and extrinsic motivation have been provided by Rummel and Feinberg (1988), Wiersma (1992) and Tang and Hall (1995). The meta-analyses by Cameron and Pierce (1994) and Eisenberger and Cameron (1996) – they essentially consider the same experiments and should therefore be counted as one meta-analysis only – have received most attention. In contrast to the three other meta-analyses mentioned above they conclude that the undermining effect of intrinsic motivation by rewards is a 'myth' (Eisenberger and Cameron 1996, p. 13) and that the corresponding theories should therefore be 'abandoned' (Cameron and Pierce 1994, p. 396). The most recent meta-analysis has been undertaken by Deci,

Koestner and Ryan (1998) who include all the studies in the previous meta-analyses as well as experiments most recently undertaken. They thus include 59 articles, 68 experiments and 97 effects covering the period from 1971 to August 1997. On the basis of a very careful scrutiny of the previous meta-analyses as well as of the experiments included (and in which they are able to identify serious errors and omissions in the studies by Cameron, Pierce and Eisenberger[5]) they reach a 'remarkably clear and consistent [result]: Tangible rewards have a strong negative effect on intrinsic motivation for interesting tasks' (Deci et al. 1998, p. 44). All these meta-analyses consider laboratory experiments only, whose results cannot simply be transformed to actual conditions.

However, the existence of the crowding effect is also supported by numerous field studies. For example, in an econometric study of 116 managers in medium-sized Dutch firms, Barkema (1995) found that work morale (measured by the number of hours worked in the company) decreased with the intensity of the personal control effected by superiors, which means that intrinsic motivation was crowded out by the interventions. Another real-life case is provided by the so-called 'token economies' where people living in old-age institutions were induced to undertake certain tasks in exchange for vouchers. As a consequence, after some time, they were only willing to do anything at all if they received compensation. The intended activation of the aged proved to be a failure (Kazdin 1982).

The crowding effect refers to the consequence of an external intervention on intrinsic motivation. But an external intervention normally also has a direct price effect. Thus, for example, a material reward represents a positive price for performing a task; this is the incentive effect based on extrinsic motivation normally (and exclusively) considered in economics. In the case of crowding out, the two effects work in an opposite direction, and the total outcome depends on which effect is larger. Thus, a material reward for work reduces work input only if the crowding-out effect dominates the normal price effect.

The size of the crowding-out effect, as we may have seen, differs strongly according to circumstances. Moreover, when the outside intervention is perceived by the actors concerned to be supportive rather than controlling, a 'crowding-in effect' takes place. Schumpeter (1936) pointed out long ago that many entrepreneurs consider profits as an indicator of success. A monetary reward thus perceived raises work motivation. This explains why successful economic agents often relentlessly pursue their high work input even when they have earned more money than they can sensibly spend. In principle, commands can also crowd in work morale. This is the case when they are perceived by the addressees as expressing an appreciation of their intrinsic motivation. The possibility of commands to serve that purpose constitutes an important advantage of hierarchical institutions, in particular firms, over the market (see in more detail Osterloh and Frey 1998).

National planning and commands undertaken in Soviet economies are far from fulfilling a supportive function and thus have not crowded in intrinsic motivation. Efforts to establish all sorts of nonmonetary rewards such as orders ('Hero of the Soviet Union' and so on) and rankings ('Most productive worker of the province', for example) were unable to compensate for the undermining effects on work morale of rigid planning.

Our analysis suggests that a command economy is at a clear disadvantage relative to the market as the guiding decision-making system. Command economies are not only less efficient but also more damaging to work morale and civic virtue than the price system. The same type of analysis undertaken here for the market and for commands could be done for other social decision-making systems such as decisions by bargaining, tradition or random mechanisms (lotteries). In all these cases, one would have to consider intrinsic motivation as an endogenous and dynamic factor in addition to the traditional efficiency aspects.

DISCIPLINE VERSUS TRUST

Discipline

Constitutional rules serve to prevent 'knaves' from exploiting the other members of society. They should be strict enough to deter rational and egoistic individuals from acting as free riders or to take advantage of co-citizens. Individuals are generally assumed to act in an opportunistic way, 'seeking their self-interest with guile' (as Williamson, 1985 or 1993, puts it). This assumption is not claimed to be realistic but serves to construct institutions which are able to restrain the activities of the worst members of society.

This concept has been the foundation of constitutional economics beginning with Hume ([1742] 1963) and John Stuart Mill ([1861] 1996), to the modern formulations in Buchanan (1987), Brennan and Buchanan (1985) or Mueller (1995). It has become part of the theory of economic policy and need not be spelled out further here.

Trust

A different approach to constitutional economics puts faith in the citizens. They are not only assumed to be capable of making reasonable decisions. More importantly, citizens are assumed in principle to have good will. While they dislike being exploited by others, they are considered to have a good measure of civic virtue.

This view of human nature has been championed by scholars such as Cooter (1984), Kelman (1987), Dryzek (1992) or Mansbridge (1994). It has been concluded that in order to support the existing civic virtue, and to help to raise it further, the constitution should be benevolent towards the citizens. The constitution should put trust in the citizens (this is a different type of trust from that discussed above which was the trust citizens had towards government and society). This trust is reflected by giving individuals many direct participation rights. Citizens should be given the right not only to elect their representatives but also to participate directly by voting on issues (Frey 1997a).

There exists considerable empirical evidence that this view of human nature is realistic and not overly optimistic. Individuals are not grabbing any opportunity to take advantage of others, as a large number of experiments indicate (see Bohnet 1997 and Bohnet and Frey 1997 for surveys; Frey and Bohnet 1995 for specific experiments). Econometric studies for Swiss cantons and cities reveal that the more developed the institutions and the higher the participation possibilities for the citizens are, the lower is tax evasion and the greater is fiscal responsibility (that is, the less likely is the budget to be in deficit), and the higher is per capita income, all *ceteris paribus* (see the survey by Feld and Kirchgässner 1997, and the specific study by Feld and Savioz 1997). The assumption that a significant amount of civic virtue exists among citizens, and that it is crowded in by a constitution that puts faith in its citizens is thus warranted.

This does not mean that constitutions should only consider participation rights. As experimental evidence (public good or prisoner's dilemma experiments are especially relevant here, see, for example, Hey 1991, chapter 11; Kagel and Roth 1995, chapter 3.A; Fehr and Gächter, forthcoming; see also experiments in the ultimatum game setting, for example, Güth, Schmittberger and Schwarze 1982) as well as everyday observations clearly indicate, it is important to prevent individuals from perceiving themselves to be systematically exploited by others. If they have this feeling, they would quickly start behaving in an egoistic way in an attempt to guard their position. A good constitution balances these two considerations.

MORAL SUASION AND DIRECT INTERVENTION

Moral Suasion

On the basis of Crowding Theory, the role of moral suasion as an economic policy device must be reconsidered. The major function of psychological appeals is to support the intrinsic motivation of those persons who act according to the principles of civic virtue. This point has eluded economists who deal only with extrinsic incentives. But it has been appreciated long ago by legal scholars who argued that laws may be valuable even if they cannot be monitored and obeyed because they still indicate what is 'right'. Once a wider perspective on human motivation is adopted, moral suasion has a role to play in economic policy. Obviously, this instrument must be used with care and is no substitute for other policy actions. In particular, moral appeals lose their motivating force if they are used too often or under circumstances where following them would mean risking one's position.

But moral suasion has been empirically shown to affect people's behaviour in a significant way in times of crisis (see, for example, Baumol and Oates 1979).

Direct Intervention

One of the insights gained by crowding theory is that government interventions are less effective than expected, following the relative price effects, when intrinsic motivation is thereby induced to fall. This effect is particularly relevant in two policy areas.

1. *Environmental policy*   Direct interventions are still the most prominent instrument used to influence the quality of the natural environment (Hahn 1989; OECD 1994). Empirical evidence confirms that individuals have some amount of environmental morale especially if the corresponding costs are not high (see, for example, Diekmann 1995). The use of commands then risks crowding out intrinsic motivation if the persons concerned perceive that their own efforts to safeguard the environment are not appreciated by the policy makers. In that case, the same effect must be expected if market instruments such as environmental taxes, tradable licences or other incentives are used. But for the reasons given above, the crowding-out effect is likely to be less pronounced.

The crowding-out effect may help to explain why environmental policy is often less effective than economists expect on the basis of the relative price effect.[6] At the same time it explains why the environment sometimes improves without much government intervention.

2. *Regulatory policy*   Government intervention via regulations can be seen as a generalization of most environmental policies. It can be applied to a very large range of areas, for instance, with respect to work conditions.

The economic approach evaluates the extent to which regulations are followed by using the model of expected utility maximization. In the economics of crime (Becker 1968), individuals are assumed to be rational egoists and to observe regulations only to the extent that it is to their own benefit. Careful empirical work has established, however, that this approach is unable to explain the *level* of the disregard for the law in a satisfactory way. The level of tax evasion, for example, cannot be accounted for by the expected utility approach (as championed by Allingham and Sandmo 1972; for surveys, see Pommerehne 1985, Roth, Scholz and Witte 1989, or Cuccia 1994): the size of the expected punishment is simply too low even if individuals are quite risk averse.[7] After an extensive and careful analysis of the American Internal Revenue Service (IRS) Taxpayer Compliance Measurement Programme, Graetz and Wilde (1985, p. 358) were forced to conclude that 'the high compliance rate can only be explained either by taxpayers' . . . commitment to the responsibilities of citizenship and respect for the law or lack of opportunity for tax evasion'. The same authors (as well as Reinganum and Wilde 1986) attribute the observed falling tax compliance to the erosion of tax morale (see also Reckers, Sanders and Roark 1994, or Kaplan, Newberry and Reckers 1997).

Nor does the expected utility model fare too well with respect to explaining marginal effects on tax evasion. A large number of econometric studies have found that the partial coefficients of the probability of detection and the penalty rate, while often having the expected negative sign, are not statistically different from zero (see, for example, Pommerehne and Weck-Hannemann (1996) for Switzerland and their references on p. 164 to other countries and time periods).

The discussion suggests that intrinsic motivation in the form of civic virtue has an important systematic effect on how government regulations work. Moreover, the corresponding state interventions may crowd out, and sometimes crowd in, this motivation depending on whether the addressees perceive them to be controlling (which is normally the case) or supporting. Empirical research in the area of work, environmental and health regulations (see, for example, Bardach and Kagan 1982) are consistent with these conclusions.

OTHER AREAS OF CURRENT POLICY

Agricultural Subsidies

The support of farmers via guaranteed high food prices undertaken in many countries, has led to huge distortions. A large oversupply of agricultural goods was produced but the hard work on the farms nevertheless induced many peasants to move to more suitable occupations, often located in cities. The policy thus resulted in a considerable waste of human resources (as well as in negative effects on the environment through the pollution of the soil by chemical products) and did not reach the officially proclaimed goal of maintaining the traditional rural way of life.

In view of this failure, and based on efficiency theory, economists have long argued that price support should be replaced by direct income support of farmers. Some countries such as Switzerland have heeded this advice and now hand out direct income transfers to their farmers. There can be little doubt that this policy prevents the production of excess supply because price distortions are reduced and, at least ideally, completely removed. From the point of view of crowding theory the policy looks less favourable. The transfer of money just for being a farmer may well undermine the intrinsic motivation of being a farmer. The subsidy for 'being like a farmer' is likely to affect their self-perception negatively: they now behave like farmers because they are paid for that. Many people will argue that this removes the essential reason for supporting people working in this sector. At the same time, keeping individuals and families on the farms will become more and more expensive in tandem with the speed with which the farmers lose their former intrinsic motivation. They now expect compensation according to the inconveniences of the 'job' (for example having to work long hours during the day and at night). Over the long run, voters and politicians will realize that this policy tends to destroy what it originally claims to support. Together with the large cost increases this may well lead to such strong political resistance that the direct support programme has to be scrapped. This analysis helps us to explain why the agricultural lobbies tend to oppose the switch from price to income supports. They possibly sense that such a development might take place and try to prevent it because it also undermines their own position as an interest group.

Volunteering

Psychological aspects such as crowding effects are of particular importance in the social area where intrinsic motivation can be expected to play a larger role than in many other sectors of the economy. For the sake of concreteness, I shall consider only a specific activity, volunteering, which is responsible for about 40 per cent of total work offered in the social service nonprofit economy (Weisbrod 1988, p. 131). Volunteering for charitable nonprofit institutions has grown more rapidly than employment elsewhere (ibid., p. 132) so that it is becoming an increasingly important activity.

Neoclassical economics based on the relative price effect is able to make a number of sharp predictions (Menchik and Weisbrod 1987; Weisbrod 1988). With respect to the supply side, it makes four hypotheses: (i) the higher the wage rate or income, the less voluntary work is offered due to the higher opportunity cost; (ii) individuals either volunteer or donate money but not both. People who are more productive on the market, and are willing to help others, should work more and donate the money to a charitable or nonprofit institution; (iii) a complete substitution is also expected to take place between husband and wife, that is either he or she, but not both, offer voluntary work; and (iv) on the other side of the market, economists normally assume a perfectly elastic demand for volunteers by the respective institutions.

Menchik and Weisbrod (1987) find that these hypotheses are supported by the data for the United States. A very careful and recent study by Freeman (1997) with new data for the US, however, finds that they are clearly refuted. He generally concludes that the standard labour supply theory explains only a minor share of empirical reality. In particular, volunteers have a significantly higher personal and family income than nonvolunteers, thereby contradicting hypothesis (i) (see also Vaillancourt 1994, for Canada). Hypotheses (ii) is also rejected because a volunteer normally donates money at the same time. Neither is there substitution between husband and wife, as hypothesis (iii) claims, but both typically work as volunteers.

This does not mean that relative price effects have no explanatory power, but it does so only at a secondary level. While a higher wage rate is associated with more volunteering such people put in less hours than those earning less on the market. Also, because there is no substitution between volunteering and donating, higher-income families contribute relatively less hours and give relatively more in cash.[8]

These results (which have been gained using the state-of-the-art theory and econometrics) strongly suggest that traditional economic theory misses something important. A good candidate for filling this gap is the concept of intrinsic motivation and its dynamization by crowding theory. The positive association between income and volunteering may be attributed to the fact that poorer people can less afford to pursue their intrinsic motivation than richer ones. This is exactly Berthold Brecht's statement in the *Dreigroschenoper: 'Zuerst kommt das Fressen, dann die Moral!'*, which is supported by sound empirical evidence (for example, Lane 1991, part 5). The positive association between volunteering and donating holds because the major underlying motivation for both actions is intrinsic motivation, thereby rejecting any substitutive relationship. Rather, people who are intrinsically motivated to help others have an urge to help by all means. Actually, only economists and probably a few other people would even consider the relationship between volunteering and donating to be substitutive. Finally, the positive association of voluntary work by husband and wife can be explained by positive sorting with respect to intrinsic motivation, and also by the person doing voluntary work, educating and motivating the other to do likewise. Freeman (1997, pp. 159–65) offers a narrower explanation, namely 'the importance of being asked' to volunteer. This explanation is not inconsistent with an explanation in terms of intrinsic motivation. It has been emphasized throughout this chapter that intrinsic motivation is not exogenously given but can be triggered by being asked to act according to this motivation. On the other hand, Freeman is careful to admit that people do not simply volunteer when they are asked but only if they consider it a worthy cause, and if the demand comes from trustworthy people. Thus, being asked is perhaps a necessary but not sufficient factor to explain volunteering.

Empirical research on the demand side also suggests the importance of intrinsic motivation (see Duncombe and Brudney 1995). There are considerable costs involved for organizations using volunteers and therefore they do not exhibit a perfectly elastic demand as claimed by hypothesis (iv). The costs actually go far beyond recruiting and training; volunteers are different from paid workers because they are more difficult to steer according to the wishes of the management. The concept of intrinsic motivation is again helpful in explaining this phenomenon. As volunteers are (mainly or exclusively) motivated by *their own* concept of what has to be done, they are less willing to conform to the demands of management compared to paid staff. From the managers' point of view 'paid staff . . . may be more productive and provide higher quality service' (ibid., pp. 359–60). Consequently, the managers make an effort to have a suitable balance between paid workers and volunteers which is reflected in a statistically significant negative elasticity of demand for volunteers (ibid., p. 371; also Steinberg 1990).

Infrastructural Policy

Everyone considers a good infrastructure to be an important prerequisite for economic development. However, the earthworks and buildings necessary for roads, railway tracks, airports and so on as well as the risks involved with projects such as nuclear power plants and depositories and prisons normally meet with heavy resistance by the local communities affected. Such undertakings meet the criteria of NIMBY phenomena, that is the desire to have those projects 'not in my backyard' (for example, Easterling and Kunreuther 1995). Economists have a handy tool to solve this problem, namely to compensate those communities that are prepared to host such an infrastructural project (for example, O'Hare 1977 or Portney 1991). The best way to determine the required compensation efficiently is by auction (Kunreuther and Kleindorfer 1986). Such a move is made possible because the projects produce by definition positive net benefits for society as a whole so that the winners can compensate the losers. Empirical evidence, however, shows convincingly that the compensation strategy does not work (for the United States, see Easterling and Kunreuther 1995, or Carnes et al. 1983; for Switzerland, see Oberholzer-Gee 1998). Indeed, it has been found that the willingness to accept a nuclear waste repository in Switzerland fell from 50.8 to 24.6 per cent of the population when a sizeable compensation was offered. This reaction, which contradicts the relative price effect, was attributed to the crowding-out effect (Frey and Oberholzer-Gee 1997).

The siting of infrastructural projects is another important instance where economic policies based solely on the relative price effect do not work, and may even worsen the situation. Rather, psychological elements such as the crowding effect have to be taken into account.

CONCLUSIONS

The discussion has endeavoured to establish seven propositions by relying on analytical and empirical evidence. The main goal was to show that psychological factors are indeed of great practical importance for economic policy making (proposition 1). It has been argued that to 'psychologize' economics in a general way is of little use, but that concrete and empirically well-supported elements have to be *integrated* into economics. In this chapter a particular psychological factor, the crowding effect, has been identified (proposition 2) and its substantial quantitative and qualitative relevance for economic policy at the level of the constitution (proposition 3) and for the current policy process (proposition 4) has been demonstrated. It has turned out that the concepts of intrinsic motivation and of motivational crowding help us to explain phenomena with respect to tax evasion, volunteering and infrastructural siting, which appear paradoxical from the point of view of traditional neoclassical theory (proposition 5).

The intention of this chapter is not to criticize existing economic theory and policy without presenting an alternative approach. What is proposed here is an extension of economic theory while completely accepting the crucial importance of the relative price effect. An economic policy which takes the possibility of crowding effects seriously is less interventionist than present economics prescribes because it takes into account that adverse effects on intrinsic motivation occur under identifiable conditions. What is suggested here as a general policy rule is that individuals are reasonable human beings whose intrinsic motivation can be put to good effect, that motivation should therefore be taken care of (proposition 6).

It would be a misunderstanding to assume that intrinsic motivation is always welcome. It is neither generally good nor bad. While intrinsic motivation in the form of work or environmental morale, solidarity in the private and civic virtue in the public domain are often most desirable, these same features are undesirable if they are put to bad use such as when working for a fraudulent firm, exerting nepotism or supporting a criminal political regime. It is crucial to face the issue *where* we need *what* motivation (proposition 7). So far, we have only quite limited knowledge in this regard. Hopefully what has been established here is that to disregard intrinsic motivation and crowding effects is perilous and may lead to costly policy errors. At the same time, an alternative to present policy design based on faith in human nature has been suggested.

NOTES

1. A partial exception is Frank and Cook's (1995) call for raising taxes on high-income recipients to reduce the unproductive race for positional goods.

2. For a formal treatment, see Frey (1997b). This book also extensively discusses the psychological and institutional conditions under which the crowding-out effect takes place. A behavioural rationale for the emergence of a crowding-out effect in the case of the voluntary provision of a public good has been formally developed by van Dijk and van Winden (1997). They argue that the public provision of a public good under some conditions leads to a decrease in total provision because it impedes the development of social ties. In Frey (1997b) personal relationships have indeed been identified as a crucial condition for supporting intrinsic motivation.
3. There is a large psychological literature on creativity that is relevant here. Most of it argues strongly that intrinsic motivation is necessary for creativity, in particular concerning the idea-generating stage of creativity (Amabile 1988) but there are also divergent views (for example, Torrence 1970, or Winston and Baker 1985). This literature is discussed and put into an economic context in Frey (1998).
4. Important contributions are Gambetta (1988), Coleman (1990), Putnam (1993), Fukuyama (1995), Kramer and Tyler (1996), and Nye, Jelikow and King (1997).
5. See also the critique by Kohn (1996), Lepper, Keavney and Drake (1996), Ryan and Deci (1996) and the answer by Eisenberger and Cameron (1997).
6. Another, by now well-researched, reason is the political factors preventing an effective environmental policy.
7. Following Alm, McKee and Beck (1990, p. 24), calculations of empirical magnitudes for the US show that taxpayers would have 'to exhibit risk aversion far in excess of anything ever observed for compliance predicted by expected utility theory to approximate actual compliance'.
8. A staunch supporter of traditional economics might argue that this shows that the theory is correct after all, provided it is correctly applied. This is a typical *ex post* argument and essentially states that the traditional theory is flexible and coherent enough to be adjusted to the empirical evidence. This is certainly a useful exercise (it allows us to determine where the theory works well and badly) but it is of little use for predictive purposes.

REFERENCES

Akerlof, G.A. (1984), *An Economic Theorist's Book of Tales*, Cambridge: Cambridge University Press.
Allingham, M.G. and A. Sandmo (1972), 'Income tax evasion: a theoretical analysis', *Journal of Public Economics*, **1** (November), pp. 323–38.
Alm, J., M. McKee and W. Beck (1990), 'Amazing grace: tax amnesties and compliance', *National Tax Journal*, **43** (1), pp. 23–38.
Amabile, T.M. (1988), 'From individual to organizational innovation', in K. Gronhang and G. Kaufmann (eds), *Innovation: A Cross-Disciplinary Perspective*, Oslo: Norwegian University Press, pp. 139–66.
Bardach, E. and R.A. Kagan (1982), *Going By the Book: The Problem of Regulatory Unreasonableness*, Philadelphia: Temple University Press.
Barkema, H.G. (1995), 'Do top managers work harder when they are monitored?', *Kyklos*, **48** (1), pp. 19–42.
Baumol, W.J. and W.E. Oates (1979), *Economics, Environmental Policy, and the Quality of Life*, Englewood Cliffs, NJ: Prentice-Hall.
Becker, G.S. (1968), 'Crime and punishment: an economic approach', *Journal of Political Economy*, **76**, pp. 169–217.
Becker, G.S. (1976), *The Economic Approach to Human Behavior*, Chicago: Chicago University Press.
Blanchard, O. (1996), 'Theoretical aspects of transition', *American Economic Review*, **86** (2), pp. 117–22.

Bohnet, I. (1997), *Kooperation und Kommunikation. Eine ökonomische Analyse individueller Entscheidungen*, Tübingen: Mohr (Siebeck).

Bohnet, I. and B.S. Frey (1997), 'Rent leaving', *Journal of Institutional and Theoretical Economics*, **153** (4), pp. 711–21.

Bös, D. (1986), *Public Enterprise Economics. Theory and Applications*, Amsterdam: North-Holland.

Brennan, G. and J.M. Buchanan (1985), *The Reason of Rules. Constitutional Political Economy*, Cambridge: Cambridge University Press.

Buchanan, J.M. (1987), 'Constitutional economics', in J. Eatwell, M. Milgate and P. Newman (eds), *The New Palgrave: A Dictionary of Economics*, vol. 1, London: Macmillan, pp. 585–8.

Buchanan, J.M. (1991), *Constitutional Economics*, Oxford: Basil Blackwell.

Bushnell, J. (1979), 'The new Soviet man turns pessimist', *Survey*, **24** (Spring), pp. 1–18.

Cameron, J. and W.D. Pierce (1994), 'Reinforcement, reward, and intrinsic motivation: a meta-analysis', *Review of Educational Research*, **64** (Fall), pp. 363–423.

Carnes, S.A. et al. (1983), 'Incentives and nuclear waste siting', *Energy Systems and Policy*, **7** (4), pp. 324–51.

Coleman, J.S. (1990), *Foundations of Social Theory*, Cambridge, MA: Harvard University Press.

Cooter, R.D. (1984), 'Prices and sanctions', *Columbia Law Review*, **84**, pp. 1523–60.

Cuccia, A. (1994), 'The economics of tax compliance: what do we know and where do we go?', *Journal of Accounting Literature*, **13**, pp. 81–116.

Deci, E.L. and R. Flaste (1995), *Why We Do What We Do. The Dynamics of Personal Autonomy*, New York: Putnam.

Deci, E.L. and R.M. Ryan (1985), *Intrinsic Motivation and Self-determination in Human Behaviour*, New York: Plenum Press.

Deci, E.L., R. Koestner and R.M. Ryan (1998), 'Extrinsic rewards and intrinsic motivation: a clear and consistent picture after all', University of Rochester, Department of Psychology: mimeo.

Diekmann, A. (1995), 'Umweltbewusstsein oder Anreizstrukturen? Empirische Befunde zum Energiesparen, der Verkehrsmittelwahl und zum Konsumverhalten', in A. Diekmann and A. Franzen (eds), *Kooperatives Umwelthandeln. Modelle, Erfahrungen, Massnahmen*, Chur und Zurich. Rüegger, pp. 39–68.

Dryzek, J.S. (1992), *Discursive Democracy: Politics, Policy, and Political Science*, New York: Cambridge University Press.

Duncombe, W.D. and J.L. Brudney (1995), 'The optimal mix of volunteer and paid staff in local governments: an application to municipal fire departments', *Public Finance Quarterly*, **23** (3), pp. 356–84.

Earl, P.E. (1990), 'Economics and psychology: a survey', *Economic Journal*, **100** (402), pp. 718–55.

Easterling, D.H. and H. Kunreuther (1995), *The Dilemma of Siting a High-level Nuclear Waste Repository*, Boston: Kluwer.

Eisenberger, R. and J. Cameron (1996), 'Detrimental effects of reward. Reality or myth?', *American Psychologist*, **51** (November), pp. 1153–66.

Eisenberger, R. and J. Cameron (1997), 'Rewards, intrinsic task interest, and creativity: new findings', Paper presented at the Society of Experimental Social Psychology, Toronto.

Fehr, E. and S. Gächter (forthcoming), 'Cooperation and punishment – an experimental investigation of norm formation and norm enforcement', University of Zurich: Institute for Empirical Economic Research.

Feld, L.P. and G. Kirchgässner (1997), 'Public debt and budgetary procedures: top down or bottom up. Some evidence from Swiss municipalities', University of St. Gallen: Volkswirtschaftliche Abteilung, mimeo.

Feld, L.P. and M.R. Savioz (1997), 'Direct democracy matters for economic performance: an empirical investigation', *Kyklos*, **50** (4), pp. 507–38.

Frank, R.H. (1985), *Choosing the Right Pond*, New York: Oxford University Press.

Frank, R.H. (1988), *Passions within Reason. The Strategic Role of the Emotions*, New York: Norton.

Frank, R.H. and P.J. Cook (1995), *The Winner-Take-All Society*, New York: Free Press.

Freeman, R.B. (1997), 'Working for nothing. The supply of volunteer labor', *Journal of Labor Economics*, **15** (1), pp. 140–66.

Frey, B.S. (1983), *Democratic Economic Policy*, Oxford: Blackwell.

Frey, B.S. (1992), *Economics as a Science of Human Behaviour*, Boston, Dordrecht and London: Kluwer.

Frey, B.S. (1997a), 'A constitution for knaves crowds out civic virtues', *Economic Journal*, **107** (443), pp. 1043–53.

Frey, B.S. (1997b), *Not Just for the Money. An Economic Theory of Personal Motivation*, Cheltenham, UK and Brookfield, USA: Edward Elgar.

Frey, B.S. (1998), 'State support and creativity in the arts: some new considerations', Paper presented at the Association for Cultural Economics International, Barcelona.

Frey, B.S. and I. Bohnet (1995), 'Institutions affect fairness: experimental investigations', *Journal of Institutional and Theoretical Economics*, **151** (2), pp. 286–303.

Frey, B.S. and F. Oberholzer-Gee (1997), 'The cost of price incentives: an empirical analysis of motivation crowding-out', *American Economic Review*, **87** (4), pp. 746–55.

Frye, T. and A. Shleifer (1997), 'The invisible hand and the grabbing hand', *American Economic Review*, **87** (2), pp. 354–8.

Fukuyama, F. (1995), *Trust: The Social Virtues and the Creation of Prosperity*, New York: Free Press.

Furnham, A. and A. Lewis (1986), *The Economic Mind. The Social Psychology of Economic Behaviour*, Baltimore and Brighton: Wheatsheaf Books, Harvester Press.

Gambetta, D. (ed.) (1988), *Trust: Making and Breaking Cooperative Relations*, Cambridge: Cambridge University Press.

Goldman, M. (1994), *Lost Opportunity: Why Economic Reforms in Russia have not Worked*, New York: Norton.

Graetz, M.J. and L.L. Wilde (1985), 'The economics of tax compliance: facts and fantasy', *National Tax Journal*, **38** (3), pp. 355–63.

Güth, W., R. Schmittberger and B. Schwarze (1982), 'An experimental analysis of ultimatum bargaining', *Journal of Economic Behaviour and Organization*, **3** (4), pp. 367–88.

Hahn, R.W. (1989), 'The political economy of environment regulation: towards a unifying framework', *Public Choice*, **65** (1), pp. 21–47.

Hanson, P. (1984), 'The Novosibirsk Report: comment', *Survey*, Spring, pp. 83–7.

Hey, J.D. (1991), *Experiments in Economics*, Oxford: Blackwell.

Hume, D. (1742), 'Of independency of parliament', in *Essays Moral, Political and Literary*, vol. 1, reprinted 1963, London: Oxford University Press, pp. 117–18.

Jöhr, W.A. (1972), 'Zur Rolle des psychologischen Faktors in der Konjunkturtheorie', *Ifo-Studien*, no. 18, pp. 157–84.

Kagel, J.H. and A.E. Roth (eds) (1995), *Handbook of Experimental Economics*, Princeton, NJ: Princeton University Press.

Kaplan, S., K. Newberry and P. Reckers (1997), 'The effect of moral reasoning and educational communications on tax evasion intentions', *Journal of the American Taxation Association*, **19** (2), pp. 38–54.

Katona, G. (1975), *Psychological Economics*, Amsterdam: Elsevier.

Kazdin, A.E. (1982), 'The token economy: a decade later', *Journal of Applied Behavioural Analysis*, **15**, pp. 431–45.

Kelman, S. (1987), *Making Public Policy: A Hopeful View of American Government*, New York: Basic Books.

Kirchgässner, G. (1991), *Homo Oeconomicus: Das ökonomische Modell individuellen Verhaltens und seine Anwendung in den Wirtschafts- und Sozialwissenschaften*, Tübingen: Mohr (Siebeck).

Kohn, A. (1996), 'By all available means: Cameron and Pierce's defense of extrinsic motivators', *Review of Educational Research*, **66**, pp. 1–4.

Kramer, R.M. and T.R. Tyler (eds) (1996), *Trust in Organizations*, Thousand Oaks: Sage.

Kunreuther, H. and P.R. Kleindorfer (1986), 'A sealed-bid auction mechanism for siting noxious facilities', *American Economic Review*, **76** (2), pp. 295–9.

Lane, D. (ed.) (1986), *Labour and Employment in the USSR*, New York: New York University Press.

Lane, R.E. (1991), *The Market Experience*, Cambridge: Cambridge University Press.

Lea, S.E.G., R.M. Tarpy and P. Webley (1987), *The Individual and the Economy. A Survey of Economic Psychology*, Cambridge: Cambridge University Press.

Leibenstein, H. (1976), *Beyond Economic Man. A New Foundation for Microeconomics*, Cambridge, MA: Harvard University Press.

Lepper, M.R. and D. Greene (eds) (1978), *The Hidden Costs of Reward: New Perspectives on the Psychology of Human Motivation*, Hillsdale, NY: Erlbaum.

Lepper, M.R., M. Keavney and M. Drake (1996), 'Intrinsic motivation and extrinsic rewards: a commentary on Cameron and Pierce's meta-analysis', *Review of Educational Research*, **66**, pp. 5–32.

MacFadyen, A.J. and H.W. MacFadyen (eds) (1986), *Economic Psychology: Intersections in Theory and Application*, Amsterdam and New York: North-Holland.

Mansbridge, J. (1994), 'Public spirit in political systems', in H.J. Aaron, T.E. Mann and T. Taylor (eds), *Values and Public Policy*, Washington: Brookings, pp. 146–72.

Menchik, P.L. and B.A. Weisbrod (1987), 'Volunteer labor supply', *Journal of Public Economics*, **32** (2), pp. 159–83.

Mill, J.S. (1861), 'Considerations on representative government', in *Essays on Politics and Society*, reprinted in J.M. Robson (ed.) (1996), *Collected Works of J.S. Mill*, vol. 18 & 19, London: Routledge & Kegan Paul.

Mueller, D.C. (1995), *Constitutional Economics*, Cambridge: Cambridge University Press.

Murrell, P. (1991), 'Can neoclassical economics underpin the reforms of the centrally planned economies?', *Journal of Economic Perspectives*, **5** (4), pp. 59–76.

Nye, J.S., P.D. Zelikow and D.C. King (1997), *Why People Don't Trust Government*, Cambridge, MA: Harvard University Press.

O'Hare, M. (1977), 'Not on my block you don't: facility siting and the strategic importance of compensation', *Public Policy*, **25** (4), pp. 409–58.

Oberholzer-Gee, F. (1998), *Die Oekonomik des St. Florianprinzips. Warum wir keine Standorte fuer nukleare Endlager finden*, Basel: Helbing & Lichtenhahn.

Organization for Economic Cooperation and Development (OECD) (1994), *Integrating Environment and Economics: The Role of Economic Instruments*, Paris: OECD.

Osterloh, M. and B.S. Frey (1998), 'Managing motivation and knowledge in the theory of the firm', University of Zürich: Institute for Research in Business Administration and Institute for Empirical Economic Research, mimeo.

Persson, T. and G. Tabellini (1994), *Monetary and Fiscal Policy. Vol. I: Credibility*, Cambridge, MA: MIT Press.

Pommerehne, W.W. (1985), 'Was wissen wir eigentlich über Steuerhinterziehung?', *Revista Internazionale di Scienze Economiche e Commerciali*, **32** (12), pp. 1155–86.

Pommerehne, W.W. and H. Weck-Hannemann (1996), 'Tax rates, tax administration and income tax evasion in Switzerland', *Public Choice*, **88** (1/2), pp. 161–70.

Portney, K.E. (1991), *Siting Waste Treatment Facilities: The NIMBY Syndrome*, New York: Auburn House.

Putnam, R.D. (1993), *Making Democracy Work*, Princeton, NJ: Princeton University Press.

Rabin, M. (1998), 'Psychology and economics', *Journal of Economic Literature*, **36** (1), pp. 11–46.

Reckers, P., D. Sanders and S. Roark (1994), 'The influence of ethical attitudes on taxpayer compliance', *National Tax Journal*, **47** (4), pp. 825–36.

Reinganum, J.E. and L.L. Wilde (1986), 'Equilibrium verification and reporting policies in a model of tax compliance', *International Economic Review*, **27** (3), pp. 739–60.

Roth, J.A., J.T. Scholz and A.D. Witte (eds) (1989), *Taxpayer Compliance*, Philadelphia: University of Pennsylvania Press.

Rummel, A. and R. Feinberg (1988), 'Cognitive evaluation theory: a meta-analytic review of the literature', *Social Behavior and Personality*, **16**, pp. 147–64.

Ryan, R.M. and E.L. Deci (1996), 'When paradigms clash: comments on Cameron and Pierce's claim that rewards do not undermine intrinsic motivation', *Review of Educational Research*, **66**, pp. 33–8.

Sachs, J.D. (1993), *Poland's Jump to a Market Economy*, Cambridge, MA: MIT Press.

Sachs, J.D. and W.T. Woo (1994), 'Structural factors and economic reforms in China, Eastern Europe, and the Former Soviet Union', *Economic Policy*, **9** (18), pp. 101–45.

Schmölders, G. (1962), *Volkswirtschaftslehre und Psychologie*, Berlin: Reinbek.

Schumpeter, J. (1936), *The Theory of Economic Development*, Cambridge, MA: Harvard University Press.

Scitovsky, T. (1976), *The Joyless Economy: An Inquiry into Human Satisfaction and Dissatisfaction*, Oxford: Oxford University Press.

Shleifer, A. (1997), 'Government in transition', *European Economic Review*, **41** (3/5), pp. 385–410.

Simon, H.A. (1983), *Reason in Human Affairs*, Oxford: Blackwell.

Steinberg, R. (1990), 'Labor economics and the nonprofit sector: a literature review', *Nonprofit and Voluntary Sector Quarterly*, **19**, pp. 151–69.

Tang, S.-H. and V.C. Hall (1995), 'The overjustification effect: a meta-analysis', *Applied Cognitive Psychology*, **9**, pp. 365–404.

Thaler, R.H. (1992), *The Winner's Curse. Paradoxes and Anomalies of Economic Life*, New York: Free Press.

Theil, H. (1968), *Optimal Rules for Government and Industry*, Amsterdam: North-Holland.

Tinbergen, J. (1956), *Economic Policy: Principles and Design*, Amsterdam: North-Holland.

Torrence, E.P. (1970), *Encouraging Creativity in the Classroom*, Dubudque, IA: Brown.

Vaillancourt, F. (1994), 'To volunteer or not: Canada, 1987', *Canadian Journal of Economics*, **27** (4), pp. 813–26.

Van Dijk, F. and F. van Winden (1997), 'Dynamics of social ties and local public good provision', *Journal of Public Economics*, **64** (3), pp. 323–41.

Van Raaij, W.F., G.M. van Veldhoven and K.E. Wärneryd (eds) (1988), *Handbook of Economic Psychology*, Dordrecht: Kluwer.

Weisbrod, B.A. (1988), *The Nonprofit Economy*, Cambridge, MA: Harvard University Press.

Wiersma, U.J. (1992), 'The effects of extrinsic rewards on intrinsic motivation: a meta-analysis', *Journal of Occupational and Organizational Psychology*, **65**, pp. 101–14.

Williamson, O.E. (1985), *The Economic Institutions of Capitalism. Firms, Markets, Relational Contradicting*, New York: Free Press.

Williamson, O.E. (1993), 'Opportunism and its critics', *Managerial and Decision Economics*, **14** (2), pp. 97–107.

Winston, A.S. and J.E. Baker (1985), 'Behavior analytic studies of creativity: a critical review', *Behavior Analyst*, **8**, pp. 191–205.

World Values Study Group (1994), *World Values Survey, 1991–1993*, Ann Arbor, MI: Inter-University Consortium for Political and Social Research.

11. Interpreting institutions: the case of international public law

Ernst Mohr*

INTRODUCTION

When an economist leaves his or her autopoetic circle he or she is soon confronted with the complaint of scholars of other social sciences that economic arguments invade and dominate the societal discourse. The irony in this experience is that the economist is inclined to retort that although this is how it indeed should be, in the real world the economic argument all too often fades away unheard. If we accept that the economist is the better empiricist we face an intriguing puzzle: if the economic argument loses out all too often in having little or no practical impact on the course of public issues why is it then such a pain in the neck of other sciences which compete with economics in public debates? If we further accept that the economic argument is indeed frequently the better point we face a follow-up question: why is it then not taken up to a greater extent by other sciences? Tackling these puzzles cannot but help economists in handling the transfer of their economics into other social science disciplines.

A problem with making an economic point on the turf of other sciences is that it is often seen as an invasion. The family illustrates this point. Few noneconomists would challenge that the family also serves some economic purpose. Few economists would challenge that it contains facets which escape economics. The stage is thus perfectly set for a noninvasive economic analysis. However, there are perhaps few other subjects of economic investigation which entice noneconomists to fiercer critiques of economics.

My impression is that problems of this sort arise because of the particular way in which economists structure issues usually covered by other disciplines: economists structure many if not most of these issues as economic institutions. The family, law, social norms, religion, professional standards, to name but some,

* I thank Uwe Schneidewind, Tobias Stoll, Jonathan Thomas and Andreas Ziegler for comments and discussions on various issues which affected the chapter. However, none would presumably subscribe to it entirely.

are all interpreted as institutions. The invasive touch comes into this interpretation because the economic research programme reduces these institutions to their pure economic function. This programme, innocent and helpful as such, has often fatal consequences when it comes to communicating economic findings to other sciences as it leaves them little room to breathe.

Drawing heavily on an example, the purpose of this chapter is to investigate how economics treats other disciplines while addressing issues these disciplines concern, thereby shedding light on to the issue of why economic arguments are often ill-received and commenting on what economists could do to perform better when communicating their ideas.

The example taken is the case of international public law (IPL). To be precise, I analyse how economists treat IPL as a legal science by analysing how economics treats IPL as an object of investigation. IPL as a science interprets the set of legal relations between states. This set is IPL as an institution. Both IPL as a science and economics therefore take IPL as an institution as an object of investigation. The point of departure of the analysis is the observation that these interpretations of the same object of investigation appear to be obviously incompatible.

The example is of some importance. Many policy issues involve the cooperation of states such as, for example, trade, intellectual property rights or environmental protection. Lawyers as well as economists support the policy process with their interpretations of these issues. The fate of economic arguments therefore also depends on how they relate to legal ones and how convincing, provoking or off the point they seem to lawyers.

IPL is a good example to investigate because it illustrates how far the economic view can differ from the perspective of the 'native' discipline when the economics programme is put to work. As always, the economics programme is in this case to interpret IPL (as an object of investigation) as an economic institution and to reduce it to its economic function. But when economists cannot discover an economic function of an institution, the consequent application of the economics programme is to ignore it because institutions without an economic function are deemed without impact. I argue in the subsequent section that much of the economic literature dealing with issues of international cooperation bluntly ignores IPL as a relevant institution. For economists, advancing the ideas developed in this literature, IPL (as a science) is simply redundant. It takes no great experience in communication to grasp that this is not a good point to start from when trying to advance an economic argument in legal circles.

IPL is a good example to tackle the issues at hand because it also illustrates how intricate the communication of interpretations of institutions can be. In those cases in which the economic perspective is simply misleading, the therapy commendable to economists is equally simple: change your view. I argue below, however, that in a sense to be made precise the economic view of ignoring IPL (as an institution) is not off the point. Indeed, it is right but right for the wrong reason. The problem of communicating the economic perspective to lawyers is therefore rather one of motivation than one of conclusion. The challenge is to explain to them *why* for an economic point it is admissible to treat IPL as a redundant institution, not to insinuate that IPL is a redundant science.

The chapter is organized as follows. The next section develops the traditional economic interpretation of IPL. In the following section it is shown how to cope with certain translation problems facing two scientific languages covering the same issue. Subsequently an alternative economic interpretation of IPL is given. This section draws heavily on the analysis of Mohr and Thomas (1998a). The subsequent section draws conclusions from this interpretation as to how economic arguments concerning state cooperation should be advanced. The last section hazards a guess as to how economic arguments could fuel other scientific disciplines in general.

IS THE STATE ABOVE OR BELOW THE LAW?

Game theory provides the tools with which many economists prefer to address the issue of state cooperation. Their empirical motivation is reference to state sovereignty as they understand it. They understand state sovereignty as a lack of higher authority which invites them to model state conduct as rational opportunism before and after the conclusion of a treaty. Accordingly a state is deemed free to engage in cooperation and terminate it at will, even if this implies a breach of obligation. The comparison of gains with costs of breaching a treaty is all that counts to an economist when predicting the fate of cooperation. A treaty is worth the paper it is written on only if the costs of violating it in the most advantageous way exceed the gains from doing so. The Folk Theorem of repeated game theory provides the framework for an evaluation of the potential for cooperation: a treaty which is a success is believed to have the properties of a perfect equilibrium or an even stronger equilibrium concept.

The economic analysis of international environmental cooperation is a point in case. One example which assumes that states can commit themselves to environmental cooperation is Black, Levi and de Meza (1993), whereas the dominant institutional assumption, such as in Barrett (1994), Heal (1994), Hoel (1991, 1992), Carraro and Siniscalco (1997), Cesar and de Zeeuw (1996), is that the conclusion of a treaty in no way affects the set of feasible actions of states.

The fundamental problem with this game-theoretic perspective from the point of view of IPL (as a science) is that treaties, once in force, become part of (treaty) law and are binding under Article 26 of the Vienna Convention on Law of Treaties. Therefore, if an economist maintains the claim that rational opportunism guides the behaviour of states after it becomes a party to a treaty, he or she claims that the state is factually above the law.

This contradicts the fundamental dogma in IPL (as a science) that the law is in a substantial sense above the state.

> It is *communis opinio* of the contemporary international society of States that a State by virtue of its sovereignty is not *iure gentium solutum* but, in exercising its sovereignty, is bound by international law. . . . Absolute sovereignty would mean the very denial of the idea of an international legal order of mankind . . . (Steinberger 1987, p. 414)

IPL (as a science) maintains the view that *pacta sunt servanda* because 'limitations of sovereignty are not presumed, but may be agreed to' (Castro Rial 1987, p. 477) and 'international law and morality set apparent and real limits to power politics' (Schwarzenberger 1986, p. 309).

Translated into economic language the dogma says that the community of states started out in anarchy (defined as absolute sovereignty) but states had and still have available an instrument of commitment which transforms the nature of the game. This instrument is IPL (as an institution) which evolves and governs ever more facets of state conduct whenever a new treaty comes into force.

The dogma holds beyond treaty law and also applies to general IPL such as customary law (Bernhardt 1984) thus enlarging the dynamic capacity of transforming the nature of the game. For example, under the dogma a binding obligation of a state is deemed to emerge simply because it did not openly object to repeated claims of other states or obeyed it only in a private spirit of voluntaryism which, however, was not detectable by others.

To a lawyer the game-theoretic approach to analysing state cooperation is as if since the time of anarchy states had never ratified a treaty, and never maintained a form of conduct which became a custom. To the lawyer the game-theoretic approach is blatantly ignorant of facts. On the other side, to an economist nothing substantial has changed since the time of anarchy; nothing substantial *can* change. Perhaps economists' reservations about the view that the rules of the international game are changeable by law arise from a perceived problem of infinite regress. If in the state of anarchy there is no authority above the state how can compliance with 'law' ever be anything but voluntary?

The discrepancy between the legal and the economic perspectives of state cooperation could hardly appear greater. In view of this it comes as no surprise that the scope for mutual understanding is limited, that the policy proposal voiced by the economist is challenged by the lawyer and perceived to be inconsistent with the realities of the world. The conflict is aggravated in substance as the economic position undermines the self-image of the lawyer. If one argues, without convincing explanation as though IPL as an institution did not exist one might just as well say that IPL as a science is redundant. The identified fundamental difference in perceived perspectives explains why lawyers and economists sometimes manoeuvre themselves into opposite camps in policy debates.

A superficial analysis of the transfer process of economic knowledge in as far as the involvement of IPL is concerned could stop here with the statement that if these fundamental differences exist there is little one could do about it. In the following I argue, however, that this transfer problem is much more intricate and, behind a maze of misperceptions, offers much more scope for agreement than would appear at first sight.

LANGUAGE AND THE TRANSLATION OF COMMON THEORY

Listening, say, to immunologists, economists are not surprised that they do not understand them because their own field of research is different from that of immunologists. Listening to lawyers of IPL should be much easier as state cooperation is a common field of interest. Views may differ but one would expect economists to readily grasp what they hear and subsequently understand what lawyers mean. First experience is, however, very likely a frustrating one. Perhaps it is much the same the other way around. Lawyers of IPL and economists may sit on the same panel but they have little to say to each other because they hardly understand each other.

It takes quite a long time to discover that the difficulty with making sense of a string of legal arguments does not so much hinge on what appears as an endless invention of ever-new words. The real problems are the economic terms the economist uses when he or she is confronting a lawyer with an economic point, and the lawyer's legal terms which the economist believes he readily knows what they mean to the lawyer. The result is that there is no distinction made between the terms when they are used in different contexts, and misinterpretations can lead to serious misunderstandings. The following examples illustrate the point.

- The legal term 'cooperation' includes what in IPL is called 'procedural cooperation' (Stoll 1996, pp. 54 ff.), which in economic language means 'contact and talk'. To an economist used to thinking of cooperation in terms of impact on expected discounted average payoff, legal parlance of procedural cooperation may indeed quickly appear as cheap talk. In turn, to a lawyer used to a richer concept of cooperation, economic parlance of cooperation may quickly appear as loose talk, and when talking to a lawyer the economist should express what he or she means by cooperation with the legal term 'cooperation in substance'.

- Sometimes it is the really innocent words which provoke an argument. When the economist uses the term 'normative', the reference is to something which is preferred over something else and therefore should be sought. The lawyer, however, refers to an obligation when calling something 'normative'. Hence if the economist uses that term, for example in the sentence 'normatively, state cooperation is needed' the lawyer may object, referring to the principle of the freedom to contract.

- 'Sanction' is a word used both in IPL and in economics. It means roughly the same in both fields, but only roughly. To the economist, it means the equilibrium conditional continuation game subject to a prior defection from cooperation by a state, having the property that that state's conditional expected discounted average payoff is smaller than the unconditional one. Loosely speaking, the economist uses the term in the sense of any loss in welfare emanating from a punishment of a defective state. To the lawyer the precise meaning of 'sanction' is the withdrawal of resources from a state *other* than the drain of resources caused by compensation owed (Bothe 1996, p. 19), which to the lawyer is of crucial importance when making a judgment on the legality of punishment.

Sometimes a term calls for translation but the translation is wrong. 'Self-executing' as a legal term refers to the fact that treaties cannot implement themselves domestically and therefore need transposition into national law (ibid., p. 16). The hasty economist may translate 'self-executing' into 'self-enforcing', referring to a crucial stability property of a treaty when the state is above the law. The context in which the lawyer uses the term, then, will likely make no sense to the economist.

The list of terms having a different connotation in economics and in IPL could easily be extended to the size of a small dictionary. Given the maze of words which are used in both languages but which have a different meaning, the appropriate translation technique cannot be, of course, to search for unfamiliar vocal expressions and then to translate them using the context of familiar vocal expressions. The appropriate technique from theoretical linguistics is rather Willard Van Ormand Quine's *radical translation* (Quine 1964) to be used when we visit the indigen without an interpreter or a dictionary. The only objective data available for translation are the forces we observe an impact on the surface of the indigen and the subsequent observable vocal and other behaviour.

Obviously it helps if economists use the correct legal language when making a point on state cooperation in the presence of lawyers, just as it helps to order a meal in the language of the waiter. But this is not the main point made in this chapter. The main claim is that a careful translation of the language of IPL (as a science) into the language of economics helps reveal a common theoretical denominator behind both sciences. That common denominator helps us to demolish many of the incongruities between IPL (as a science) and economics when interpreting IPL (as an institution).

The common theoretical denominator becomes apparent when we attempt to translate legal terms on the assumption that they are *concepts* of an interpretation of IPL (as an institution). Surprisingly, one can translate a number of these legal concepts in a way which makes them the legal twin (in legal science) of important game-theoretic concepts (in economics). For example, frequently the best translation into economic language of the legal concept of 'reciprocity' when applied to the dynamics of state conduct is 'subgame-perfectness'.[1]

Existence of a concept used in both disciplines raises a doubt and a question. The doubt concerns the perceived incongruity of the legal and economic perspectives of state cooperation. If both sciences (behind high language barriers) apply several or even many of the same concepts for analysis and interpretation, their perspectives of state conduct cannot be so different after all. My claim is that IPL (as a science) is a source of game-theoretic wisdom by featuring many concepts which can also be found in game theory, and IPL (as an institution) is an attempt to codify economic efficiency.[2] This claim is substantiated in the following section. A follow-up question is why IPL (as an institution) can be interpreted in game-theoretic terms and why it codifies economic optimality. The answer cannot simply be that lawyers and economists as interpreters of a given institution are equally intelligent on average and hence must come to the same conclusion however different the language that they use. A more subtle answer will be given below.

EFFICIENCY OF SANCTIONS AND ITS CODIFICATION IN INTERNATIONAL PUBLIC LAW

If the state is above the law, then state cooperation is appropriately analysed within the Folk Theorem framework of repeated games.[3] In this framework, cooperation is sustainable through credible threats of sanctioning states which consider exploiting the cooperative conduct of other states. Sanctions are thus, for lack of availability, (imperfect) substitutes for authorities or institutions which are above the state. The availability of credible and appropriate sanctions is the essential precondition for the feasibility of cooperation in anarchy. However, should the law be indeed above the state, then a natural benchmark for judging its efficacy, in terms of bringing about cooperation, is to compare the legal reactions to breaches of cooperation with the sanctions states would want to execute in anarchy.

If the law is above the state and makes sanctions mandatory which otherwise would be incredible then IPL extends the set of sustainable cooperation compared to anarchy. If the law is above the state but makes sanctions nonobligatory upon noncompliance, and sets legality constraints on sanctions which constrain the economic optimum, then IPL constrains the set of sustainable cooperation compared to anarchy. Lastly, if the law is above the state and makes sanctions nonobligatory but sets legality constraints such that the sanctions supporting economic efficiency fully exploit what is legally admissible, then the fact that the law is dogmatically above the state has no effect on state conduct. In this case the predictive capacity of the economic approach concerning state cooperation is not weakened if IPL is ignored as an institution. A careful comparison between economically efficient sanctions and legal norms concerning sanctions is therefore of crucial importance for understanding the legal and economic position *vis-à-vis* each other.

Legal sanctions – or *countermeasures*, which is a more appropriate legal term for the concept (Conbacau 1986, p. 340) – have to comply with a few general principles of customary international law, but more specific rules about sanctions may be stipulated in the relevant treaty itself (Heister et al. 1997, p. 35), thereby becoming a norm under treaty law. It is important to note that the set of these rules possesses the properties of conventional constraints in economic maximization problems: legal sanctions have limits but there is nothing in customary law which makes the execution of sanctions obligatory to states.

If sanctions are to prevent defection from cooperation, then efficiency of sanctions is a sensible concept only under certain conditions. For example, in a world where players have perfect control over their actions and act perfectly rationally, sanctions simply must be sufficiently severe. More severe sanctions are just as good because sanctions enter the expected discounted average payoff with probability zero since they must never be executed. In this case one can seek minimal sanctions which sustain a given degree of cooperation (for example, Cave 1987), but this has no bearing for welfare. Hence efficiency (and optimality) of sanctions is a sensible concept only if the probability of having to execute them is positive.

Mohr and Thomas (1998a) investigate efficient sanctions *vis-à-vis* legal sanctions in a version of the Fudenberg, Levine and Maskin (1994) framework. They consider a symmetric two-state (-player) partnership game whose stage game is a variant of the prisoner's dilemma game. Outcomes of stage games are public knowledge but imperfect signals of states' motivations and dispositions. In particular, states are modelled as exhibiting farsighted rationality most of the time but possessing a small probability in each stage of the game of behaving as if they were myopic and thus maximize the stage game payoff instead of the expected discounted average payoff. In this framework, sanctions can prevent farsighted rational opportunism. Sanctions are, however, unable to prevent defection arising from shortsightedness. Because, by inference from public signals, rational opportunism and accidental shortsightedness are indistinguishable, the prevention of rational opportunism occasionally requires the punishment of the unlucky innocent who happened to be shortsighted once too often. Hence sanctions enter the expected discounted average payoff with positive probability even if they are severe enough to prevent rational defection. Efficient sanctions are defined as sanctions supporting the symmetric (and hence unique) strongly renegotiation proof (in the sense of Farrell and Maskin 1989) perfect public (in the sense of Fudenberg, Levine and Maskin 1994) equilibrium.

In the following subsection, properties of efficient sanctions supporting this equilibrium are compared with legality constraints on sanctions.

Compensation and Decomposability on Hyperplanes

The equilibrium supported by optimal sanctions is solvable by backward induction. This permits a decomposition of the equilibrium payoff vector on a hyperplane which represents the impact of sanctions on the welfare of states after a defection has taken place.[4] If we require that the equilibrium be (at least weakly) renegotiation proof, then the values of the different continuation games, if different states are responsible for defection, must be Pareto-unrankable. The intuition is simple. In the wake of executing sanctions, resources should not be unnecessarily destroyed but handed back and forth, or else at least some of the sanctions could be negotiated away. Efficient sanctions are therefore redistributive rather than destructive.

IPL favours redistributive sanctions. Although the primary purpose of reparations is *restitutio in integrum*, this may neither be achievable nor bring about an advantage to the injured party. Legal writers therefore stress the consequences of reparations owed, among which is compensation for damages suffered (Wolfrum 1987, p. 352 or Thomsen 1987, p. 376), and Dolzer (1985, p. 219) observes, in the context of compensation for illegal expropriation, a tendency to compensate in 'utility-compatible currency'. We therefore observe a tendency in IPL to bring about redistributive sanctions which avoid an unnecessary destruction of resources. This is a necessary condition for efficient sanctions.

Presumptive Evidence and Statistical Inference

With spurs of irrationality a defection from cooperation can have either of two causes: occasional inadvertent shortsightedness or farsighted rational opportunism. Hence, the observable outcome of stage games is only an imperfect signal of motivations and dispositions of states. This raises the problem of on which evidence to base the decision to sanction a party, public signal or personal motivation? With several partners and a wish to hand resources back and forth, an additional problem arises. Parties have to know or make an educated guess as to which party has defected. The perfect public equilibrium approach resolves this by making sanctions contingent on statistical inference obtained only from the history of public signals. Hence it bases sanctions on outcomes and not on motivations.[5]

Legally, the production of appropriate evidence of a wrongful act is a *conditio sine qua non* for the legality of sanctions. Private information, which in dispute settlements such as those before the International Court of Justice is considered 'claim against claim', is usually inappropriate. Some objective evidence such as that extractable from public signals is desirable if available. Statistical inference appears in that respect compatible with IPL. The crucial question is, however, whether legal sanctions can be based on presumptive evidence or need the proof of malicious intentions. What in IPL is generally relevant for the constitution of a wrongful act

> is not the psychological attitude of the individual but the objective conduct of the subject of international law (whose) responsibility does not require an act of malice; it may equally consist of a general defect or failure in the organization of the subject concerned and be entirely divorced from any subjective intention. (Wolfrum 1987, p. 275)

In conclusion, presumptive evidence produced in an objective way, such as by statistical inference, as is required by the perfect public equilibrium concept, appears to be admissible under the law.

Efficiency of Sanctions and Renegotiation Proofness

The game-theoretic notion of renegotiation proofness is a refined concept of perfectness ensuring that at least one party will want to veto any proposal to forget the sins of the past and cancel the execution of sanctions. It thereby makes sanctions credible. Renegotiation proofness is a reasonable condition to impose in economic analysis both if the state is above or below the law. IPL is concerned only with the right to take countermeasures and restrictions thereon, but no obligation to execute sanctions exists in general IPL and such obligations are usually absent in treaty law. Ress (1994, p. 283) writes that 'the entire system of international treaty law is more similar to a system of reciprocal *do ut des* or, in better circumstances to a system of permanent renegotiation than to a system where clear-cut final legal decisions are taken and implemented'.

There are various alternative definitions of renegotiation proofness and strategies for bringing it about (for a survey, see Pearce 1992). The widely used concept of Farrell and Maskin (1989) contains a de-escalating mechanism as sanctions are imposed only for a sufficient but finite number of rounds, thereby allowing for an eventual return to normal play. The incentive constraint on feasible continuation games requires in this case that the punished party maintains throughout an incentive to cooperate in its own punishment. Some legal interpreters of IPL maintain a legal theory which mirrors even such rather sophisticated game-theoretic concepts. For example, Conbacau (1986, p. 339) writes that 'the sanction is thus a technique of compulsory enforcement in which the State voluntarily though not freely of course decides to return to the proper course of conduct'.[6]

Legality Constraints on Reprisals and the Incentive Constraint

Economic equilibrium concepts call for the imposition of sanctions only upon a defection from cooperation. In general IPL, *reprisal* is a legal sanction against a *wrongful act*, which is the inducing act which must be a violation of international law (for example, Partsch 1986a, p. 334). A violation of the rights of third states is a violation of international law itself (ibid., p. 332).

In the legal model a reprisal is an interference in a right, which to be legal must not only be preceded by an illegal interference with another right but it also must be proportional. The *principle of proportionality* is legally binding within the law of reprisals (Delbrück 1984, p. 398). Hence, compensation brought about by reprisal must also be proportional. If the state is below the law the principle of proportionality imposes a constraint on the game similar to the economic incentive constraint supporting normal play. However, it imposes an upper bound on sanctions supposed to prevent a sanction excess, whereas the incentive constraint imposes a lower bound. If the legal constraint is tighter than the economic constraint requires, then cooperation is not sustainable as an equilibrium of the game if the law is above the state. In this case all sanctions are illegal which suffice to support cooperation.

However, legal writing supports the view that the legality constraint does not obstruct the existence of equilibria. To see this, one has to observe that IPL distinguishes a twin purpose of reprisal in the legal model: giving incentives and undoing harm done by providing sufficient compensation (Simma 1984, p. 403). In the IPL literature there appears to exist a preponderance of the compensation objective over the incentive objective in giving proportionality a precise meaning.[7] The distinction is important because if the set of feasible stage game payoff vectors is a convex set, as it is in partnership games consisting of repeated prisoner's dilemma games, full compensation of the betrayed party requires more severe sanctions than is necessary to maintain incentives. In other words, the preponderant school in IPL accepts that the defective state is not indifferent concerning compliance versus noncompliance, but regrets *ex post* each incidence of noncompliance. If proportionality is defined by the compensation objective, then there exist sanctions which give sufficient incentives and which are legal. Therefore, the legality constraint does not interfere with the existence of 'legal and stable' cooperation.

As legal sanctions strive for redistribution, the parties having a right to reprisals wish to exhaust what they are entitled to. They thus induce sanctions which from the incentive point of view are unnecessarily severe. This implies, however, that executed sanctions are economically inefficient, that is excessive in the partnership game with spurs of irrationality because sanctions supporting the symmetric strongly renegotiation proof perfect public equilibrium are minimal such that a state is indifferent between normal play and maximizing its stage game payoff by defecting from cooperation (Mohr and Thomas 1998a).

General IPL, that is the set of norms not codified in treaties, therefore heeds the economic incentive constraint which supports normal play. But it endows compliant states with rights against noncompliant states which are unnecessarily welfare destructive in expected discounted average payoff terms. If institutions evolve towards efficiency one would expect IPL (as an institution) to adapt until the full welfare potential of cooperation, available in the economic model, is realized under the law.

Self-contained Regimes and Restoration of Optimality

Legal writers observe a 'modern trend of limiting reprisals as far as possible' (Partsch 1986a, p. 332). One method of achieving this is the codification of sanctions pending in a treaty. Treaty law prevails over customary law with the exception of *ius cogens* (Bernhardt 1984, p. 62). In principle, states can set norms in a treaty which can either extend or narrow down the legality constraint as they wish and wish to agree upon. Usually, the stipulation further constrains legal sanctions compared to what is admissible under general IPL (Heister et al. 1995, p. 53). "These regimes of dispute settlement may be "self-contained" in so far as they do not allow the participating States to have recourse to the normal sanctions against a treaty breach, such as reprisal' (Ress 1994, p. 285).

Self-contained regimes can therefore be interpreted as legal innovations correcting the right of applying economically excessive reprisals as they would emerge from the principle of proportionality under general IPL.

Nonbinding Agreements and Retorsion

In the economic model, state cooperation is measured on the scale of expected discounted average payoff. This impact orientation is not matched by the legal model. The law distinguishes cooperation which might have the same welfare effect on states but which differs in legal status. Cooperation need not take the form of concluding a treaty in order to fall under the law. So-called '[s]oft law comprises (if it exists) rules which are neither strictly binding nor completely void of any legal significance' (Bernhardt 1984, p. 62). *Nonbinding agreements* such as gentlemen's agreements or declarations of policy (Münch 1984, p. 354) have a legal status in so far as they affect which countermeasures are legal in response to an act which obstructs cooperation. IPL qualifies acts which obstruct a nonbinding agreement as unfriendly. An *unfriendly act* is disadvantageous to another state but it is not wrongful in that it does not interfere in a right of that state because the nonbinding agreement did not create rights in the first place (Weber 1981, p. 252). *Retorsion* is the legal countermeasure against unfriendly acts. As the action to which it responds is itself not a violation of law, retorsion must therefore itself not interfere with any right of the other party but 'the rule of proportionality valid for reprisals does not apply' (Partsch 1986b, p. 336). Dimensions of international relations covered by nonbinding agreements are therefore burdened with the opportunity to impose sanctions which are excessive even beyond proportionality.

One is inclined to take this legal design as a point against the thesis upheld in the present chapter. If IPL (as an institution) evolves so as to codify economic efficiency, should this design not be threatened by extinction? Indeed, one argument in defence of my thesis is that ever-more dimensions of international relations fall under treaty law. Another argument maintains that a suitable combination of nonbinding agreements and self-contained regimes may be a design which codifies efficiency in a world in which states simultaneously interact in many dimensions.

Optimal Legal Design of Multidimensional Cooperation

If different games are simultaneously played between the same players, then the situation changes not only in scale but also in nature. Continuation games in one game can now be made contingent on signals emerging from another game. Folmer, Van Mouche and Ragland (1993) show that a transformation of several independently played games into a single ('tensor') game by such cross-game contingencies can be welfare-improving. Borrowing and lending of sanction capacity across dimensions can reduce the overall incentive to rationally defect from cooperation (Mohr 1995), and sovereignty risk-pooling across dimensions of international interaction can be welfare-improving (Mohr and Thomas 1998b). Special legal provisions are required under IPL to accommodate this welfare-increasing potential. Without these provisions it may be a violation of Article 60 of the Vienna Convention on the Law of Treaties to interfere with a right of a party in a dimension in which that party has not violated law.

> Safeguards against disputes of this kind can be seen in the opportunity to combine in one and the same treaty several and different obligations, so that the disregard of one of them entitles the partners to suspend the other obligations too and with the argument that the whole treaty itself is obsolete if it is not fully accomplished. (Doering 1994, p. 311)

With such *cross-default arrangements* a sanction programme can be codified which turns several otherwise independent treaties into one covering all associated dimensions of international relations.

However, considering the costs of negotiating a mega treaty, covering some if not many or even all dimensions of international relations, suggests a less ambitious design, but one which may be more efficient. One such design is the combination of self-contained regimes covering some dimensions, with nonbinding agreements covering other dimensions. The design implies that a violation of treaty law can be answered with an unfriendly act, that is with retorsion, in a dimension covered by a gentleman's agreement because 'measures not affecting the rights of another State can be taken in response either to an unfriendly act or to a violation of international law committed by another State' (Partsch 1986b, p. 335). The design therefore allows even for a concentration of all sanctions in one or a few dimensions covered by nonbinding agreements because retorsion is not constrained by the principle of proportionality and the self-contained regimes can stipulate that sanctions in these dimensions shall be limited to 'peace talks' only. Mohr and Thomas (1998a) argue that this design can be welfare-improving if dimensions differ with respect to the probability with which states act irrationally. Hence the prevalent existence of nonbinding agreements or other forms of cooperation not protected by treaty law is no proof of the inefficiency of IPL as an institution. It simply may be the expression of economic efficiency in a form which protects the internal consistency of legal principles.

EXTENSION OF ECONOMIC INSTITUTIONALISM: INTERPRETING IPL AS AN INSTITUTION AND A SCIENCE

To the surprise of the casual observer a good deal of game-theoretic wisdom can be found in IPL. General IPL contains concepts which match game-theoretic concepts considered important in characterizing equilibrium cooperation in an anarchic world. It contains sufficient flexibility not to obstruct economic efficiency by making efficient sanctions legal. Although it is far stretched to conclude from this evidence that IPL codifies economic efficiency precisely, treaty law can be interpreted as a body of norms which trims down sanctions which are economically, but not legally, excessive. Beyond that, IPL produces designs which legally accommodate complicated contingency plans for sanctions which approximate or sustain efficiency under multidimensional international relations.

From this evidence the conclusion seems not too far stretched that IPL is an institution which, perhaps among other things, legalizes what is efficient in anarchy. Furthermore, bearing in mind the growing proliferation of treaty law, which constrains sanctions below the level of what is permissible under the principle of proportionality, one can even conclude that IPL as an institution seeks to codify economic efficiency.

An important follow-up conclusion from this is that, in so far as predictions are concerned, it is not essential whether the law is above or below the state. Economists do not lose much of their precision in prediction when they ignore IPL as an institution. In this sense they are right to do so – but they may be right for the wrong reason. At least their reason is wrong if they believe that IPL is without a function.

If IPL seeks to codify economic efficiency, then the body of norms it has accumulated over centuries is a source for orientation when planning costs cannot be ignored. Bernholz (1994, p. 308) has already claimed that a function of IPL is to guide states to an equilibrium when there are many. The claim made here is, however, that IPL tries to guide states not to any one of several existing equilibria but to an efficient one.

If IPL as an institution possesses this information function and performs smoothly, then economists are right in ignoring this institution only because of the lucky coincidence that their models tend to abstract from planning and information costs. This assumption is in itself, of course, the result of just such costs and part of an appropriate frame of analysis only *because and in so far* as IPL succeeds in trimming down these costs.

I consider evidence that IPL as an institution actually seeks to codify economic efficiency at least as interesting as the provision of an explanation why this might be so because there is an institutionalistic explanation readily at hand: institutions survive only if they evolve so that they accommodate incentives provided by an environment which they essentially fail to control. Accordingly, in an anarchic environment, IPL had only the opportunity to enshrine into law what states wished to do anyway, and to make illegal what states did not wish to do, including during the period after adopting an obligation.

What, then, in the institutionalist's perspective is IPL as a science? Who are the lawyers? If IPL as a science seeks internal consistency in the body of principles and dogmas with which it interprets IPL as an institution and if IPL as an institution seeks to codify economic efficiency, then the lawyer is the economist's best friend: the lawyer behaves as if he or she were an economist him- or herself.

If one took the institutionalist's view that step further, one could ask why this might be so. Is it reasonable to transpose the rules governing the evolution of institutions to the world of scientific disciplines? If this is indeed admissible, then the same rules can be applied to IPL as a science: the hypothesis then is that the noneconomic interpretative institution, a science, evolves following the same principles as its object of investigation. If IPL as an institution accommodates incentives and constraints provided by an environment which it cannot affect, so does IPL as a science. The economic institutionalist's conclusion then is that IPL is the legal science of anarchic cooperation and all is governed by the same economic factors.

This radical institutionalism then leads the economist to where he or she departed from: IPL is irrelevant and redundant. On second thoughts such a conclusion would, however, be an act of unwarranted scientific imperialism because the comparison undertaken of the economic and the legal models of international sanctions simply showed that both match to a surprising degree. The only feasible conclusion, therefore, is that economic rationale follows legal rationale as much as it does the other way around.

We must therefore be careful with the claim that a revealed compatibility of seemingly 'incongruent' scientific approaches permits their epistemologic ranking. One must, instead, face the possibility of the existence of forces which tend to make incongruent scientific bodies match, at least as far as a common object of investigation is concerned.

Knowledge about such forces would enhance the management of the communication problem. However, such knowledge requires a positive theory of science, as opposed to the normative orientation of epistemology. The comparison of the legal and economic models of state cooperation suggests that meta-rules are in force which tend to make scientific approaches converge in substance. In conclusion, Feyerabend's programme that 'anything goes' (Feyerabend 1975) may give rise to the expectation of scientific chaos, but the practice of science seems to produce more order than one might expect on the basis of such postulates. That order, and these meta rules, promise to give guidance when serious consideration is given to the communication challenge across disciplines.

CONCLUSIONS: A KUHNIAN APPROACH TO COMMUNICATION

Thomas Kuhn's positive theory of science provides a platform from which to address the communication problem (Kuhn 1962). In Kuhn's theory, science is a special type of social organization. (Normal) science is a consensus system which is characterized by the following:

1. Members form an invisible college, sharing common interests, commitments and interaction.
2. Members of the invisible college solve problems.
3. Members work on problems of detail.

4. Members share an understanding of what the interesting questions are and the general nature of their solutions. This is the result of common training.
5. Only the judgement of other members of the same college is accepted.
6. The college never runs out of interesting and tractable questions of detail.

This is a shorthand version of Benjamin Ward's summary of Kuhn's concept of normal science. Ward concludes that both neoclassical economics and law easily qualify as normal sciences in Kuhn's theory (Ward 1972). How, then, should our economist and our lawyer communicate their views, belonging to two different invisible colleges?

Item 3 ensures that they can easily fail to understand each other even if, deeply hidden in the basements of their colleges, they share something in common. Item 5 ensures that they will fail to understand each other unless something exceptional happens, and item 6 ensures that this will last for ever. So the solution to the communication problem must be found in items 1, 2 and 4.

Item 1 ensures that a communication strategy which works with one addressee will likely work with all members of a given college. Item 2 ensures that one can gain someone's attention if one takes his or her solution to the problem seriously. The problem here is item 3, again, but getting one's ideas across requires getting interested in the details to be solved in the other college. Given that interest, the chances of succeeding rest exclusively with the handling of item 4. Item 4 is the body of shared problems of interest and shared admissible solution concepts. It is here that the meta-rules which produce order within methodological chaos (across colleges) seem to support communication.

For example, the economist wants to get across the message that the Montreal Protocol on the protection of the ozone layer should not impose deadweight and excessive sanctions on noncompliant parties while the lawyer may be concerned with the compatibility of some norms created by that treaty with the GATT rules, say. Because of a meta-rule at work in between game theory and IPL (as a science), it would be void and even counterproductive to follow the impulse of wanting to challenge the entire body of solution concepts of the invisible IPL college by developing a string of arguments as though that college was irrelevant. It is likely that the opposite strategy will be successful. The economist could simply trust that the legal solution would suffice for much of what is important economically. Alternatively, the economist could ask for information concerning the legal principles which govern the legal solution to the sanction problem, and then demonstrate bit by bit that what makes economic sense is compatible with law or can be made compatible if an advantageous legal design is chosen. There is little which could prevent this strategy from being successful, except the temptation to insist that states anyway do what they think fit, irrespective of law.

Is the example taken here a singular exception or are there other such examples where a meta-rule produces compatible solution concepts across invisible colleges? Is that even the rule rather than the exception? We do not know, but we must find out. At least, the example nourishes the hope that the communication of economic institutional analysis beyond economics can be more successfully accomplished than it presently is.

NOTES

1. I characterize a word by the term 'concept' to emphasize its capacity of bringing into a relation other words which could not be related if the word that is a concept did not exist. For example, without the concepts of 'reciprocity' or 'subgame-perfectness' one could only speak of a state's advantage from cooperation as compared to another's, whereas 'reciprocity' and 'subgame-perfectness' introduce a relation between the two advantages which permits us to think of them in terms of being 'mutually advantageous'. It is only the existence of words being concepts in two scientific languages which are identical relational operators which permit us to infer a common theoretical denominator behind the two sciences.
2. The term 'codification' is used in a nonlegal, more general sense. In IPL (as a science) codification refers, for example, to the act of writing an obligation into a treaty. Treaty law is codified law, customary law is not. Concerning economic aspects, no distinction is made here between treaty law and general IPL and codification of, for example, economic efficiency is meant to refer to the whole set of legal norms in general.
3. For a survey of the literature, see Pearce (1992).
4. For details see, for example, Fudenberg, Levine and Maskin (1994, Section 4).
5. A sufficient condition for the availability of statistical inference is the pairwise full rank condition. See Fudenberg, Levine and Maskin (1994, Section 5).
6. Similar economically sophisticated interpretations can be found in Ress (1994, p. 289). Ress tries, however, to bridge the gap to economics and it is not clear whether his interpretations refer to the legal or the economic dogma.
7. Evidence can be found, for example, in Akehurst (1984, p. 508), Partsch (1986a, p. 331), or Wolfrum (1987, p. 352).

REFERENCES

Akehurst, M. (1984), 'Treaties, termination', in R. Bernhardt (ed.), *Encyclopaedia of Public International Law*, Instalment 7, Amsterdam: North-Holland, pp. 507–10.
Barrett, S.A. (1994), 'Self-enforcing international environmental agreements', *Oxford Economic Papers*, **46** (supplement), pp. 878–94.
Bernhardt, R. (1984), 'Customary international law', in R. Bernhardt (ed.), *Encyclopaedia of Public International Law*, Instalment 7, Amsterdam: North-Holland, pp. 61–6.
Bernholz, P. (1994), 'Ex ante safeguards against ex post opportunism in international treaties', *Journal of Institutional and Theoretical Economics*, **150** (1), pp. 304–9.
Black, J., M.D. Levi and D. de Meza (1993), 'Creating a good atmosphere: minimum participation for tackling the "greenhouse effect"', *Economica*, **60** (239), pp. 281–93.
Bothe, M. (1996), 'The evaluation of enforcement mechanisms in international environmental law', in R. Wolfrum (ed.), *Enforcing Environmental Standards: Economic Mechanisms as Viable Means?*, Heidelberg: Springer, pp. 13–38.

Carraro, C. and D. Siniscalco (1997), 'R&D cooperation and the stability of international environmental agreements', in C. Carraro (ed.), *International Environmental Negotiations: Strategic Policy Issues*, Cheltenham, UK and Brookfield, US: Edward Elgar, pp. 71–96.

Castro Rial, J.M. (1987), 'States, sovereign equality', in R. Bernhardt (ed.), *Encyclopaedia of Public International Law*, Instalment 10, Amsterdam: North-Holland, pp. 477–81.

Cave, J.A.K. (1987), 'Long-term competition in a dynamic game: the cold fish war', *RAND Journal of Economics*, **18** (4), pp. 596–610.

Cesar, H.S. and A.J. de Zeeuw (1996), 'Issue linkage in global environmental problems', in A.P. Xepapadeas (ed.), *Economic Policy for the Environment and Natural Resources: Techniques for the Management and Control of Pollution*, Cheltenham, UK and Brookfield, US: Edward Elgar, pp. 158–73.

Conbacau, J. (1986), 'Sanctions', in R. Bernhardt (ed.), *Encyclopaedia of Public International Law*, Instalment 9, Amsterdam: North-Holland, pp. 337–41.

Delbrück, J. (1984), 'Proportionality', in R. Bernhardt (ed.), *Encyclopaedia of Public International Law*, Instalment 7, Amsterdam: North-Holland, pp. 396–400.

Doering, K. (1994), 'Ex ante safeguards against ex post opportunism in international treaties', *Journal of Institutional and Theoretical Economics*, **150** (1), pp. 310–14.

Dolzer, R. (1985), 'Expropriation and nationalisation', in R. Bernhardt (ed.), *Encyclopaedia of Public International Law*, Instalment 8, Amsterdam: North-Holland, pp. 214–21.

Farrell, J. and E. Maskin (1989), 'Renegotiation in repeated games', *Games and Economic Behaviour*, **1** (4), pp. 327–60.

Feyerabend, P. (1975), *Against Method. Outline of an Anarchic Theory of Knowledge*, Frankfurt am Main: Suhrkamp.

Folmer, H., P. Van Mouche and S. Ragland (1993), 'Interconnected games and international environmental problems', *Environmental and Resource Economics*, **3** (4), pp. 313–53.

Fudenberg, D., D. Levine and E. Maskin (1994), 'The Folk Theorem with imperfect public information', *Econometrica*, **62** (5), pp. 997–1039.

Heal, G.M. (1994), 'Formation of international environmental agreements', in C. Carraro (ed.), *Trade, Innovation, Environment*, Dordrecht: Kluwer, pp. 301–22.

Heister, J., E. Mohr, W. Plesmann, F. Stähler, T. Stoll and R. Wolfrum (1995), 'Economic and legal aspects of international environmental agreements', *Kiel Working Paper*, No. 711, Kiel Institute of World Economics.

Heister, J., E. Mohr, F. Stähler, T. Stoll and R. Wolfrum (1997), 'Strategies to enforce compliance with an international CO_2-treaty', *International Environmental Affairs*, **9** (1), pp. 22–53.

Hoel, M. (1991), 'Global environmental problems: the effects of unilateral actions taken by one country', *Journal of Environmental Economics and Management*, **20** (1), pp. 55–70.

Hoel, M. (1992), 'International environment conventions: the case of uniform reductions of emissions', *Environmental and Resource Economics*, **2** (2), pp. 141–59.

Kuhn, T.S. (1962), *The Structure of Scientific Revolutions*, Chicago: University of Chicago Press.

Mohr, E. (1995), 'International environmental permit trade and debt: the consequences of country sovereignty and cross-default policies', *Review of International Economics*, **3** (1), pp. 1–19.

Mohr, E. and J. Thomas (1998a), 'Are legality constraints on international sanctions a codification of economic optimality?', University of St. Gallen, mimeo.

Mohr, E. and J. Thomas (1998b), 'Pooling sovereign risks: the case of environmental treaties and international debt', *Journal of Development Economics*, **55**, pp. 171–88.

Münch, F. (1984), 'Non-binding agreement', in R. Bernhardt (ed.), *Encyclopaedia of Public International Law*, Instalment 7, Amsterdam: North-Holland, pp. 353–8.

Partsch, K.J. (1986a), 'Reprisal', in R. Bernhardt (ed.), *Encyclopaedia of Public International Law*, Instalment 9, Amsterdam: North-Holland, pp. 330–35.

Partsch, K.J. (1986b), 'Retorsion', in R. Bernhardt (ed.), *Encyclopaedia of Public International Law*, Instalment 9, Amsterdam: North-Holland, pp. 335–7.

Pearce, D.G. (1992), 'Repeated games: cooperation and rationality', in J.-J. Laffont (ed.), *Advances in Economic Theory Sixth World Congress*, vol. 1, Cambridge: Cambridge University Press, pp. 132–74.

Quine, W.V. (1964), *Word and Object*, Cambridge, MA: MIT Press.

Ress, G. (1994), 'Ex ante safeguards against ex post opportunism in international treaties: theory and practice of international public law', *Journal of Institutional and Theoretical Economics*, **150** (1), pp. 279–303.

Schwarzenberger, G. (1986), 'Power politics', in R. Bernhardt (ed.), *Encyclopaedia of Public International Law*, Instalment 9, Amsterdam: North-Holland, pp. 305–10.

Simma, B. (1984), 'Reciprocity', in R. Bernhardt (ed.), *Encyclopaedia of Public International Law*, Instalment 7, Amsterdam: North-Holland, pp. 400–404.

Steinberger, H. (1987), 'Sovereignty', in R. Bernhardt (ed.), *Encyclopedia of Public International Law*, Instalment 10, Amsterdam: North-Holland, pp. 397–418.

Stoll, T. (1996), 'The International Environmental Law of Cooperation', in R. Wolfrum (ed.), *Enforcing Environmental Standards: Economic Mechanisms as Viable Means?*, Heidelberg: Springer, pp. 39–93.

Thomsen, S. (1987), 'Restitution', in R. Bernhardt (ed.), *Encyclopaedia of Public International Law*, Instalment 10, Amsterdam: North-Holland, pp. 375–8.

Ward, B. (1972), *What's Wrong With Economics?*, London: Macmillan.

Weber, H. (1981), 'Unfriendly act', in R. Bernhardt (ed.), *Encyclopaedia of Public International Law*, Instalment 4, Amsterdam: North-Holland, pp. 252–3.

Wolfrum, R. (1987), 'Reparation for internationally wrongful acts', in R. Bernhardt (ed.), *Encyclopaedia of Public International Law*, Instalment 10, Amsterdam: North-Holland, pp. 352–3.

Index

Abraham, Katharine 47
academia, employment of economic
    majors 113
academic economists 51–2
Ackley, Gardner 81
Advanced Executive Program 145
advisory process, institutional factors
    77–80
advocacy 80–1
aggregate demand functions 20, 21
agricultural subsidies, crowding theory
    175–6
Albert, Hans 24
amateurs 75
Aninat, Eduardo 48
applied economists, making of 103–22
Austria, culture of policy advice 56t, 59t,
    63t

backward induction 194
backwardation 137
balkanization, in training 55
bank capital regulation 134
Bank for International Settlements (BIS)
    61
banks, influence of institutional investors
    131
Banque de France 50
behaviour, economic model of 13, 19
behavioural finance 147
Belgium
    culture of policy advice 56t, 57, 58,
      59t, 63t, 65
    institutional factors, policy advice 78
benefits, option pricing models 140–1
bias, scientific statements 26
Black-Scholes, option pricing model
    125, 133, 137, 146
budget policy, German research
    institutes 96
Bundesbank 50, 112

bureaucratic capture, of policies 41
bureaucratic-authoritarian states 36

Cairncross, Sir Alec 74–5
campus education 155–9
capital asset pricing model 139–40,
    140–1, 146
Cavallo, Domingo 47–8
censorship 64
central banks 50, 51
certification, financial postgraduate
    education 144
chalkboard methods, teaching 119
Chicago Board Options Exchange
    (CBOE) 133
Chicago school, markets work
    perspective 3, 9, 10, 11, 12
civil servants 58–60, 75
class notes 120
client-adviser relationship 81–3
coherence, in undergraduate curricula
    117–18
commands, crowding theory 168–70,
    171
communication
    economic education 116–17
    Kuhnian approach 201–3
    skills, need for 122
communitarian arguments, opposition to
    markets 4, 9
comparative advantage argument, misuse
    of 37, 39
compensation 194
competence, policy advisers 53
competencies, on-campus learning
    155–6
competition
    among researchers 64
    financial innovation 129–30
comprehensive exams 55

computable general equilibrium models
    (CGE) 33
computerized learning 120
Conseil de l'analyse économique 50
constitutional economics, discipline
    versus trust 172–3
constitutional policy, public choice 9–11
constraints, and preferences 166–7
continuity, financial postgraduate
    education 145–6
controversies
    among economists 85
    dealing with 66–7
conventional thinking 55
cooperation
    see also state cooperation
    legal terminology 190–1
    universities and institutes 92–3, 96, 97
corporate governance, influence of
    institutional investors 131–2
corruptibility, of economists 26
costs, distance learning 154
Council of Economic Advisers (CEA)
    49, 50, 66, 79, 81, 82
counterarguments 67
countermeasures 193
courses, for policy advisers 55–7
creative destruction, opposition to
    markets 4, 9
credit risk management 130–1
crime, regulatory policy 174
crowding theory 166–7, 170–1
    agricultural subsidies 175–6
    direct interventions 174–5
    infrastructural policy 178
    moral suasion 173–4
    volunteering 176–8
curriculum, designing postgraduate 143–4

data mining 132
debates, about policy advice 16, 69
decomposability, on hyperplanes 194
demand, for policy advisers 58–68
Denmark, culture of policy advice 49,
    55, 56t, 58, 59t, 63t
deregulation 129–30
derivatives
    characteristics of 135–8
    innovative power of 133–4, 138–9
design, of research institutes 95–6

Deutsche Börse 131
developing countries
    policy advice 52
    social capital, measured as trust 169
    use and abuse of theory 32–42
direct interventions, crowding theory
    174–5
discipline, versus trust 172–3
discussions, on policy advice 24
distance learning 152, 154, 156

earmarked funding, Germany 94, 95
ecological taxes 21
econometric methods, finance curricula
    146
economic councils 50–1
economic degrees
    cycles and trends in 104–10
    implications of decline in 111–13
    teaching, views on 113–18
    universities as franchisers of 157–8
economic education
    see also postgraduate education;
        undergraduate curricula
    advisory work 85–6
    chances and challenges for suppliers
        of 151–61
    culture of policy advice 54–7, 68–9
economic knowledge
    financial innovation 135–42
    transfer of
        by research institutes, Germany
            90–8
        finance sector 125–48
    use and abuse of theory 32–42
economic science, policy perspectives
    8–9
economic teams 78–9
economic theory, and policy advice 20–3
economics
    complaint of detachment 114, 121
    perceptions and status 69
    recognising limits of 53
    science or party line 62–4
economics departments, decline of
    economics degrees 111–12
economists
    see also academic economists; applied
        economists
    controversies among 85

corruptibility of 26
in government 77–8
international standards for 158
legal cases 80–1
as policy advisers 14–16
reputation of 17
Economists as Policy Advocates 80
education *see* economic education
electronic networks, finance sector 132
empirical economics, Germany 96–8
empirical work, finance curricula 146–7
employers, undergraduate curricula 114
entrepreneurs, profits as indicators of
    success 171
environmental cooperation, among states
    188
environmental policy, direct
    interventions 174
Eurex 131
Europe
    culture of policy advice 49, 50, 51, 55,
        68
    institutional factors, policy advice 78
European Central Bank 112
European Commission 58, 61–2
Everything for Sale 3
examinations 55–7, 144
exchange economies, economic theory
    21–2
executive education
    financial innovation 142–8
    Switzerland, early eighties 127
experts 24–6, 75, 84
external interventions, intrinsic
    motivation 166–7, 171
externalities 21
extra-curricular activities, students 57
extrinsic motivation, and intrinsic
    motivation 170–2

factional states 36
faculty members, impact of new media
    158–9
family, economics of 13
finance, Switzerland, early eighties
    126–9
financial innovation
    and evolution of know-how,
        Switzerland 129–35

implications for postgraduate
    education 142–8
financial modelling, postgraduate
    education 146
Finland, culture of policy advice 50, 51,
    56t, 58, 59t, 63t
Fit for Finance 143–4
folk theorem, state cooperation 188–90,
    192–9
Ford, Gerald 82
formalism, in training 54
Foundations of Finance 127
France, culture of policy advice 50, 51,
    55, 56t, 57, 58, 59t, 60–1, 63t, 64–6
Frankel, Jeffrey 47
Freiburger Schule 98

game theory, state cooperation 188–90,
    192–9
Gaulle, Charles de 65
generalists, Civil Service 75
German Science Council, evaluation of
    research institutes 91–3
Germany
    culture of policy advice 49, 51, 55,
        56t, 57, 58, 59t, 63t, 65
    economic knowledge transfer,
        research institutes 90–8
    institutional factors, advisory process
        79
    new media and learning process 153
    trends in economics degrees 105,
        107f, 108
Giavazzi, Francesco 48
globalization
    and competition 112
    through deregulation 130
good theory, misapplication of 37–41
government
    development policy 36–7
    economists in 77–8
grades, economic education 119–20
Greece, ideology 65
Gutachten 49

Harding, Warren 82
Hayekian-Austrian perspective, on
    markets 3
hidden cost of reward 170
honesty, in policy advisers 53

horizontal communication, economic
     education 116–17
hyperplanes, decomposability on 194
hypotheses, testing of 19

ideology, impact of 64–6
implementation issues, financial
     modelling 146
impossibility theorem 3
incentive constraint 196–7
income, and volunteering 176
independence, of researchers and
     research institutes 94
individualization, of learning 153
infant industry argument 37–8
influence
     loss of, German economists 98
     and the media 67–8
information, policy advice 23–4
infrastructural policy 178
innovations
     finance sector, Switzerland 129–35
     in teaching 120
institutions
     advisory process 77–80
     influence of economic reasoning
          112–13
     innovative power of 131–2
     international public law 186–203
     of policy advice 48–52
     policy consultation 93–5
interactive teaching 153–4
international cooperation, research
     networks 97
International Monetary Fund (IMF) 51,
     58, 61
international organizations
     culture of policy advice 61–2
     research 79–80
international public law (IPL) 186–203
     economic interpretation 188–90
     efficiency of sanctions 192–9
     as institution and science 199–201
     translation problems 190–2
international standards, for economists
     158
intrinsic motivation
     commands 168–70
     direct interventions 174–5
     for economic degrees 114

and external interventions 166–7
and extrinsic motivation 170–2
monetary incentives 167–8
volunteering 177, 178
investment policies, universities 160
Ireland, culture of policy advice 56t, 59t,
     63t
Israel, central bank 50
Italy, culture of policy advice 50, 56t, 57,
     58, 59t, 63t, 65
ivory tower syndrome 57

Japan, culture of policy advice 56t, 58,
     59t, 60–1, 63t
job prospects, economic degrees 114–15
Johnson, Lyndon B. 82
Jöhr, Walter Adolf 90
journals, financial 145
JurLINK 153

Kennedy, John F. 82
Keynes, J.M. 98
Kloten, N. 90
Kuhn, Thomas, approach to
     communication 201–3

language
     publications 57–8, 97
     translation of common theory 190–2
lawyers, and state cooperation
     discrepancy with economic
          perspective 189–90
     language and translation problems
          190–2
learning
     see also computerized learning; on-
          campus learning
     differences in 119
     new media 152–5
lectures 119
legal cases, economists in 80–1
legal design, multidimensional
     cooperation 198–9
literature, on economic policy 48

macroeconomic theory, policy makers 35
magic asterisk 83
mainstream 55, 64, 66
market
     for economic advice 83–4
     versus command 167–72

market failure
  decline in economic majors 113
  role of government 36
markets
  defence of 3, 9, 10, 11, 12
  matrix representation, policy
    perspectives 5–8
  opposition to 4, 10
Marxism 65
matrix representation, policy
  perspectives 5–8
media
  barriers to change, in learning 156–7
  impact on faculty and research staff
    158–9
  influence on policy making 67–8, 73
  innovation in universities 160
  and learning process 152–5
meta-analyses, intrinsic and extrinsic
  motivation 170–1
microeconomic theory, policy makers
  34–5
mistakes, with derivatives 137–8
model approach, bank capital regulation
  134
models
  see also capital asset pricing model;
    computable general equilibrium
    models; option pricing models
  in policy analysis 32–4
  recognising performance and benefit
    of 140–1
  versus procedures 141–2
modularity, financial postgraduate
  education 145–6
monetary incentives, intrinsic motivation
  167–8
moral suasion 165, 173–4
multiple-choice test scores 118–19

negative results, in theorizing 39–40
Netherlands, culture of policy advice 49,
  50, 56t, 58, 59t, 63t
New York University 143
Nixon, Richard 82
nonbinding agreements 197–8
normative, economic terminology 191

objectivity 17–18, 24, 25–6, 27
official advice 76

on-campus learning 155–9
one-minute paper 120
option pricing models
  Black-Scholes 125, 133, 146
  innovative power of 139–40
  performance and benefits of 140–1
  risk management 137
  transfer of knowledge 136–7
Organization for Economic Cooperation
  and Development (OECD) 58–60,
  61
over-the-counter derivatives 137

parliaments, demand for policy advisers
  62
part-time jobs, graduate students 57
participants, executive teaching 144
Pechman, J.A. 90
performance, option pricing models
  140–1
personal development, on-campus
  learning 155–6
Pigouvian taxes 21
policies
  bureaucratic capture of 41
  design, psychological aspects 165–79
policy advice
  culture of 47–69
  opportunities and limitations 74–86
  political economy of 13–27
policy advisers
  client relationships 81 3
  necessary qualities 52–3
  supply and demand 53–68
policy consultation
  institutional aspects of 93–5
  need for 92–3
policy makers, mind-set of 33
policy perspectives, public choice 3–12
policy reform, economic teams 78–9
political discourse, process of policy
  advice 24, 27
political parties
  demand for policy advisers 62
  policy advice 52
politicians
  demand for policy advisers 62
  policy advice 13, 14
politics fail perspective 3, 9, 11
Popper, Karl R. 18, 55

portfolios, diversification through
    technology 132
Portugal, ideology 65
postgraduate education, financial
    innovation 142–8
preferences, constraints and 166–7
presentation, of ideas 52
Presidents, relationships with economic
    advisers 81–3
presumptive evidence, legal sanctions
    194–5
principal-agent theory 168
principle of proportionality 196
problem-solving skills, need for 121–2
procedural cooperation 190
process-orientated view 147
product design, in derivatives 137
product differentiation, through
    deregulation 130
product-orientated view 147–8
professional structures 57–8
protection, developing countries 38, 39
psychological aspects, policy design
    165–79
public choice, alternative policy
    perspectives 3–12
public discourse, process of policy
    advice 24
publications
    attitudes to 97
    language 57–8

qualitative factors, asset management
    141
qualities, in political advisers 52–3
quality
    of policy advice 64, 76–7, 84
    of research 92
    scientific advisory boards 94–5
    university degrees 157–8
quantitative information 141

rational opportunism 188–9, 193–4
rational resource allocation 35–6
Reagan, Ronald 82
reasoning, policy advisers 52
redistributive sanctions 194
regulatory policy, direct interventions
    174–5

regulatory pressure, financial innovation
    134
relationships, client-adviser 81–3
renegotiation proofness 195
reprisals, legality constraints on 196–7
reputation 17, 25
research
    financial postgraduate education 145.
    international organisations 79–80
research departments, policy advice 51
research institutes, Germany 90–8
researchers
    censorship 64
    impact of new media 158–9
    mind-set of 33
    tenure contracts, Germany 95
residual socialist perspective 4, 10
retorsion 197–8
risk management, model-based 142
risk perception 130–1
Role of the Economist 90
Rosy Scenario 83
Royal Economic Society 57

Sachs, Jeffrey 48
Sachverständigenrat 15, 16, 49, 79, 90
sanctions
    economic terminology 191
    efficiency of 192–9
scholarship 57
*Schweizerische Zeitschrift für
    Volkswirtschaft und Statistik* 128
Schweizerisches Institut für Banken und
    Finanzen 143–4
science, economic policy advice 17–19,
    24–6
Science as Profession 90
scientific advisory councils, Germany
    94–5
scientific discourse 19
scientific method 64
scientific reports, objectivity of 25–6
securities trading
    influence of institutional investors 131
    technology 132
self interested behaviour 13, 14, 16, 19,
    25, 26
self-contained regimes 197
signalling, unversity degrees 157
Singer, Hans 90

single European currency 112–13
social capital, measured as trust 169–70
social welfare, democracies 14
society, decline of economics degrees
    112–13
sociology, economic policy advice 84–5
SOFFEX (Swiss Options and Financial
    Futures Exchange) 132, 138
solutions, policy advisers 52
sources, of economic advice 76–7
Soviet economies, intrinsic motivation
    168–70
Spain, culture of policy advice 50, 55,
    56t, 59t, 63t, 65
special studies 51
specialists, Civil Service 75
Staatsgarantien 133
stability, economic theory 20, 21, 22
standardized contracts, derivatives 137
state cooperation 188–90
    and sanctions 192–9
state sovereignty 188
statements, of economic theory 20–3
statistical inference, and legal sanctions
    194–5
Stein, Herbert 81
Stern School, New York University 143
Stillhalteroptionen 131
students
    decline in numbers 103–4
    extra-curricular activities 51
    impact of new media 159
    views on undergraduate curricula
        114–15
stylized facts, policy formulation 33–4,
    40–1
substitution, economic theory 20, 22
Summers, Larry 47
supply, of policy advisers 54–8
Sweden, culture of policy advice 49, 51,
    56t, 58, 59t, 63t, 65
Swiss Banking School 145
Swiss Exchange 131
Swiss Federal Diploma for Financial
    Analysis and Portfolio
    Management 143
Swiss National Bank 112
Switzerland
    culture of policy advice 55, 56t, 58,
        59t, 63t, 65

finance
    in early eighties 126–9
    innovations and evolution of
        know-how 129–35
financial services industry 125–6
undergraduate curricula 108–9, 110f,
    115

tax evasion, regulatory policy 174
teachers
    impact of new media 158
    on undergraduate curricula 115–16
teaching
    changes in, Germany 97
    and learning process 153
    methods of 118–20
    views on 113–18
technology 132
technopols 78–9
terminology, international public law
    190–2
theoretical pluralism 19
theory, use and misuse in transfer
    process 32–42
think-tanks 51–2
three factors model 37
token-economies 171
trade theory, negative results 39–40
training, of policy advisers 54–5, 69, 72
transfer process
    research institutes, Germany 90–8
    use and misuse of theory 32–42
treaties, state cooperation 188–90
trust
    discipline versus 172–3
    social capital 169–70
truth, policy advice 27

UN agencies, demand for policy advisers
    61
unanimity, in policy advice 66–7
undergraduate curricula 103–22
    decline in economic degrees 111–13
    summary and proposal 120–2
    teaching methods 118–20
    trends in economic degrees 104–10
    views on teaching 113–18
uniform tariffs 39–40
United Kingdom
    computerized learning 120

culture of policy advice 50, 55, 56t,
    57, 58, 59t, 60, 63t
  institutional factors, advisory process
    79
United States
  adviser-client relationships 81–3
  culture of policy advice 49, 50, 51, 55,
    56t, 58, 59t, 63t, 68
  institutional factors, advisory process
    79
  undergraduate curricula 104–5, 106f
  volunteering 177
universities
  cooperation with institutes 92–3, 96,
    97
  decline of economics degrees 112
  on-campus learning 155–9
  strategic choices for 159–61
University of Münster 153
University of Phoenix 152

University of St Gallen 74, 108–9, 110f,
    113, 114, 117, 118, 119, 120, 142
useful theory 34–7

valuation models 136–7
value judgements 80
vertical communication, economic
    education 117
Viñals, José 48
virtual learning 152
volunteering 176–8

Weber, Max 17, 24, 90
Weinstein, Michael 80–1
Wertfreiheit 17–18, 24
WinEcon project 120
Wissenschaftsrat, evaluation of research
    institutes 91–3
World Bank 51, 58, 61
World Trade Organization (WTO) 61, 112